What is typography?

"True spontaneity, however, seems to come from *working by rule, but not being bound by it.*"

Edward Johnston, Writing, & Illuminating, & Lettering. **1906.**
(Johnson's emphasis)

RotoVision

A RotoVision Book

Published and distributed by RotoVision SA
Route Suisse 9
CH-1295 Mies
Switzerland

RotoVision SA
Sales and Editorial Office
Sheridan House, 114 Western Road
Hove BN3 1DD, UK

Tel: +44 (0)1273 72 72 68
Fax: +44 (0)1273 72 72 69
www.rotovision.com

10 9 8 7 6 5 4 3 2 1

ISBN: 2-88046-822-1

Art Director: Tony Seddon
Designer: David Jury
Reprographics in Singapore by ProVision Pte. Ltd
Tel: +65 6334 7720
Fax: +65 6334 7721

Printing in China by Midas Printing International Ltd

Right: Book cover
Typography has always been
more than the quiet, efficient
purveyance of words. Authors
also want authority, prestige,
integrity, and solemnity.
Published 1956.

BLACKWELL'S FRENCH TEXTS

VOLTAIRE

Lettres Philosophiques

Edited by F. A. TAYLOR

BASIL BLACKWELL · OXFORD

Foreword

I was intrigued by a catalog I found of an exhibition that took place at the Museum of Modern Art, New York, 1964/1965. Its title is *Architecture without Architects*. The introduction, written by Bernard Rudofsky, attacked the conventional view of architecture which "presents us with a full-dress pageant of 'formal' architecture. The discriminative approach of the historian as we know it is equally biased on the social plane … amounting to little more than a who's who of architects who commemorate power and wealth … with never a word about non-pedigreed architecture. This is so little known that we don't even have a name for it but, we can call it vernacular, anonymous, spontaneous, indigenous, rural, as the case may be." The beauty of the dwellings came directly from the natural, local materials which were utilized with a minimum of intervention.

Digital technology has changed the nature of typography by making it something everyone does almost every day. The fact that most people doing typography (both in a professional capacity and recreationally) have no "formal" concept of what they are doing does not make it meaningless or valueless. Quite the opposite. Ad-hoc signs and messages have been, of necessity, concocted by workmen, emergency services, businesses, lovers, and vandals ever since time immemorial. Such material is all around us and, as the title of this book asks the question "what is typography?", I have taken this opportunity to explore the overlaps, the formal and informal, between typography produced by typographers and typography produced without typographers.

Below: Exhibition catalog
The cover and spreads from the
catalog accompanying Bernard
Rudofsky's exhibition at The
Museum of Modern Art,
New York, 1965.

by courtesy of The Museum of Modern Art (MoMA), New York, 2006

ARCHITECTURE WITHOUT ARCHITECTS
by Bernard Rudofsky

Issues

Anatomy

Portfolios

Etcetera

What is typography?

If we were to consider the normal, everyday activities that consume our lives, it would quickly become apparent that typography is ubiquitous and inescapable. For the most part, this material is routine and boring. But it is also, for the most part, essential.

Typography has been traditionally associated with design and, in particular, with the printing industry. However, owing to the universal access to digital technology,[1] the word "typography" is increasingly used to refer to the arrangement of *any* written material and is certainly no longer restricted to the work of a typographer. Everyone is a typographer now...

"Written" implies first and foremost "handwritten," but there are clearly many ways of presenting written language using technologies such as the printing press, text messaging, e-mail, ink-jet printer, and even the standard typewriter. The word "typography" subsumes all these methods of communication.

Typography and writing have, quite naturally, always been closely entwined: typography being the discipline and professional practice that mediates between the contents of the message and the receiving readership. Therefore, to understand the grammar of typography, one must also gain a knowledge and understanding of language and how it is adapted to function in various social contexts.

Authority
A sense of authority has little to do with size and a lot to do with precision. This sign above is small, but it is rule governed and, therefore, entirely consistent.

Opposite, top: Centering words is often far from easy. The writer of this sign began with the idea of drawing each letter on a separate plank, but realized after drawing the "P" that he had misjudged the alignment. To rectify his error and maintain the symmetrical arrangement, he intended to squeeze two letters onto each plank but, after misdrawing the "N," realized the game was up!
Opposite, bottom: Even when a sign "reiterates precision" it will lose authority if it is not maintained.

Elementary typographic conventions are introduced in schools. However, little thought is put into explaining where these conventions originate or what exactly they aim to achieve.

Nevertheless, these conventions do carry, if blindly, sound principles: how to draw and then write letterforms clearly; how to present words, sentences, and paragraphs; how to arrange text on a sheet of paper; and how to provide emphasis where required. A few specific tasks, such as how to lay out a letter and address an envelope, are also achieved, but little more. Even the most elementary principles of visual language are usually ignored and, as a result, most people, when faced with the task of designing a poster or a flyer, discover (often to their surprise) that neither they nor their computer is able to convey the message in the manner they intended.

Consistency of rhythm
Rhythm is a key factor in good typography. This stems directly from those characteristics that make "good" handwriting: equal spaces within and between letterforms.

Right: *Typographica 15* cover with photogram by Brian Foster, 1958.
Opposite: Page from the *Payson, Dunton and Scribner Manual of Penmanship*, New York, 1873.

Typographica 15

Movement Exercises.

By contrast, there are several specialist areas of research where studies into various aspects of typography have been undertaken in considerable detail. In particular, there has been minute analysis of the letters of the alphabet and the thousands of forms these letters take. Such specialists include type designers, type manufacturers, historians of printing, historians of inscriptions (epigraphers) and handwriting (paleographers), art and design historians, linguists, psychologists, philosophers, forensic scientists, graphologists, and, of course, typographers. Others (publishers, editors, writers, cartographers, draughtsmen, typists, etc.), whose work requires the organization of information, will also have interesting views on typography.

Although all of these specialists share an interest in the same subject, each has their own rich and complex terminology to explain what they are doing, looking for, and/or finding.

The typographer deals with all matters that affect the appearance of type on the page (or screen, or any other flat or 3-D substrate) and all matters that contribute to the effectiveness of typographic information or discourse. These will include considering the shapes, weights, and sizes of individual letterforms, diacritics, punctuation marks and special symbols (or sorts), the amount of space between characters, words, and punctuation as well as the space between lines, the size of margins, and the position, size, and weight of page headings and associated

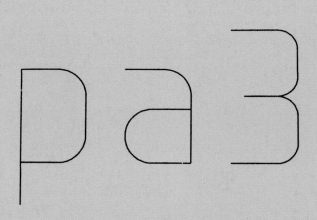

Letter	Strokes	Letter	Strokes
A	∧	N	N
B	B B	O	O O
C	C	P	P P
D	D D	Q	O
E	Ɛ	R	R R
F	Γ Γ	S	S
G	G 6	T	⅂
H	h	U	U
I	I	V	V V
J	J	W	W
K	⋌	X	X ⋈
L	L	Y	Ƴ Ƴ
M	m m	Z	Z
Space	—	Back Space	→
Carriage Return	/	Period	tap twice

1   8 INCH CAKES
1   REG COFFEE

page numbers therein, the selection of textual headings and subheadings, reference figures, and reference material. There may also be diagrams or tables to design which will require captions. In addition, the typographer will normally expect to choose the method of printing, the paper, and all matters relating to print finishing such as laminates, spot varnishing, creasing, folding and diecutting, binding, etc.

If the typographer is to create an appropriate ergonomic arrangement of, for example, a complex scientific textbook or a business card, it is helpful to recognize the relationship of social practice and spoken language to typography. Words and images, as well as graphic and typographic conventions, habits, and prejudices, are culturally and historically determined, and together form what we characteristically call "visual language." The effectiveness (or otherwise) of a form or, more particularly, an understanding of why so many people hate filling in forms, is important to the work of a typographer.

Joseph Moxon, in one of the earliest printing manuals, *Mechanick Exercises* (1683), wrote "A good [typographer] is ambitious as well to make the meaning of his Author intelligent to the Reader, as to make his Work shew graceful to the Eye, and pleasant in Reading: Therefore if his Copy be Written in Language he understands, he reads his Copy with consideration; so that he may get himself into the meaning of the Author, and consequently considers how to order his Work the better both in the Title Page, and in the matter of the book: As how to make his indenting, Pointing, Breaking, Italicking &c. the better sympathise with the Author's genius, and also with the capacity of the Reader."[2]

In attempting to answer the question "What is typography?", this book will discuss the various ways in which it functions, how it functions, and how these influence the way it finally appears. Typography is a very different subject from what it was just 20 years ago. Digital technology has not only changed how typography is done but also who does it. In the process it has also required the typographer who wishes to "challenge the way we read" instead to "challenge the way we don't read."

The everyday world in which typography plays an important part is largely invisible. (Until the reader falters at a typo!) For the most part, this is how it should be. This book will emphasize how type hides itself from view by communicating essential and mundane information effectively. In so doing I hope to make strange again that which we have learned too well.[3] The point is not so much to discuss this fundamental, if elusive subject, as to make such a discussion possible; that is, by means of inquiry, to indicate pathways for further investigation.

Function and technology
Type is often influenced by the technology and purpose for which it is designed.

Opposite, above: Characters from patternmaking software as used in the fashion industry.
Opposite, below: A cash register receipt with characters produced from a dot-matrix configuration.
Opposite, right: Information provided with a Palm Pilot describing how the owner should "write" letterforms in order to be correctly interpreted by the device.

The nature of typography

So many aspects of typography—the terminology, technology, its apparent rule-bound conventions, and micro-attention to barely perceptible details —give laypeople who investigate the subject the impression of a discipline of daunting precision. It is even more daunting to then discover that there appears to be so little about typography that can, in fact, be specifically pinned down.

The basic range of characters likely to be necessary for any lengthy text will include capitals, lowercase, lining and nonlining numerals, punctuation, small capitals, diacritic characters (acute [ó], breve [ê], tilde [ñ], etc.), mathematical characters (fractions, plus, minus, and multiplication symbols, decimal point, @, etc.), currency symbols (pound, dollar, yen, etc.), referral characters (raised or superior numerals and reference ideographs [* † ‡ ¶ §], etc.), graphic sorts (bullet, brace, fist, etc.), abbreviations (&, etc.), and ligatured characters (fi fl, etc.). All of these will be required in both roman and italic and, at the very least, in two weights.

Yet there is no standard which describes precisely what might constitute a font. A display font might consist of just 26 characters plus a few punctuation sorts. A comprehensive text font, however, including various weight options, can easily amount to more than 1,000. Consequently, when considering which font to buy, it cannot be assumed that all of the above will be included, although some will contain more. The requirements for which the font is intended should be fully examined before purchase.

However, there are also no standards concerning weight of character—or how many different weights, or how these varying weights might be measured or described. Similarly, the angle of the italic will vary from typeface to typeface. The italic characters might be true italic with a number of their own specific characters, or simply a sloped version of the roman characters.

The type designer not only designs the characters but also the spacing between the characters. When set, the spaces allocated will give some typefaces a closer, denser, and darker texture than others. Although most type designers go to great lengths to design the space between every character combination, there is every likelihood that a few of the more unlikely combinations will be missed. Most common oversights are roman/italic combinations.

Flexible type
Designed by Gerrit Noordzij. The variants of one character can be seen along three axes. Digital technology has made the morphing of typefaces and/or weights a relatively simple matter.

View of body inclined to show the face.

Letter H, from a type of canon body.

Face of the letter on the body.

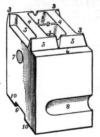

1 counter.	6 shoulder.
2 hair-line.	7 pin mark.
3 serif.	8 nick.
4 stem, or body-mark.	9 groove.
5 neck, or beard.	10 feet.

Spaces of Pica

| Hair. | Five to em. | Four to em. | Three to em. | En quad-rat. | Em quad-rat. | Two-em quadrat. | Three-em quadrat. |

Dimensions of Bodies

| Non-pareil. | Min-ion. | Bre-vier. | Bour-geois. | Long-primer. | Small-pica. | Pica. |

Inflexible type
Page from a book by Theodore Low De Vinne, describing the physical nature of typography, circa 1900.

Although there is agreement that the size of a typeface is taken as being the height of the body, the visible perception of two different typefaces of the same body size can be very different. This is because the x-height (the height of a lowercase x) is set at the whim of the type designer. For example, 24pt *Helvetica* will appear larger than 24pt *Caslon*.

The apparently arbitrary nature of font design is the result of various factors, sometimes historic and cultural, and sometimes related to technological changes affecting their manufacture, but most often it relates to the function for which the font was designed. This can be confusing for the novice, but there are good reasons for these variations. The nature of such basic typographic elements does not reflect an ambiguous or imprecise activity; in fact, it is quite the opposite.

But the typographer needs to know something about the individual typefaces that might be used. The function for which they were designed will be reflected in their appearance and will always be the reason for the proportion of x-height to body size; for a specific range of weights; for the particular characteristics of the italics, numerals, and ligatures; and for the existence of particular or unusual characters and additional symbols.

For the typographer, every new message presents a unique problem. Choice of typeface, size, fit, and arrangement cannot be arbitrary. Type must be made fit for its purpose.

Knowledge, experience, and practical limitations are what have regulated typography. The activity, while shrouded in empiricism, leaves much open to interpretation.

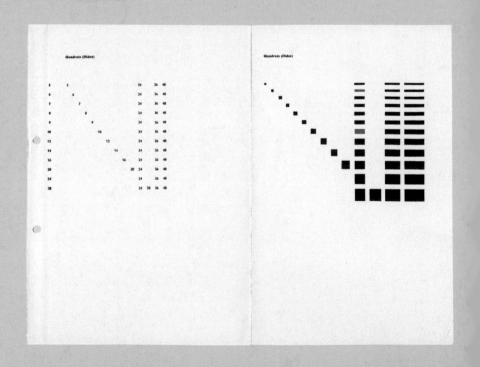

In the past, the profession has actively "promoted a facade of exactness."[1] Precision is something that everyone can understand and most are willing to pay for. When typography was the responsibility of several specialists, including the author, editor, compositor, proofreader, and printer, it encouraged standards which could be measured, readily recognized, and assessed by all.

Today, many typographers, taught at schools of art and design, have been encouraged to be less reticent in the language used and to acknowledge that emotive responses have a function and that texts can be designed with passion. Technology has played an important part in this transformation by making the typographic process more insular, providing independence and the opportunity to experiment.

And yet the rules, the conventions, have not in themselves changed (besides, there are really very few of these); it is the language, the words used to define and promote the rules that have changed. The precision that is associated with typography is more to do with the perception of it being rule bound when really it is common sense, experience, and practical limitations that have regulated typography.[2] Today, passion permeates the language used to describe what typography is, or might be, because the workplace is now the design studio ("express yourself") rather than the printers' workshop ("no flashy stylists here!").[3]

Contrasting aims
The nature of typography offers the widest possible range of attitudes and opportunities. When Anthony Froshaug took up his teaching post at the Royal College of Art, London, it was in the throes of a burgeoning Pop Art movement. Nothing could be further from the ideals held by Froshaug. His stay was short.

Left: Anthony Froshaug, *Typographic Norms*, Kynoch Press/Designers and Art Directors Association, 1964.
Right: *Ark*, journal of the Royal College of Art, London, designed by Melvyn Gill, 1963.

JOURNAL OF THE ROYAL COLLEGE OF ART   SUMMER 1963   3 SHILLINGS 75 CENTS

ARK 34

Speaking and typography

We do not generally write to each other if there is the alternative of speaking directly. Speaking is a relatively informal, relaxed activity because there is little or no emphasis on efficient use of the language. "Meaning" can be repeated, rephrased, or elaborated on using a range of highly regulated physical gestures and facial expressions as well as the use of stock phrases (know what I mean?) or sounds (erm…) whose function is generally to fill time while struggling to find a more helpful, more appropriate word or phrase. Speaking generally is an interactive activity that includes interjections and all manner of alternative responses, physical as well as oral, which are acceptable, valuable, and helpful communication aids.

Writing is generally a more formal activity than speaking. It requires an efficient use of language and a logical and systematic expression. Unlike spoken communication, where a response (verbal or visual) will indicate if the chosen words are understood or not, written communication should function by, and of, itself, and for this reason the author's choice of words should normally avoid vagueness and ambiguity.

The printed word has tended to reinforce this. In fact, less than 50 years after Europe's first book had been printed from movable type (Gutenberg's *42-Line Bible*) circa 1455, the quality and accuracy of scholarly work, notably by Jenson and Aldus Manutius in Venice, had established the printed word as the medium of authority—the one that could be trusted above all else. The relative permanence of the printed medium certainly makes it ideally suited for such functions as recording facts and explaining complex ideas because the reader can conveniently return to the text as many times as is necessary.

But because writing is, on the whole, more formal, it should not necessarily be considered more accurate or even more correct than the spoken word. It has long been argued that as speech is the primary medium of communication among all peoples, it should, therefore, be the primary subject of linguistic, historic, and sociological study. Today, with the technology to directly record speech (rather than relying on a written transcript), the spoken word has a far more important function in all aspects of education and general information storage than ever before, and its influence will inevitably increase.

Oral records have also led to a growing interest in local dialects. Here, the spontaneity and lack of "correctness" provide the words with a candid and distinct expressive advantage in establishing the authenticity of a personal account of a given event. It was for these very same reasons that transient, everyday spoken language was, for many years, ignored or even condemned as a subject unworthy of study. It was considered careless, chaotic, and unstructured. Unstructured was mistaken for aimless and, therefore, considered to be lacking in value.

As recently as the 1970s, children were encouraged, generally with little effect, to speak "properly," to follow the "correct norms" as described in the standard books on grammar and the manuals of written style of the day. The written language printed in book form was the main plank on which the prescriptive tradition rested. Today, this formal approach has been relaxed. This is due to several factors, but must certainly include the influence of "real-life" television programs and movies. It is generally acknowledged that there are differences between spoken and written language and that regional dialects are not substandard but nonstandard. But although there is far greater flexibility in the acceptance of nonstandard vocabulary, nonstandard spelling is generally not acceptable.

And yet, even in a relatively formally prepared situation, such as a teacher addressing a class, the structure of the language that is spoken will bear little resemblance to that found in writing. Those who have attended a lecture that is delivered entirely from a written paper will understand how different (and often lifeless) such a talk can be.

Although typographers deal, in the main, with the written word, they will be aware that the way we use inflections, pace, and volume in our voices to provide emphasis, expression, or clarification can be interpreted visually to provide graphic expression to the printed word.

Describing speech
Left: Transcript and visual interpretation of *Silence*, a John Cage "lecture on nothing," Calder and Boyars, London, 1968. Typographer uncredited, presumably set to instructions provided by John Cage.

Below: Designed by R. Buckminster Fuller with Jerome Agel and Quentin Fiore. The use of a speech bubble and hand gestures emphasize the informal nature of the text.

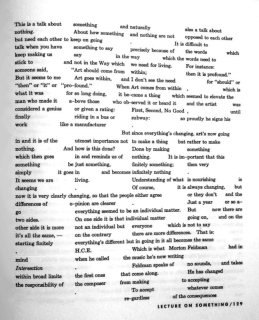

Reading and typography

Studies into what actually happens when we read have always been controversial because it is so difficult to obtain information about what precisely is taking place. Monitoring eye movements does not explain how we extract meaning from graphic symbols. Similarly, testing people after they have read something will tell us something about what has been read (and retained), but not how they read it. Besides, all experimental situations are likely to produce abnormal results simply because they ask the reader to do abnormal things (or normal things in abnormal circumstances).

However, what has been established is that during reading, the eyes do not follow a line of words in a smooth, linear manner, but proceed in a series of movements, called saccades, from the French "the flick of a sail." Where the eye momentarily lands is called a fixation. We usually make three or four fixations per second. Although such fixations are short, tests have proved that in just one-hundreth of a second the eye and brain can recall three or four individual letters or even between two and three short words.[1]

The visual perceptual span at each fixation, using 12pt type, is approximately 10 or 11 characters from the center of vision, although information about word length and general shape could be perceived from a further distance.

The fact that individual, random letters take far longer to read than letters that make up words suggests that we identify common groupings of letters and shorter whole words principally by their arrangement of counters, ascenders, and descenders. In other words, a reader will take less time to recognize bag than agb. (If the three random letters are given more space: a g b, or better still: a, g, b, then the reader will immediately recognize that these three letters are not a word and therefore quickly read them as individual letters.) Because reading is more efficient if the eye can identify more rather than fewer letters in each fixation (up to approximately 2¾ in [70 mm] in length), this suggests that the size of type should not be any larger than necessary. It is a misconception to imagine that because type is large it is easier to read. But obviously, there is also a limit as to how small type can be effectively read. (See also Legibility and Readability.)

The optimum size for continuous (or linear) text is generally held to be between 10pt and 12pt. But the notion of standard "sizes" in relation to the size of type is rather meaningless because although all typefaces share common body sizes, the x-height of each different typeface will vary.

A typeface with a larger x-height will appear larger even though all body sizes are identical. However, a larger x-height leaves less space for

1   2   3   4   5

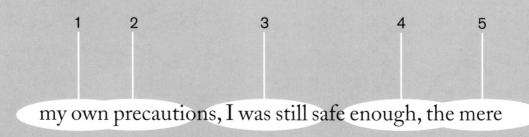

my own precautions, I was still safe enough, the mere

abcdefghijklmnopqrstuvwxyz

abcdefghijklmnopqrstuvwxyz

Variable x-height
Opposite: Letter groups as perceived within individual "fixations." The letter f is one of the easier characters to recognize and can easily be identified even when at the periphery of a fixation.
Above: *Caslon* and *Helvetica.*
Left: The distance between these two horizontal lines represents the difference in x-height (approximately 20%) between *Caslon* and *Helvetica.*

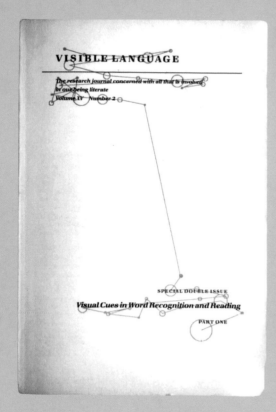

ascenders and descenders. Remembering that the eye tends to recognize common character combinations and word shapes rather than individual letters, it is argued that distinctive ascenders and descenders help the reader to identify word shapes, particularly where these appear at the edges of fixation spans. However, a typeface with a large x-height (and, therefore, shorter ascenders and descenders) can be made more effective by providing a little more space between the lines of type to provide clearer word shapes.

So that the maximum number of letters can be recognized at each fixation point, the setting of text should be tighter rather than looser. Tighter setting will also help word shapes to be recognized. "Tight but not touching" used to be a common request to the typesetter.

Research into reading and the effectiveness in the design of text is often criticized for dubious methodology, imprecise definitions of reader abilities, a lack of concern for the influence of type design, and the effects of variable standards of typographic setting. But it has tended, on the whole, to confirm several fundamentals which constitute good practice: close setting, equal spacing between characters, equal spacing between words, approximately 10–12 words per line, and a little more leading (interline spacing) for typefaces with larger x-heights (and shorter ascenders and descenders).

However, what is considered good practice can, and over time, does change. There are many examples of innovative design in which traditional notions of conventional standards have been knowingly flouted. John Baskerville (1706–1775) had many critics during his working life. The contrast of line (from thick to thin) in his types, the blackness of his ink, the whiteness and

Fixations
Above: Cover of *Visible Language*, Volume xv, No.2. Movement, direction, and fixation points are recorded and printed on the cover of this issue dedicated to "visual cues and word recognition in reading."

Rationalization
Opposite, top: The changing contrast of line (from thick to thin). *Caslon*, from the type-specimen sheet of 1734; *Baskerville* from the type-specimen sheet of 1762; and *Bodoni*, from the *Manuale Tipografico*, 1818.
Opposite, bottom: These attempts at rationalizing type design influenced Baskerville and Bodoni. A drawing by Verini, 1527 (left), and design for the *romain du roi*, circa 1692 (right).

> Quousque tandem abu
> tere, Catilina, patienti
> noſtra? quamdiu nos e·

> T ANDEM aliquando,
>   tes! L. Catilinam fur
> audacia, ſcelus anhelante
> A B C D E F G H I J K L

> dono puro di Dio e felicità ̀
> ra, benchè spesso provenga d
> esercitazione e abitudine, ch·
> difficili cose agevola a segno

smoothness of his paper, and the lack of decorative elements caused his fiercest critics to claim that reading his books would cause blindness. But although Baskerville has since been vindicated, Giambattista Bodoni (1740–1813), who was celebrated in his own time for his neoclassical types and typographic arrangement, has been regarded ever since as an archetypal example of a typographer falling prey to a combination of passing fashion and self-indulgence.

Today, the flouting of convention is not uncommon, especially where nonstandard views might be expressed or where specialist audiences can be trusted to participate in the visual debate. Such examples will always be open to criticism and this is, at least in part, its purpose.

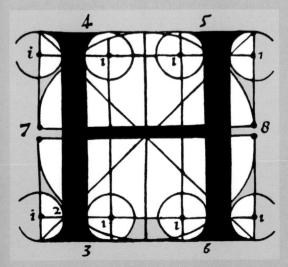

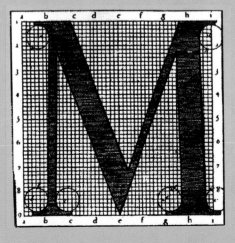

Writing and typography

The arrangement of a text on a page—the grouping and subgrouping of its individual parts and its hierarchical detailing—are taught at school from a very early age.

Children are asked, for example, to keep the left-hand margin clear to provide space for the teacher's comments. This also ensures that the left side of the handwritten column is both straight and vertical: a valuable aid to the reader. The letterforms should be open and evenly spaced as should the spaces between the words. The paper provided will be lined (to enable the children to write in straight lines) and the lines will be far enough apart to ensure that the size of the writing allows about 10 or 12 words to fit comfortably on each line.

The text itself will be broken down into paragraphs, indicated by indenting the first line of a new paragraph. The title will be given added emphasis by underlining it with a ruler. A ruled line is also often used to signify the end of the text. Unfortunately for the children, these prescribed writing procedures have little meaning beyond accuracy of spelling, neatness, and obedience; they are not concerned with objectives of readability or legibility, nor, of course, how these might be achieved or evaluated.[1]

The connection between writing and typography is fundamental. Typography is idealized writing adapted for a special purpose.[2] In fact, writing, in many ways, is the primal basis of everything the typographer does.

Writing is studied by several specialists. Paleographers study handwritten documents, typically Greek and Latin, ancient and medieval. Epigraphers study inscriptions; texts engraved, carved, or embossed into hard, durable materials which include objects such as seals, rings, medals, coins, clay vessels, etc. The aim of paleographers and epigraphers is generally to decipher the meaning of surviving written material to gain information about historic events and the daily life and business activities of past civilizations.

Calligraphy is the art and study of handwriting itself, or penmanship as it was once (and occasionally still is) called. Calligraphy, which means "beautiful writing" in Greek, remains a major art form in eastern Asia, China, Korea, Japan, and in Arabic-speaking countries. Rosemary Sassoon defines calligraphy as normally having to require two elements "first, the writing be carefully crafted, and second, that it should add a dimension of its own to the message."[3] This definition could also be applied to typography, although the purpose and influence of the second requirement will vary depending on the context of the text.

Although handwriting is allowed a cursory appearance on the school curriculum, interest in the nature and craft of handwriting continues to decline, excused in educational documentation by "a greater emphasis being placed on content."[4] In this way, we are told that bad handwriting is a sign of "good" education. Pedagogy is the art of presenting the failures of education as its virtues.

To support such sophistry, the material that is available to teachers who are required to teach handwriting today suggests a relaxed approach, with no emphasis on craft and little on accuracy. Repetitive marks such as loops, circles, obliques, crosses, and lines undulating and zigzagging are presented, but there is no evidence that the writers of such documents have any idea about what the child might learn about letterforms. Instead, the purpose appears to be focused entirely on (a rather low level of) dexterity.

How to Write Your Own CV
A twenty-first century equivalent to the nineteenth-century handwriting manual. The page below, described as "sophisticated," is appropriate for someone seeking a job in creative media and advertising.

Example 8 – The Creative CV

Paula Smith
250 Cuckoo Lane, Somewhere
Tel: 010 0202 0202
Moblile: 077 0202 2020

Personal details

DOB: 10th March (year)
Place of Birth: Anytown, Southshire
Nationality: British
Marital Status: Single
Driving Licence: Current (clean)

Education and Qualifications

Impressive University, Large City, Southshire
Sept (year) – July (year)
June (year) BA Hons Media Studies (2.2)

Impressive School, Smaller City, Southshire
Sept (year) – July (year)
June (year) 8 GCSEs (1A, 4Bs and 1C)
June (year) 3 A Levels (2Bs and 1C)

Training and work experience

Ace Media Ltd
Sept (year) Windows 195
Nov (year) Word 5000
Dec Customer Service (2 weeks)

And yet, writing is certainly the mode of communication most utilized in schools. Written material is easiest to assess formally and, therefore, easiest to standardize. Speech plays a relatively minor role and visual communication, once reading classes commence, becomes almost nonexistent.

The writer has considerable power because of the freedom of expression the process of writing allows. Although writing (and language in general) is bound by conventions to a remarkable degree, it is paradoxically still possible for the author to feel entirely free and unrestricted by the means and process of writing. This is because written and oral language are rigorously taught and, more importantly, constantly practiced throughout our lives. In contrast, visual communication is rarely touched on between preschool and graduate-level education. For this reason, for visual communication—including typographic communication—to work efficiently, it generally requires clarity rather than complexity, the expected rather than the unexpected. Uniqueness slows down the communication process. For these reasons, typography is generally expected (by the author, editor, and publisher) to be conventional.

Alignment and grids
Left and below: Seven-year-old children painting patterns as a preparation for writing lessons. Marion Richardson, *Writing & writing patterns: teaching book*, 1935.
Right: The character "death," written by the Japanese Zen philosopher Hakuin (1685–1768) is accompanied by an inscription: "He who has penetrated this is beyond danger."Despite intensive post-War industrialization, Japan has revived the art of *sho*, Japanese calligraphy.
Below right: The common grid, used by all in the west.

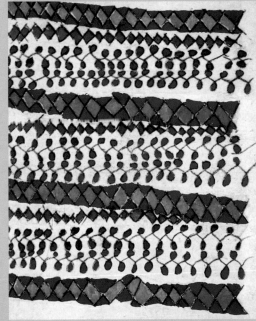

Change and typography

The physical appearance of type has changed little since 1470. This is because the act of reading is one of the most rule-governed of all human activities and if something different, no matter how discreet or subtle, causes an unplanned distraction for the reader then it must be considered a typographic fault. As we already have many typefaces that have proved to be such excellent models, the perennial question is "why do we need another typeface?"[1]

The experimental typographer is almost always a young typographer. The more talented, the more dedicated, the more energetic he is, the more contempt he tends to have for the design establishment and for orthodoxy. It is not only inevitable but also generally accepted (certainly in the West) as a good thing. This, of course, is because the design establishment is often composed of older ex-avant-garde typographers.

Innocence is what allows conventions to be so fearlessly questioned. But after working in a chosen field for 20 years, it is impossible to remain innocent. Students are often told by their tutors that they are being taught the conventions so that they can better understand what they are *not* doing. In this way, and in the true ethos of the art school, students are encouraged to make a difference by creating change.

In fact, it is difficult to imagine a worse fate for a design student than to be "like everyone else" because in their mind, that comprises the mediocre—too often considered to mean the same as conventional. But being taught the meaning of typographic conventions and the function of predictability should not be shirked. It will not crush the creative spirit. For a lively mind, working within parameters whose meaning and function have been made clear will be invigorating, not restricting.

With experience, typographers develop convictions. But experience need not, of necessity, lead to resistance or indifference to change. The process of design requires an inquiring and generous attitude and the opportunity to experiment with the process should certainly be included in the learning process. But this should include intellectual rigor, an understanding of what the consequences might be. Typographers who lose sight of standards and become evermore cynical as they grow older are usually those who followed trends without shaping or understanding them and then simply got left behind. In other words, they never had any standards of their own to lose.

The inevitability of change suggests that the practice of design consists of the pursuit of an ever-swinging pendulum. However, the work of the responsible typographer must surely be based on something more than the reaction of one generation against the work of the preceding one. Today, it seems natural that each generation will try to make its own voice heard.

Encouraging change
The Next Call, edited and designed by H.N. Werkmann, Gröningen, circa 1925. Most of Werkmann's texts were in Dutch, but he gave a number of his projects English titles. *The Next Call* was a small review, the main purpose of which was to establish a new field of communication, "neither a luxury nor an elegant object, but a journal for spiritual use and the exchange of ideas."

the next call 9

THE

WORKS

OF

Dr. Jonathan Swift,

Dean of St. PATRICK's, Dublin.

VOLUME VII.

LONDON,

Printed for T. OSBORNE, W. BOWYER, C. BATHURST,
W. STRAHAN, J. RIVINGTON, J. HINTON, L. DAVIS
and C. REYMERS, R. BALDWIN, J. DODSLEY,
S. CROWDER and Co, and B. COLLINS,

MDCCLXVI.

Conventions of authority
What is considered
conventional and authoritative
changes with time. Centered
arrangements were, and still
are, considered to be the
appropriate way of presenting
a text of distinction. While the
printing of this book is poor,
its age lends added prestige.
Printed in London, 1766.

During the experiments of the 1920s and 1930s,
typographers were trying to create a new, freer,
more flexible, visible means of communication
that would enable them to respond to challenges
without indulging in past stylistic affectations.
Here is the first (of six) statements that the
Czech avant-garde typographer Karel Teige wrote
in his manifesto, *Moderní typo* [Modern Type]
1927, in which he describes what Constructivist
typography stood for. "A liberation from traditions
and prejudices: overcoming archaisms and
academicisms; an elimination of any decorativism.
A disrespect for those academic and traditional
rules which are not supported by concrete
optical reasons and which represent only rigid
formulas, such as the golden section, or the
unity of typefaces."[2]

Although the avant-gardists were content to
break the rules, the designers/teachers of the
Bauhaus, being educationalists, had to *rewrite*
them. Max Bill, a tutor at the Bauhaus, later
(in 1946) described rules as "recipes" whose
sole purpose was to provide a security blanket
for (he suggests) the weak-willed typographer.
The Bauhaus, in fact, simply replaced the schema
of the sixteenth century with a schema for the
twentieth century.

Change is inevitable in an open, secular
society. It is a force. It drives both commercial
and public institutions and is itself pushed along
by cultural and technological developments and
financial imperatives. The easiest way to suggest
dynamic management is to instigate change. We
have surely all witnessed this depressing, often
vacuous process take place. But the visual
communications professions depend on change
generally being considered a good thing.
If nothing needed changing, nothing would
need designing.

Nicolete Gray

LETTERING ON BUILDINGS

270 illustrations

The Architectural Press London

Perceived levels of skill
During the early part of the
twentieth century, ranged left
setting was associated with
elementary levels of
technology (the typewriter, for
example) and skill: centered
typesetting by hand was
considerably more demanding
than ranged left. This gave it
a utilitarian aspect that some
authors and typographers
(particularly after World War II)
felt lent transparency, a down-
to-earthness appropriate for
what was intended to be
factual information. Nicolete
Gray, *Lettering on Buildings*,
The Architectural Press,
London, 1960.

This can lead to designers being commissioned for projects that no one needs. The concept of excess has become an important notion in a society that promotes freedom to choose. Something useless—designed on a whim and for an ill-conceived, ill-researched purpose—is a sign of a society with more than it needs. This is its comfort zone.

This is a relatively new phenomenon. Until the Industrial Revolution in the nineteenth century, change was considered to be something vulgar.

A book, for example, would always be designed to look like every other book. The more "bookish" attributes it had, the better its design. The best design was that which was invisible and typography was certainly no exception.[3] If there was any criticism, it would generally be about the quality of the materials and the skill of the printer and the binder.

There is a different attitude today, possibly because of the influence and range of alternative media available from which to glean information. Inflatable book covers, polystyrene containers, inventive bindings, and paper engineering are all used to test how far the concept of the book can be stretched before it ceases to be a book. But although such projects attract the specialist media (which, too often, is what they are designed to do), there is far more typography of far more value that is working quietly and effectively to inform and enrich our normal daily lives.

Authority and convention

Authority is linked with validation. It is established through a prescribed set of conventions that validate the reader's expectations. An authoritative text will, therefore, use a range of typographic elements that the reader has learned to expect.

Authority comes from several factors. The reputation of the author, publisher, and (occasionally) the typographer will provide a document with authority. An authoritative text (in the academic sense) is expected to include footnotes, captions, running heads, references, biographies, illustration lists, indexes, introduction, and contents pages. Optional extras might include a foreword and, perhaps, even a dedication. Less obvious to the casual reader will, perhaps, be the use of a more comprehensive range of characters. (It should also be informative!)

Authority can also be insinuated by the language used. Many readers will be discouraged by the widespread use of unusual words or words used in unusual contexts, particularly where this seems unnecessary. In such circumstances, the author's intention to establish his/her authority can actively inhibit the reader. As the author must know this, the reader will assume that making the subject difficult is part of the author's chosen form of rhetoric. In other words, the author wants the reader to struggle. Professionals in specialist fields of study defend their use of technical and complex language (jargon) as being a means of expressing technical and complex ideas. It might be that some also consider it to be an effective method of both elevating and insulating the authority of an individual, a profession, or an organization.[1]

Authority is sometimes reflected or enhanced in the materials used. A book, well bound, protected by hard covers, and printed on carefully chosen paper with traditional sewn and glued binding, will provide a sense of authority because the substance and quality of such materials suggest longevity. The same sense of purpose and esteem will also generally be the result if words are cut into stone. Weight generally equates with substance, both physically and intellectually.

Formality is almost inseparable from authority, and lettering whose purpose is to convey power or status generally becomes the formal lettering

The prestige of age
Age, perhaps more than anything, provides authority. Indeed, something that is very old must have been expertly made from good-quality materials to have lasted for so long.

Right: Leather-covered boards with gilt edging. Printed in London, 1766.

Opposite: Lettering at the base of the Trajan Column, carved AD 114. The materials used and the formal arrangement of these letterforms bespoke the power of the Roman Empire at its peak. The government required stone carvers to adhere to strict rules so that each script maintained a uniform appearance.

SENATVSPOPVLV
IMPCAESARIDIVI
TRAIANOAVGGE
MAXIMOTRIBROT
ADDECLARANDVMQ
MONSETLOCVSTAN

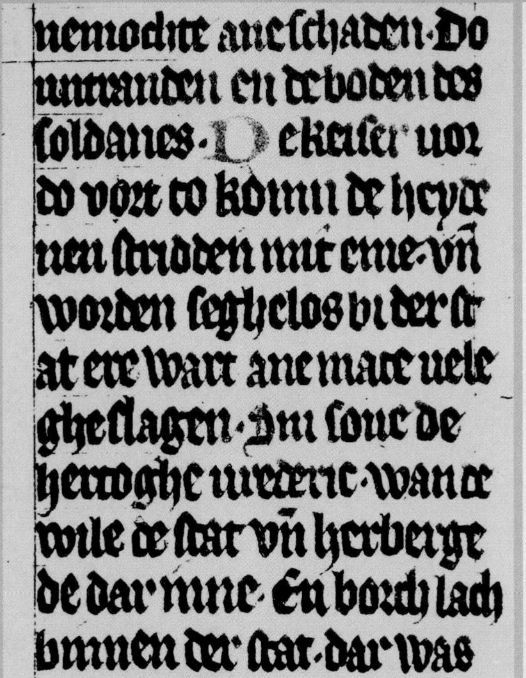

nemockte ane schaden·Do
untranden en de boden des
soldanes·De keiser vor
do vort to komen de heyer
nen striden mit eme·vn
worden seghelos bi der se
at ere wart ane mate vele
gheslagen·Int soue de
hertoghe wederic wan te
wile de stat vn herberge
de dar mne·En borch lach
binnen der stat·dar was
uppe de soldan vor der bor
ch laghen derxpenen also
lange·wan se den soldan
dar to dwrungen·dat he
en des gisele gaf dat se do
hadden guden vrede·vn
guden kop al vor sin lant
So de keiser dannen vor
de heidenen braken den

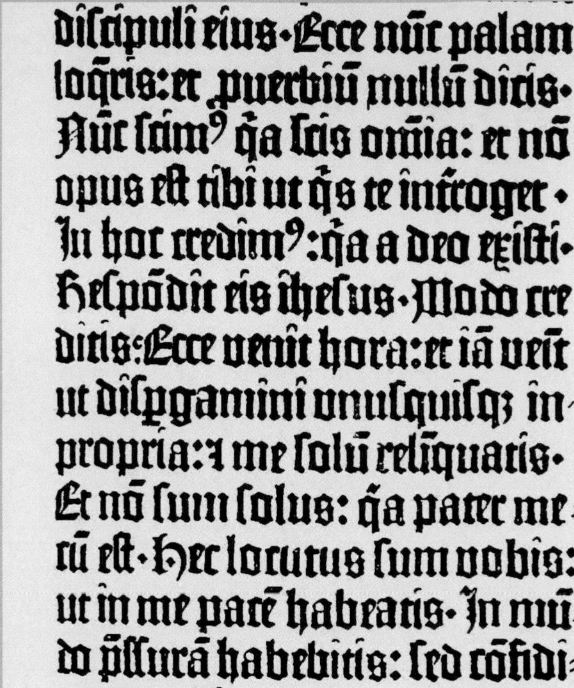

discipuli eius·Ecce nuc palam
loqris: et puerbiu nullu dicis·
Nuc scim9 qa scis omnia: et no
opus est tibi ut qs te inroget·
In hoc credim9: qa a deo exsti·
Respodit eis ihesus·Modo cre
ditis:Ecce venit hora: et ia vest
ut dispgamini onusquisqz in
propria:i me solu reliquatis·
Et no sum solus: qa pater me
tu est·Hec locutus sum vobis:
ut in me pace habeatis·In mu
do pssura habebitis: sed cofidi
te:ego vici mudu· XVII·
Hec locutus est ihesus:et sb
leuatis oculis i celu dixit·
Pater venit hora :clarifica fili
um tuu·ut fili9 tu9 clarificet te
Sicut dedisti ei potestate omiis
carnis: ut ome qd dedisti ei det
eis vita eterna·Hec est aut vita
eterna:ut cognoscat te solu deu
veru : et que misisti ihm cristu·

of the period. For example, in classical Rome, capital letters were often cut into stone on public monuments to celebrate military victories. The overwhelming sense of status is conveyed through the materials used, the position of the words both in relation to each other (centered or justified), and to the reader (above head height), and scale, whereas the letters themselves (upright, square in proportion, and generously spaced) are designed and arranged to be static and symmetrically balanced. Words presented in this way cannot be read in haste.

For a considerable time after the casting of metal type for printing had been invented and successfully applied, handwritten books remained, for many, the superior product and the preferred option. For example, while Venice, by 1500, was the renowned center for printing, the rest of Italy lagged far behind. Florence, the renowned center for the art of writing—with the famous writing schools of Niccolò dè Niccoli, Poggio Bracciolini, and others producing their best work—refused to accept any printed matter into its huge, celebrated libraries. Vespasiano da Bisticci, master scribe and famous bookseller (also the largest employer of hand-copyists in Italy) said "[In our libraries] the books are superlatively good, all are written with the pen; and were there a single printed book it would have been ashamed in such company."

If a medium or process is known to be a more economic method (cheaper, easier, and perceived to require less commitment or less skill to produce), it will be attributed low status. This was a problem that the early printers—Gutenberg, Fust, and Schöffer in Germany, and then Jenson, Ratdolt, and Aldus Manutius in Venice—had to overcome. They achieved this by their high standards of scholarship as well as their printing

Cultural precedence
Opposite: Compare the thirteenth-century, handwritten German manuscript (left) with Johann Gutenberg's *42-Line Bible* (right), the first printed book in Europe, which used metal, movable type (circa 1455, Mainz). The similarities are remarkable.

A new order of precence
Below: Aldus Manutius, *Hypnerotomachia Poliphili*, 1499. During the 45 years between Gutenberg's Bible and *Hypnerotomachia Poliphili*, the form and status of the printed word was established in a largely preliterate world through the scholarship and craftsmanship of Plantin, Ratdolt, and Manutius. They gave the book a universal structure and a state of permanence. The types and arrangements they developed continue to be models for most typographic endeavors today.

skills. The value of an exact and incontrovertible statement, moreover, a statement that can be *repeated* while maintaining the originator's intention, became an essential, interwoven part of civilized, rule-governed societies.

Many of the typefaces classified as scripts and often described as formal are actually based on informal handwriting. This is, undoubtedly, a result of our changing perceptions of what is formal. English script types first appeared in founders' type-specimen books at the end of the eighteenth century[2] and continued to be popular throughout the nineteenth and twentieth centuries for the presentation of formal social announcements. These types were based on the copperplate handwriting style that was taught

in schools at the time and was used for formal purposes such as correspondence, ledgers, and invoices. Teaching of handwriting was both rigid and rule-governed, and children were expected to produce perfect, repeated lettershapes copied from model alphabets. But by the 1920s, the typewriter had virtually replaced handwriting for the production of business accounts and correspondence, and consequently, the teaching of handwriting in schools during the twentieth century would slowly decline in importance.

Today, general perceptions of formality are based on historic precedent. Desktop publishing systems enable the layperson to emulate perceived formal arrangements (inevitably justified) that, using predigital tools and

Strong authority
Authority can be gained by finesse or by strength.

Right: *Aristocrat*, a script typeface based on "informal" handwriting.
Below: *Sans Surryphs* ornamented, Blake and Stephenson, 1838. This dour and weighty letter, with its triangular cross section, is typical of those created for the "new world" signaled by the Industrial Revolution.

abcdefghijklmn opqrstuvwxyz

ROUGH

technologies, were considerably more difficult and took more time to do well than, for instance, ranged left. There is a general although mistaken notion that by arranging the text in a centered fashion using desktop publishing software, the document will attain formality. But because such arrangements are used anywhere, everywhere, and consistently badly, the perceived formality of justified setting is quickly dissipating.

In this way, authority is affected by the inherent characteristics of the technology used. If the status of the technology wanes, so too will the authority of the message it carries. For instance, at the beginning of the twentieth century, many would have regarded a typed letter to be more authoritative than a handwritten one.

Today, a desktop published letter would be considered more authoritative than a typewritten one, whereas a handwritten letter (owing to its comparative rarity) might now, at the beginning of the twenty-first century, be considered to carry most authority of all.

Quiet authority
A book can signal its authority with minimal pretence. The Tauchnitz Edition books were an English-language reprint series, initiated in 1842 and printed in Leipzig. Careful typography and the use of utilitarian paper and binding is typical of early French and German paperbacks. These books established the conventions that Penguin Books took up in 1935.

Printing, composing, and house-style manuals

Style manuals for compositors, typesetters, printers, subeditors, proofreaders, and publishers have been in circulation since the 1890s. A few, such as *Hart's Rules for Compositors and Readers*,[1] first published in 1893 and subsequently regularly reprinted with amendments, have become an important record of the evolving conventions of typography and English usage.[2]

Printers' manuals will generally include press-work, measurement, imposition, and proofreading conventions as well as the application of printing conventions to the composition of text. Moxon's *Mechanick Exercises*, 1683, London, was the first comprehensive printing manual in any language. John Southward's *Modern Printing: a Handbook of the Principles and Practice of Typography and the Auxiliary Arts*, published in 1898, remained a standard work for apprentice printers/compositors well into the twentieth century.

Style guides or house-style guides are generally aimed at a wider readership, including authors, editors, proofreaders, and compositors, and address, for example, issues about spelling and punctuation. *Hart's Rules* comes under this heading, its original title being *Hart's Rules for Compositors and Readers Employed at the Clarendon Press, Oxford*. Books such as this explained the house (or company) rules for those areas of textual organization and English usage

where solutions to grammatical or technical problems might vary. The aim was to standardize such solutions and in so doing make the process of composition more efficient. Over a period of time such books have become "standard" works: in the UK, *Hart's Rules*; in the USA, *The Chicago Manual of Style* (the rules by which this book is edited); and in Australia, *Style Manual for Authors, Editors and Printers of Australian Government Publications*.

Notwithstanding the influence and authority of *Hart's Rules* throughout the twentieth century, the *Penguin Composition Rules*, written by Jan Tschichold in 1947 and issued to all its printers by Penguin Books, is of particular interest. This

Style manuals
From left to right: Horace Hart, *Rules for Compositors and Readers at the University Press, Oxford*, 1952. Illustrated is the 36th edition. F. Howard Collins, *Authors' and Printers' Dictionary*, Oxford University Press, 1956. *Wired Style: Principles of English Usage in the Digital Age*, HardWired, 1996.

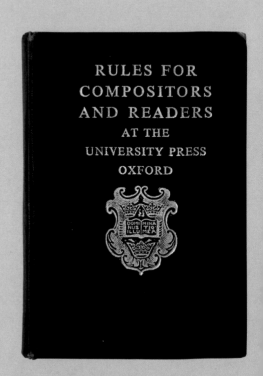

RULES FOR
COMPOSITORS
AND READERS
AT THE
UNIVERSITY PRESS
OXFORD

document is also a model of efficiency, running to just four pages.[3] Tschichold, an Austrian, and closely associated with the "New Typography" of pre–World War II Europe, became an advocate of a less doctrinaire approach to problem-solving in later life. However, he remained passionate about precision, clarity, and close setting. Herbert Spencer's *Design in Business Printing*, 1952, reinforced Tschichold's approach in what was one of the first manuals to reflect the "New Typography" in the UK. (See *Typographica*, page 6.)

Some house-style manuals are produced for specific kinds of documents. Newspapers, for example, have had their own manuals since 1907, and many publishers of books and journals provide authors with guidance on matters of style and presentation. Manuals also provide specific advice to students about how to prepare and present theses and dissertations. Some such manuals are available online.

The titles of style manuals generally suggest conformity to a prevailing standard, as with De Vinne's *Correct Composition* (1901) and *Hart's Rules for Compositors and Readers* (1893). In fact, what these "authorities" aimed to achieve was often less prescriptive than might be imagined.

John Smith in his *The Printer's Grammar* of 1755 aimed to provide a "…conformity to a standard that the consensus of opinion

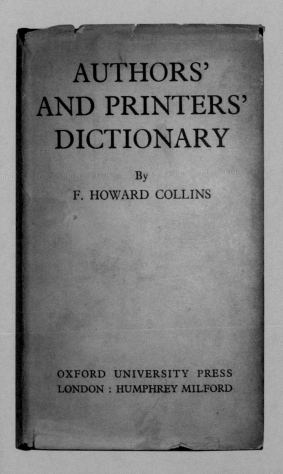

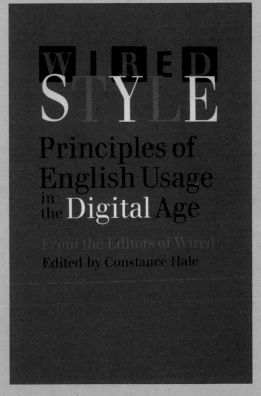

recognises as good." In 1901, De Vinne's stated intention was to define the fixed practice of the greater number of authors and printers.

What Smith, De Vinne, and Hart recognized was that there are many aspects of good typography that are the results of the typographer's craft knowledge and sensory discernment that comes from a practical understanding of the raw materials and the vagaries therein. Such knowledge is difficult to qualify or quantify, but a compositor who has it will have the status that comes with the recognition of an expert at ease with the tools and materials at his/her disposal. The deference so often signaled in the classic manuals to the compositor consistently acknowledge this fact.

Such deference exists because typographic conventions of a technical nature will always require ingenuity in their application, which,

in turn, requires that the typographer maintains the motivation to interpret such rules. The following statement is from the first edition of *The Chicago Manual of Style* in 1906 and has been reprinted in every new edition. "Rules and regulations … must be applied with a certain amount of elasticity. Exceptions will constantly occur, and ample room is left for individual initiative and discretion. [Rules and regulations] point the way and survey the road rather than remove the obstacles."

Rules and language
The language used to describe typographic activities changed little before the digital era, and many of the words still used today refer to letterpress practices. However, predigital manuals contain a remarkable amount of detailed information that is rarely covered in contemporary typography manuals.

Below: A spread from Horace Hart's *Rules for Compositors and Readers at the University Press, Oxford,* 1952.
Opposite, top: A spread from *Type and Style,* printed and published by Baldin & Mansell in 1953 as their in-house "book of instruction."
Opposite, bottom: Cal Swann, *Techniques of Typography,* Lund Humphries, 1969.

solidifying. Tin possesses the property of hardening the alloy, but not to the same extent as antimony. It is very ductile and malleable and produces toughness in the alloy, and has the valuable property of making it more fluid and easy flowing at a low temperature. Copper is sometimes added by typefounders to increase the hardness of the alloy.

Every character in the alphabet, every figure, ligature, punctuation mark, etc, is housed in varying quantities in a case which is divided into a number of compartments. These vary in size according to the frequency with which the character is used; for example, lower-case *e* is used more often than any other character in normal setting of text matter; therefore the lower-case *e* box is the largest of the character compartments. There are many layouts for the position of type in cases. A typical layout is shown above.

The parts of a type character

It is essential to have a thorough appreciation of the various parts of a type character, as knowledge of the various typefaces depends largely upon recognition of small differences or characteristics of these parts. A piece of type consists of the following three main parts: face, beard, and body.

The face consists of the printing surface of the character and other integral parts and generally contains the following:
1. The stems or main strokes, which are the thick lines usually forming the outline of the design.
2. The hairlines, which are the thinner strokes joining the main strokes to complete the outline.

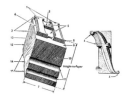

3. The serifs, which are the small strokes normally found at the tops and bottoms of the main strokes and on the ends of some horizontal hairlines.
4. The kern, which is the portion of the character overhanging the body and is mostly found in italic types.
5. The counter, which consists of the part of the type between the main strokes and is below the printing surface. It is the first part of the punch to be struck. Upon the depth of the counter depends to a large extent the printability of the type, for if the counter is shallow it will soon fill up with ink. A deep counter is needed to obtain the best results in stereos and electros.
6. The fitting, which is the space on each side of the character which prevents it from appearing too close to its fellows when assembled.
7. The set, which is the width of the type body, and consists of the width of the face and the fitting.

Justification of lines to square measures inevitably requires varying spaces on each line

In order to be capable of manipulation, lines of type must conform to the standard range of spacing material on the point system; consequently the composing 'stick' is pre-set to a suitable length measured in ems. When this measure is filled, the word spaces are adjusted as evenly as possible throughout the line to fit the measure tightly and each line is 'justified' in this manner.
In lines of normal continuous reading, containing an average of nine to ten word spaces, this spacing discrepancy from line to line is hardly noticeable, but lines averaging seven words or less should not be justified. In such cases the gaps caused by justification severely disrupt the easy movement of the eye along the line and tend to associate words together vertically rather than horizontally.

An even visual word space is achieved when lines are set as so-called 'unjustified'

The alternative to justification is for the compositor to place a constant word space throughout the line and justify at the end. The type is still justified, in fact, but the term 'unjustified' has been widely used to describe this printed effect of a ragged right-hand edge; 'fixed word space' is a more accurate description. This practice has many advantages in providing a consistent reading speed and avoiding too many word breaks and it is reasonable to assume that the fixed word space is more functional and economical than justified lines, whatever their length. In display filmsetters, it is very difficult to justify. In most cases, the line has to be set twice before the required length is obtained.

Rules and conventions

Some typographers believe that they are involved in an activity in which it is possible to make something that is right. This is a view which is less prevalent today because there are many more typographers for whom esthetics and performance are inseparable. While it is relatively easy to test the functional effectiveness of typography, when esthetic effectiveness is claimed most people will assume that what is under discussion is a matter of taste, not a matter of fact.[1]

When typography was inextricably linked to the printer, letterpress technology itself acted as an instructor. The design of all the components that make up this now largely redundant technology made assumptions as to how it would, and should, be used. This was possible because the nature of printing and the training undertaken by compositors was highly prescriptive. Outcomes would be known without the need for type and/or print specifications or even a sketch on the back of an envelope. In this sense, it was possible for all those concerned to gather around the finished item to judge and agree that the result was "right."

Typography was considered to be a discipline. Through rigid instruction, a body of knowledge was passed on while standards of excellence were set by studying the work of professional practitioners, both dead and alive. Obdurate instruction does not leave room for creativity because it is based on the principle that there is a right way of doing things and alternative ways must, therefore, be wrong. In this way, although the subject of typographic composition was infinitely more complex, it was, nevertheless, as prescriptive in nature as that experienced by the dutiful typist. Efficiency above all else was the goal for both, and avoiding the necessity to think was a great time-saver.

After World War II, a general liberalization of design education encouraged students to ask questions about the rules they were expected to learn. An individual's learning experience became

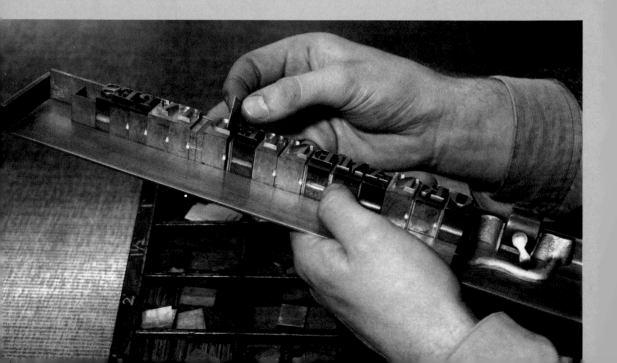

increasingly based on personal rather than external imperatives. In this enthusiasm for questioning conventions, there arose the assumption that all rules, formulas, and instruction provided to the compositor had no place in typographic education. It was never assumed that these rules were no longer correct or appropriate, but rather that it was better that students discover them for themselves as and when appropriate.

In fact, rules and formulae, in the context of a deeper understanding of typography, are simply practical, realistic, and sensible. Providing such information is common sense and, if presented in the contexts of function, history, and technology, is entirely (and efficiently) appropriate. The knowledge required to be proficient in the discipline of almost any craft is usually complex, and the transfer of knowledge from one person to another is easiest done through demonstration and structured teaching. Rules and conventions are a natural starting point.

Digital technology, with its "undo" and "save as" options, allows the typography student to test the rules to destruction in minutes, although the necessary analysis of why they are destroyed will take longer.

Too many courses teaching typography have not adjusted content and delivery to shorter timetables. This is leaving many, perhaps most, typographic practitioners with no criterion of values (either practical or esthetic) that would enable them to distinguish between the genuinely good and meritorious. What is of greater concern is that without standards of fitness derived from past or present models, typographers cannot be expected to produce not necessarily meritorious, but even intrinsically sound work.

Typography and the printer
Until the middle of the twentieth century typography was inextricably linked with the printer: until digital technology finally gave the typographer "independence," photo-composition was prevalent.

Opposite: Inserting spacing material between letterpress characters in a composing stick. (Photograph courtesy of Andrew Dunkley and I.M. Imprint.)
Above: The *'Monotype' Book of Information* (undated) was written for students training to operate Monotype equipment.

Craft and typography

In the past three centuries, the meaning of the word "craft" has changed. In the eighteenth century "craft" was used to describe political acumen and guile, a way of doing rather than making things. In some cases this still applies, for example, for Freemasons, the phrase "the craft" still has the meaning of "power and secret knowledge."[1]

The meaning of craft, in the sense that we understand it today, did not develop until the end of the nineteenth century with the Arts and Crafts movement, and although it was made up of both makers and thinkers (inspired by a crisis of social and moral conscience), craft became associated predominantly with making.

For a decade or so, at the end of the nineteenth and beginning of the twentieth century, the Arts and Crafts movement made it possible for art, craft, and design to be considered indistinguishable, and a few—notably type designer and sculptor, Eric Gill—managed to hold all three together. However, almost simultaneously, the avant-gardists declared

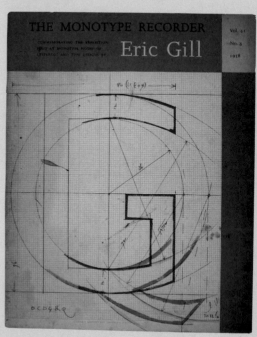

The relegation of craft
The independent craftsman/ artist as perceived by Eric Gill (1937) and the designer as technocrat (before the Macintosh gave us the MacJockey) as perceived by "business."

Above: Eric Gill in front of his relief carving for the League of Nations building in Geneva. (Photograph by Howard Coster.)
Right: Cover of The Monotype Recorder, Volume 41, No. 3, 1958, showing part of a drawing for Gill Sans C, D, G, O, and Q, dated 20.12.32.
Far right: Promotional photograph for the Crosfield and Scitex electronic display system, 1983. The hierarchy and function of the characters (including the computer, personified by the screen image) is clearly displayed.

craft to be an irrelevance. For the craftsperson, craft might represent empowerment, but for the artist, craft came to represent constraint. Indeed, for the avant-garde artists, the idea of the "artist-crafts-man" was (and largely remains) a contradiction in terms.

In the 1920s, the Bauhaus initially professed a debt to the Arts and Crafts movement declaring "there is no essential difference between the artist and the craftsman."[2] Their concept of craft sought to reinstate all disfranchised art forms in an attempt to use the dual practice of art and design as a means of supporting the struggle for human equality. However, while the theory was maintained, the notion of the handmade came to be considered antiprogressive. Equality, it was felt, could be better served with design aligned to mass production.

The consequences of the split that led to the separation of "thinking" from "doing" have been exacerbated since the advent of digital technology. As a consequence, a design student can say "I don't want craft to get in the way of my creativity," and this will be accepted as a perfectly rational statement.

For typographers, craftsmanship and technology are inseparable. The way computer technology has affected working methodologies has made some typographers pessimistic; they argue that craft has been driven out of design. However, it is a misconception that if a company invests in the best computers and the latest software then the technology will design the typography.

Having talked to many in senior management, it is clear that there is a general belief that the typographer is, essentially, a machine minder. This affects the status of the typographer, which in turn affects the way in which they are dealt with and how they are expected to work. Any time

spent improving what the software delivers can be severely criticized as time wasted "...if you want to kern, you do it in your own time, not the company's."[3]

This lack of regard for tacit knowledge echoes the business world's contempt for most craft-based activities. Has it ever been otherwise?[4] Because of this, too many design companies prefer to emphasize their use of technology to promote status rather than draw attention to the creative intelligence and craft skill of the typographer. Although such public relations tactics are understandable (if highly regrettable), a design company whose management denies the existence of its own expertise, or worse, does not recognize its own expertise, is not functioning properly.

It is impossible to improve standards of design without facing up to the politics of the workplace. Without time to think, the activity of design is not "design" at all. Unfortunately, typography, being about detail, about the barely perceptible, is at present, possibly one of the least respected of all design activities.

Typography has always encompassed the use of technology. There is a continuing debate among typographers on how far technology shapes us and how much we shape technology. Although the technology keeps changing, what is important is the level of control that the typographer has, not so much over the technology itself, but over the way it is used in the workplace. Too often it is the strategies, principles, standards, and methods that are put in place by others that have the biggest influence on the quality of the typographer's work rather than the knowledge and skills he/she possesses.

Digital technology need not drive craft out of typography; the computer is, in fact, a particularly flexible and responsive tool. But like all previous technologies, it is often the excuse, regardless of our individual desires and political or moral values, for the fall from grace of typographic craft. We have got to start talking about typography in terms of computer craft.[5]

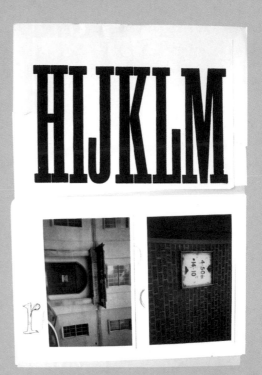

Recording tacit knowledge
Sketchbook (cover and spread) belonging to Henrik Kubel, of A2-Graphics/SW/HK. These (and many more) sketchbooks provide a record of the inextricable links between intellectual and creative thinking, and between technology and hand skills.

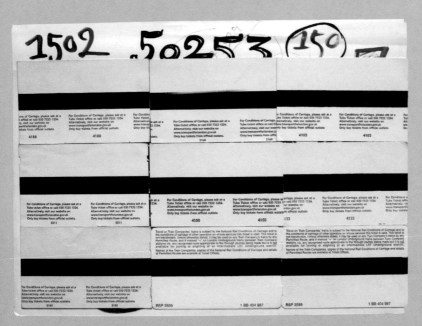

Hypermedia

The manuscript tradition on which printed books remain the standard had not been seriously challenged until about 20 years ago. Neither had the language conventions embedded in it.[1] The power of the book stems from its total integration into a cultural and social infrastructure (schools, universities, public libraries, etc.). The successful introduction of hypermedia into society is also due to the technology that drives it being fully integrated into a cultural and social infrastructure.

It is the existence of hypermedia that has caused the manuscript tradition of language and knowledge to be brought into question.

The confrontation is between the singular history of the manuscript and the tradition of the book which got us to where we are now, and the uncertain durability of hypermedia, which might get us somewhere in the future.

Initially, the speculative aspect of hypermedia was what made it so attractive. To reject the book and embrace hypermedia (this hard-line, either/or scenario is a typical stance when any new technology arrives) transforms some into adventurers, futurists, and chance-takers, and the rest into luddites. For someone with an emotive stake in the creative aspect of visual communication, the former associations are highly attractive.

The book/hypermedia debate is providing an ideal opportunity for sociologists, behaviorists, technologists, artists, and designers from all fields of specialization to get involved. Hypermedia is good at bringing such diverse groups of people together. In this way, hypermedia is certainly affecting the complementary processes through which knowledge is transferred and stored.

The initial response to any challenge to the established, dominant medium is to rebuff it. However, the history of media generally, and typography in particular, has demonstrated that each new medium has found, by public demand, its appropriate niche. These are still early days for hypermedia. In its attempt to ingratiate itself fully, as speedily as possible, into the cultural infrastructure of society, it has all too often been designed, again by public demand, to function within the comfortable conventions of the book. Many typographers are aware, however, while hypermedia continues to emulate the book, it will not escape the limitations of the book.

Surveys have found that most typographers practice in both print and screen media.[2] This is not surprising as typography in both media is still the primary means of communication.

Hypermedia is currently, surely, just a fraction of what it will be in the future and might take decades to metamorphose fully into its own visual expression. Language is, on the whole, highly conventional and, for the most part, this is how it has to be for a complex society to function. However, society is certainly also aware of the limitations that conventions impose. This is implicit in that, for example, artists, poets, and comedians are invited to circumvent or even mock the rules that make up these conventions. It is this kind of creative activity through which hypermedia might provide new insights into language and which, in turn, will require new insights into typography.

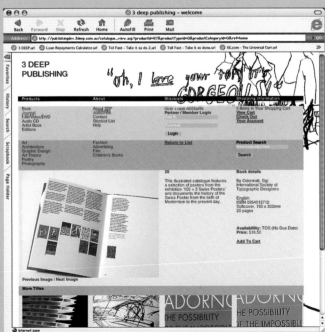

Information architecture
The conventions of the
physical book have been
applied to the architecture
of Web sites to ensure that
visitors can find their way
around. When a Web site is
preoccupied with presenting
publications, this methodology
is even more clear. Here, the
visitor can view each
document page by page while
other publications await
inspection in the panel below.
3 Deep Publishing, 2005.

Vision impairment

There are many situations affecting legibility, readability, or both, when it is necessary for the typographer to recognize that most readers have less than perfect focusing and that, for instance, one in twelve males has defective color vision.

Different eye conditions create different problems. Very few blind people see nothing at all. A minority can distinguish light from dark, but little else. Some have no central vision; others no side vision. Some see everything as a vague blur; others see a patchwork of blanks and defined areas. So some people with impaired vision will see well enough to read this text, but might have difficulty crossing a road safely.

With legibility concerning disability discrimination being introduced in many Western countries, inclusive typographic design has been placed at the forefront of modern environmental design, obliging typographers to recognize the diversity of needs their facilities and printed material have to meet.[1]

The provision of readable material for the partially sighted has been considered from time to time, particularly by teachers and those concerned with the education of children. As early as the 1880s in the UK, special large print books were published "for children with weak sight, whose eyes must be spared."[2] But the problem received little attention elsewhere because medical opinion discouraged people with poor vision from using their eyes for "close" reading, fearing it to be harmful; "residual" vision had to be "saved", not used."[3]

In addition to these developments in the educational and welfare services for the partially sighted, there has been a growing awareness of the importance of services for older people. Although medical advances have helped in reducing the number of children suffering from congenital eye defects, there has not been a corresponding decrease in the number of older people with bad vision.

With the huge improvement in the design of glasses and contact lenses (as well as a range of other optical aids), some typographers will complain that having to take account of this, admittedly small(ish) percentage of disadvantaged readers, is unnecessary. However, all of these aids are essentially magnifying devices and the mere

Issues of legibility
Cover and spread from a manual listing guidelines for inclusive signage. Designed by June Fraser, 2000.

enlargement of print is not always enough to make it legible. Remember, magnification enlarges any defects in the print, any gray letters, and indistinct outlines—it cannot improve bad typography. Second, and more obviously, magnifying aids are awkward and heavy to use, particularly for sustained periods or if the reader has difficulty holding the book and/or the reading aid in steady focus.

Another reason for including the problems of readers with impaired eyesight here is that the results from the various reports, generally provided by people who often know little about typography but a great deal about issues concerning communication, memory, and the learning processes, are, in effect, objective

critiques of the typographers' work and can tell us a great deal about readability and legibility. On the following pages, for instance, are the eight principal conclusions from the summary of the 1969 research report, *Print for Partial Sight*.4 Any of my own, brief comments follow in square brackets.

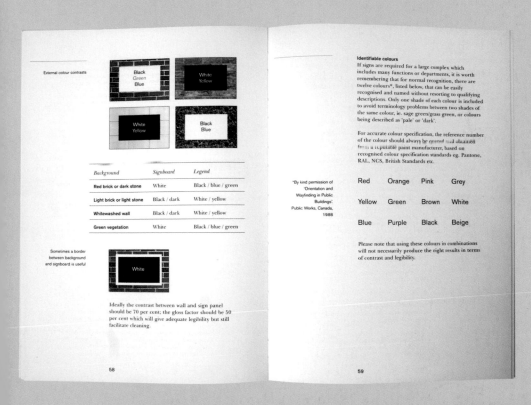

58

59

Print for partial sight

1 Differences between adults and children

Changes in typography affect adult readers much more than children (although print requirements for younger or partially sighted children might be more critical). [Adults will almost always be less tolerant of the unexpected.]

2 Type size

Size of type is one of the most important typographic factors for partially sighted readers, but this is not to say that books in extra-large print are required for all partially sighted readers, or that legibility continues to increase with successive enlargement.

There is a basic difference between adults and children in this respect. The adult often needs larger than average print, but the child, because he/she still retains powers of accommodation, can achieve adequate enlargement by bringing the print close to his/her eyes.

Enlargement much beyond the size that is necessary for the type to be seen is unlikely to increase legibility.

3 Type weight

Increased weight or boldness of type, although of secondary importance compared with size, also improves legibility for partially sighted readers. Results with children suggest that once above the lower threshold of vision, weight becomes a more important factor than size.

4 Typeface

The effect of differences between the typefaces tested (a serif and a sans serif) is of minor importance compared with the effect of size and weight. The sans-serif face was slightly more legible for the adult readers, but no measurable differences between the faces were observed with the children. [The sans serif used was *Gill Sans*, the serifed face was *Jenson*. The slight preference recorded by adults for the serifed face could be explained simply by the fact that most of their reading will have been of serifed faces.]

5 Type spacing

Changes in spacing either between letters and words, or between the words only, or between the lines only, do not appear to affect legibility. [These rather extraordinary conclusions are contrary to all other surveys on readability of texts.[5] The influence of space on both legibility and readability are discussed in the Making type work section of this book.]

6 Cause of partial sight

Legibility varies with typographic changes according to the pathologic cause of partial sight. However, there is no real conflict of interests here as typography that is helpful for one group is not positively bad for one of the other groups.

7 Amount of residual vision

There is no direct correlation between the amount of vision remaining in a defective eye and the use a person makes of it in reading. The personal attributes of the reader—willpower, incentive, and interest in reading—play as important a role as the physical amount of vision in determining whether a partially sighted person actually does much reading.

Impaired vision
Cover and images from *Print for Partial Sight*, published in 1969. The images show a good retinal image, a poor retinal image, and a poor retinal image improved by enlargement.

8 Importance of typography

Although many other factors also affect a
partially sighted person's ability to read print
easily, the part played by typography is significant,
particularly for adults: the increase in legibility
due to improvements in typography measured
in this investigation were of the order of 35%
for adult readers.

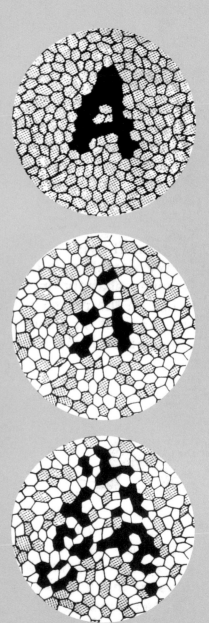

Business communication

For several generations, secretarial staff produced the correspondence and all other forms of administrative documentation required by every business and organization. The (virtually) all-female typing pool, with its own hierarchy and strict regimes, was often described as the "heart" of the organization. The personal or departmental secretary became a hybrid image of formality and efficiency—qualities that were formulated in large part by the rules of the typing manual. Secretaries and typists were trained in-house and/or at commercial college in typewriting, shorthand, business conventions, and English (with an emphasis on spelling, grammar, terminology, and punctuation).[1]

The authority of the typewritten document quickly became an essential commercial tool. The crude, mechanistic appearance of the characters punched onto the company notepaper through the inked textile ribbon was in no way detrimental to its commercial viability. Nor were the severe limitations of only 88 key options. In fact, the resulting idiosyncratic appearance of the typewritten document made it immediately recognizable, and, once established in the larger and successful companies, all other businesses, no matter how small, had to own one to present themselves to the outside world as a commercially viable manufacturer, merchant, or service.

The conventions of the typing manual were of limited interest to typographers until digital technology provided everyone with desktop publishing (DTP) software. During the 1980s, the influence of the typing manual increased considerably, while the demise of the corporate typing pool was equally dramatic. This increased influence is not so much because typists are now doing DTP work (although, of course, the few that remain still are), but that a surprisingly high

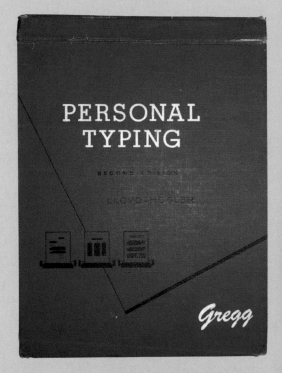

The influence of typists
Typing manuals were published in great numbers as the demand for typists increased. Between 1861 and 1911, the number of male clerical workers increased 5-fold, the number of women clerks 500-fold.

"They cannot fool FATHER TIME,
No matter how they fool their time away."

The influence of the typewritten document
Left: Cover of a four-page advertising "insert" taken from the *The Strand*, circa 1900–1916. The impact of "visible writing" machines, aided by formidable advertising campaigns, was remarkable, and the distinctive appearance of the typed document came to represent business and commerce. In contrast, the use of handwritten correspondence in a commercial context quickly came to represent a company stuck in the past, or a rank amateur. Advertising, particularly of the early nineteenth century, often represented the wasteful, inefficient methods of the past with bent old men, as here, lined up at their desks with ink pots and ledgers.

Typist and compositor
Above right: In many ways the function of the typist was similar to that of the type compositor, or later, the phototypesetter. The typist's job was to organize information, often presented in a totally chaotic manner, according to rule-governed, universally accepted standards. The type of before-and-after exercise shown was common in both typists' and printers' manuals. The printers' range of options were, of course, considerably more complex. This example is from *Typographical Layout and Design*, the Linotype technical schools series, Grade three, Linotype & Machinery Limited, London, 1930.

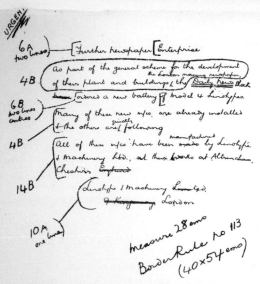

FIG. 11. ROUGH SCHEME AND COMPLETED JOB

percentage of those people who now prepare texts in the commercial sector revert to the same restrictive practices that were devised to accommodate the severe technical limitations of the typewriter.

Given the opportunity to produce printed documents using highly sophisticated DTP software, why do so many people continue to use the primitive (and entirely obsolete) conventions of the typist? Conventions such as the use of double or even triple spaces after full points, exclamation marks, and question marks; double spacing after colons and semicolons; underlining; the use of single or double prime marks to indicate quotations (rather than the turned comma and apostrophe); and the use of the hyphen for en and em dashes. The misuse of the hyphen and prime marks could be put down to a lack of knowledge of the appropriate characters, but the other

examples are surely done in the full knowledge that these are not the conventions of the printed word.[2]

The original necessity for such large spaces after certain punctuation marks can perhaps be explained by the crudity of the early typewritten document. Early machines made horizontal alignment impossible to maintain accurately and, depending on the manufacturer, some of these machines only had capitals or lowercase.

However, by 1893, when one of the first manuals was published by Pitman, these technical limitations had been effectively eliminated.

The problems common in contemporary typed documents were listed as irregularity of impression and spacing, unevenness at the beginning of lines, typing not parallel with the top of the paper, uneven spacing between lines, misuse of certain characters, bad alignment, and finger marks and smudges.[3]

Each character, whether the i or the w, is allocated the same amount of horizontal space (and the same amount of space as allocated for interword spaces), giving a line of text a loose and particularly uneven appearance. The uneven spaces within and between characters is exactly what well-designed and well-set type avoids. To ensure that this unavoidable unevenness did not interfere with the readability of the text, it was probably felt that extra spaces were required to signal, for example, the end of a sentence.

Although the mechanisms introduced to the typewriter later improved alignment both horizontally and vertically, the spring mechanism only partly alleviated the irregularity of impression. Type design and typographic layout generally aim to provide an even, visual color/texture; the idiosyncrasies of the typewriter meant that those advocating its use felt obliged to advise the use of additional clues for the reader to compensate for the irregularity of impression. Thus, double and triple spaces, just like double quotes, provided additional definition of purpose.

Looking at typed business correspondence now, such extreme procedures appear unnecessary and, once the typewriter had been accepted as an appropriate mode of communication, they became redundant. That the use of additional spaces remained the rule appears to be due to nothing more than convention—a sense of it being the "right thing to do." Interestingly, in all the technical information related to typewriters, the printer was ordered to use the spacing conventions of the typewriter manual rather than his own typesetting manual.

The advent of the typewriter provided considerable advantages to the type compositor. A typed manuscript was preferred (in fact,

generally insisted on) not only because it was easier to read, but also because each character and word space produced on the typewriter is identical. This made it a relatively easy task to calculate how many characters made up the copy (called "casting off"). From this, it could accurately be estimated, using tables provided by the leading type foundries, how many pages the copy would require in any typeface in any size or weight. Several specialist manuals were published that explained good practice for typists producing documents specifically for the printer.[4]

When phototypesetting was developed, the new technology remained, for the most part, within the print industry and so a large number of Monotype and Linotype keyboard operatives simply transferred their skills and typographic knowledge to the new technology. But when digital technology came on stream, typists simply transferred their skills, working methods, and the conventions of the typing manual from the typewriter to digital technology. Hence today, we have, for example, the aberration of texts shot through with holes.

Imperial 'Good Companion' Model T
Touch Typewriting Guide

LEFT HAND   4   4   3   2   1   1   1   2   3   4   4   4   **RIGHT HAND**

MARGIN RELEASE — 2 3 4 £5 6̄ &7 8 9 0̄ = − | | TABULAR KEY

Q W E R T Y U I O P | | |

SHIFT LOCK — A S D F G H J K L ; : | | BACK SPACER

SHIFT KEY — Z X C V B N M ?, .; %½ | SHIFT KEY

SPACE BAR *(Thumb)*

Imperial Typewriter Co. Ltd., Leicester, Eng.

Telephone 27801 (5 lines)   Agents and Service Depots in all principal towns.

Keyboard arrangements

Spreads from the *Imperial "Good Companion" Model T instruction book* (undated). The standard QWERTY keyboard arrangement dates from some of the earliest commercially produced machines (circa 1860–1870). Its design has attracted criticism on ergonomic grounds. Although most typists are right-handed, this keyboard arrangement makes the left hand do 56% of the work. Neither is finger dexterity linked to letter frequency. For example, the two strongest fingers of the right hand are used for two of the least frequent letters: j and k.

DETAILS OF FEATURES
referred to in the following instructions

1. Carriage Lock
2. Paper Supporting Arm
3. Platen Knob—left-hand
4. Platen Knob—right-hand
5. Platen Release Clutch
6. Paper Table
7. Auxiliary Paper Feed
8. Auxiliary Paper Lever
9. Carriage Release Lever
10. Paper Release Lever
11. Top Plate
12. Margin Stop—left-hand
13. Margin Stop—right-hand
14. Margin Stop Rod with Numbered Scale
15. Tabulator Stop Rod
16. Tabulator Clearing Lever
17. Platen Ratchet Release Lever
18. Line Space Lever
19. Line Space Adjusting Lever
20. Line Indicator and Card Holder
21. Margin Release
22. Shift Key—left-hand
23. Shift Lock
24. Shift Key—right-hand
25. Back Spacer
26. Tabulator Setting Lever
27. Tabulator Key
28. Space Bar
29. Colour Change and Stencil Lever
30. Left and Right-hand Ribbon Spools
31. Left and Right-hand Ribbon Spool Levers
32. Left and Right-hand Ribbon Guide
33. Ribbon Centre Guide
34. Ribbon Reversing Stud
35. Type Bar Guide
36. Baseboard Fixing Screws

4

FIG. I

5

Rural communication

Typographic decision-making begins when children start to write, although most children today also encounter DTP software from a very early age at school as well as in the home.

The use of DTP in schools as part of the writing process has the potential to provide emphasis to typographic organization. In "publishing" their documents, children are already being asked to consider how it might be used and by whom, to write with a specific purpose in mind through a process that includes drafting and editing. They are also asked to consider what would be an appropriate appearance for the finished document[1] as it is commonplace for children to be asked at school to produce newspapers, magazines, leaflets, advertisements, etc., as a means of exploring various ways of organizing text.

The problem is that for children (and teachers) their general awareness of typography stems from what they are conscious of seeing: what attracts their eye in the environment of the street and shops, on advertising boards, shop fascias, and on packaging, rather than the typography they read every day in newspapers, magazines, and books. For a child looking for ideas to help in the design of, for instance, a newspaper much of what attracts the eye is inappropriate. And even if newspapers were available in the classroom (and one must assume that in such circumstances they would be), these would require a considerable amount of detailed analysis to be of any real benefit. Teachers are given very little guidance about the potential of visual organization to enhance the meaning of text, let alone the finer points of typography.

On the community bulletin board of every village, there will be homemade notices and posters. Most amateur community notices and posters today are produced digitally, and yet,

Nonconformity
Above: The variety of signs indicating a public footpath is accepted, indeed celebrated as part of a more relaxed, less regimented way of rural life.

Symmetrical arrangement
Opposite: A village bulletin board. The variety of information and the range of technical standards is remarkably diverse and yet *every* notice or poster has a centered arrangement. In fact, the appearance of notices on village boards such as this, despite the digital revolution, has changed little. Notices remain remarkably similar to the hand-drawn versions of the 1960s and 1970s.

despite the dramatic change of tools and processes, the design of such notices remain remarkably similar to the hand-drawn versions of the 1960s or 1970s: the use of underlining, prodigious use of capitals, important words set at a diagonal, and emphasis provided for key points by the use of speech bubbles or boxes.

The persistent use of underlining is particularly interesting because of its evolution through handwritten, typewritten, and digital document making. In handwriting, it is an almost universal convention to underline headings as a means of providing hierarchic structure. This is easily achieved and will often be done as an afterthought.

For the typist, underlining was one of the few options available to provide emphasis within a typewritten text. Underlining was also used as a convention in copy preparation informing compositors to set type in italic. However, underlined characters were never part of the metal letterpress stock, although it became a possible (but rarely used) option with photo-composition. But in the 1980s and 1990s, it was a far more common sight in printed matter because it was a typing convention and many typists transferred their skills from typewriter to word processing and then to DTP software where underlining is an available option.[2]

The practice of centered arrangements for amateur bulletins and posters has also remained almost universal. Up to (and beyond) the 1960s, amateur guidebooks on lettering would suggest that typographic organization was, above all else, about balance and symmetry. Looking at advertising work up to the 1940s, there was a surprisingly high proportion of material which was essentially symmetrical, but, after World War II, the international advertising industry took

America's lead, and was transformed by more flexible asymmetric arrangements. Today, and since the 1950s in commercial poster design, asymmetric arrangements have been entirely dominant, and yet centered arrangements persistently, and perhaps appropriately, remain the norm, generation after generation, for the traditional, slower pace of life represented on the village community bulletin board.

DTP has also meant that a large amount of material for public display that would previously have been produced by the jobbing printer is produced in people's homes and offices. However, the technology has not had as big an influence on the actual appearance of local bulletins as might have been expected. With any new technology there is a period of time when the new mimics the conventions of the previous

technology. It has, however, rendered the skill of drawing letterforms and applying color unnecessary, and, of course, multiple copies mean that more information can be included.

Typography is now something everybody does, although only typographers call it "typography." For everyone else it is now considered a very common, everyday practice—a manual task requiring virtually no thought whatsoever. Thus, the fundamental significance of typography as an intellectual discipline and as a personal accomplishment has become, and probably always was, something of an enigma. But whereas, in the past, typography and printing were genuinely mysterious activities (commonly referred to as "the black art"), today everyone has access to the same tools, the same hardware and software. Typography is so familiar, so matter of fact,

that most people fail even to acknowledge its existence. In some ways, of course, this is the successful result of its invisible application by generations of printers/typographers. The proof of good typography has nothing to do with technology; it can be judged only in the reading.

Vernacular signs
Signage is often perceived to be so matter-of-fact that people fail even to acknowledge its existence. Yet, at its best, it adds greatly to the character of place and provides so many links, in its words and in the physical aging process, with its past.

Far left: This milestone in Ardleigh, UK, shows the number of miles to London, Harwich, and Colchester, and also provides a seat.
Left: Many street signs in Colchester are provided in the form of printed tiles of varying widths, each containing its own bracketed, slab-serifed letter. The tiles are cemented to building walls.

Urban communication

The extent of the urban streetscape for local pedestrians is generally the pavement, the road, and the first floor of the buildings. Off the main street, graffiti, fly posters, stickers, temporary traffic signs, and small vernacular shop fascias are an integral part of urban living and working. Much of this typographic material will have been done by amateurs, some by vandals, and some, although quite a small percentage, by designers, including professional signmakers.

Some of the "nondesigned" typography will have been made with commercial or political intent, some will be serendipitous, or simply caused by neglect. In older districts, the pedestrian can often find ad hoc remnants of businesses from previous generations, providing clues of past political and/or industrial upheaval. Most urban communication will have been the result of optimism: "a good idea," something new, exciting, and worth shouting about.

In all towns and cities a range of wayfinding signs, locational identity signs, and situational, ad hoc messages can be seen. Some of the signs are rule-governed brandings: corporate logo, name, and associated livery. Other signs are bespoke, one-off signs on fascias and vans, hand-chalked menus, and sale offers.

The amateurs' hand-drawn notice or sign attracts attention because we seem to be naturally drawn to anything different or unexpected. However, signs must attract for the right reason and certainly, in the urban commercial environment, the public are highly attuned to the way messages are relayed to them. A hurriedly drawn (informal) price sign on a market stall will not be perceived to represent a lack of concern by the stallholder for the quality of his fresh fruit, quite the opposite, because immediacy and impermanence are both qualities appropriately associated with fresh food. However, if a

Eye-catching typography
Left: Effective and attractive handwritten price signs (Colchester, UK.)
Right: This conspicuous lettering has all but obscured the buildings. Bold, expanded, outlined, and drop-shadowed sans serifs dominate as businesses fight each other for the attention of "passing trade." (Photograph taken in Auckland, New Zealand, by Alan Robertson.)

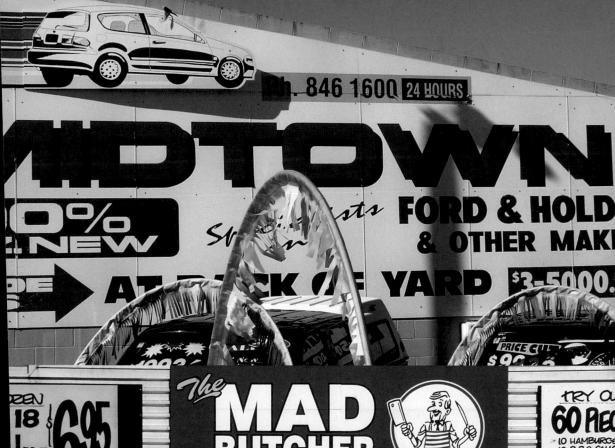

Ph. 846 1600 24 HOURS

MIDTOWN

Specialists

90% NEW

FORD & HOLD
& OTHER MAK

AT BACK OF YARD $3-5000.

The MAD BUTCHER

"We Discount the Price...Never the Quality!"

PRICE CUT

18 $6.95 EA.

60 PIEC
* 10 HAMBURGE
* 10 B-B-Q SAUS
* 20 CHICKEN N
* 10 FISH CAKE
* 10 CHICKEN V

"We Discount the Price...Never the Quality!"

13 PORK FLAVOURED SAUSAGES
$5.00

NZ HERALD
AND SUNDAY
PAPERS

ON SALE HERE

POLONI
$5.00

VISIT OU
WEBSIT
themadbutcher.co

SPORT

permanent (formal) sign, displaying the stallholder's name for example, is hurriedly (and ineptly) done, its informality will be perceived to be inappropriate. Typography, when bad, is easy to recognize, but difficult to get right.

The long-established department store generally offers a more formal persona (even if it prides itself on friendly service). A less formal method of conveying information can still be initiated for short-term events such as a sale, but this material must be disposed of the moment the event is over, so as to enable the formal presence of the business to be restored.

People understand the effort involved (if not the process) in the production of notices and signs. Something that requires time to plan and then paint or carve, print or build, will generally be considered more formal because it has gone through a process of design, making, and/or manufacture, and is already clearly intended to be in place for a considerable time. The materials chosen are very important in reflecting this. Letterforms bought "off the shelf" and fixed DIY style, either by authoritative organizations or by the individual business entrepreneur, are notorious disasters: M and W mixed up, S upside down, but more commonly, poor spacing.

In the context of hand-lettered signs, newsbills are an anomaly. Until very recently, newsbills were a hand-drawn form of public advertisement for daily newspapers sold on the city streets. It is remarkable that hand-drawn newsbills should have remained in existence for so long, especially because their function was

Utilitarian type
Far left: Small service cover set into the pavement. The raised pattern (an antislip safety requirement), applied with minimum regard for the function of the letters, has resulted in a rather crude appearance. Despite this (or perhaps because of it) I find this highly utilitarian product very alluring.
Left: In "inexperienced" hands, capital Ms and Ws can be a source of confusion.

to advertise the products of a highly sophisticated, technology-driven, newspaper media industry.

The point, of course, is that the newsbill offers urgent and topical information. The earliest specimens, dating from the beginning of the nineteenth century, contained more than 20 lines of closely printed type in various styles and sizes . Over the years, however, the tendency developed toward shorter, ever more dramatic handwritten headlines that were attention grabbing and readable at a glance.[1] Contemporary newsbills, although printed, have retained the underline and are, in this way, reminiscent of the earlier, hand-drawn newsbills.

The need for semipermanent information, often hurriedly improvised in urban streets, is generally considered to be visual clutter. In an emergency, we are reassured to see order reestablished, usually in the form of standard temporary signs, access inhibited by tape, vehicles with flashing roof lights, and uniformed personnel. Coordination in all these elements is important in providing a sense of order and authority. Disorder is stressful because change to our daily routine forces us to think about activities that we can normally take for granted.

It makes us think about what we are doing! Order allows us to form our lives into patterns, to make assumptions, to plan ahead, and use our time efficiently. When a book is opened, the reader is looking for patterns for the very same reasons.

Traffic diversion signs are unpopular because they inevitably represent a disruption or break-down of a planned journey. However, if such signs are coordinated in their appearance and placement, then they will be perceived to represent a coordinated response to a scheduled event. The driver will assume that this is a planned reroute, rather than an ad hoc, hurried, and perhaps ill-conceived emergency-induced event.

Impermanent vs. permanent typography
Right: Urgent and topical information. Newsbill, November 1990. Although printed, this bill retains some of the characteristics of a hand-written message which captures the sense of immediacy that is so important for news.
Far right: Information intended to last. Weathering has embedded this memorial into the fabric of the building.

Ad hoc signage is both celebrated and despised, depending on the viewers' circumstances. "Typographic detritus or chance art"[2] is the way that improvised urban information was described in *Typographica*. The interference by people making alternative, spontaneous additions or alterations (disregarding the best intentions of the designer) is both inevitable and a necessary aspect of urban life. Such ephemera may sometimes be ugly, but its purpose is generally to provide a valid source of information, even if it is only for a select few. Small, entirely insignificant information, the detritus of urban life, is just as valuable—more valuable some would argue[2]—to social historians than the results of grand-scale city planning.

It is a very good idea to consider how a text will be perceived (and read) in 10, 20, or 100 years' time. "Decay is the most powerful medium for the improvement of cities… Decay, not architects, adds the last touches, blackens and peels the stone, applies lichens and cracks, softens the edges, elaborates elaboration, and the hand of man works even better than the forces of nature.."[3] Similarly, a scuffed, well-thumbed book with creased page corners is the consequence of a well-used and truly useful document.

Anatomy

The title of this section suggests the specifics that enable a subject to function. But I have also included a brief introduction to specialist areas of typographic study that are undertaken by people who are not typographers.

For the practicing typographer, any interest shown in theory tends to be an indulgence restricted to "spare time." The practical process of typography is so vulnerable to the pressures of time that anyone who admits to thinking might simply be accused of not working hard enough. The problem is that theory has no *direct* bearing upon efficiency, profit margins, or any other measurable means of recording its influence. Therefore, all things theoretical, in a commercial context, are seen as having no *value*.

To those practicing typography, the unorthodox pronouncements of, for example, sociologists, linguists, or psychologists upon the subject can be galling, especially when the concluding statement is that "... typography is too important to be left to typographers."

Statements such as this occur because the practice of typography has been kept separate from the theory of typography. A statement such as "...science is too important to be left to scientists" is, after all, unthinkable. Why has the theory and practice of typography, and other areas of visual communication, not been more effectively combined to provide mutual support?

The practice of typography has, traditionally, been bound up with craft; a physical, tactile process, requiring a highly specialized range of skills that have both isolated and defended the activity of the typographer (printer and compositor) from "outsiders." This defence crumbled with the digital revolution in the 1980s.

Since then, theoretical studies relating to typography (and, in fact, all aspects of visual communication) have grown rapidly and quite separately from its practical study in the studio.

Many university art history departments renamed themselves departments of visual culture because the original title simply did not take account of the expanding syllabus. Today, visual culture includes advertising, fashion, film, photography, radio, retail, television, Web sites, and the Internet (many of which require significant input from a typographer).

A concern some typographers have with theoretical analysis is that it sets out to objectify its subject. Attempting to explain the magic of esthetics, inspiration, and creativity might be viewed as being deeply antagonistic, and, perhaps, even dangerous. It is as though understanding might break the spell and allow the subject to be appropriated by the uninitiated. Bearing in mind the current democratization of typography, perhaps this is not surprising. In the circumstances, a certain amount of resentment by typographers is understandable. But with complete power over what the theorist can theorize about, the causes of this suspicion suggest something else. Especially when it is remembered that theory must always wait for the creation of the next typographic document to ruminate over before the theoretical prognosis can progress. Theory is dependent upon practice.

Perhaps it is because theory is communicated via spoken and written language, which is very different from the way typography tends to be taught in art schools which places the emphasis on *visual* communication. And yet, during the design process, thinking and talking are both closely bound up with practice and generally encouraged. Despite this, for many practicing typographers, the notion that design might be an intellectual process carries with it negative overtones. This may be a reflection of its craft-based roots. The term heard most often in studios is "professional," defining the typographer as a solver of real problems and so aligning the activity of the typographer with the rational, realistic culture of business and commercial enterprise. It is not surprising then that the growth and development of typographic theory as a subject has been led by academics in humanity departments.

There is a persistent view among typographers and other specialists in the field of visual communication, that without practical expertise it is presumptuous in the extreme for someone to expound upon the subject. And yet, when design principles and methodologies (which might have been refined over a lifetime) are to be discussed, it would be understandable if the theorist thought it appropriate to describe such work using a mode of language that reflects the complexity of the subject. And yet, practitioners then complain that the theorist is, quite purposely, making the text difficult. Baudrillard, in the 1980s, was dubbed an "intellectual terrorist" because his texts were so intimidating. (Of course, it is also possible that an impenetrable text is due entirely to confused thinking or that certain theorists make their writing difficult because they seek a reputation for profundity.)

However, typographers, are also used to working within conventional codes, and most would consider the design of accessible information their first and most important objective. Typographers, therefore, will have little patience with a verbose writing style that appears to camouflage the meaning of the text. What is also surprising to typographers is that the product itself, and the manner of its making, are often entirely subsumed by theoretical and contextual information. So much so that a text about typography will often contain no visual references whatsoever.

Semiotics

Any activity to do with communication requires a means of conveying ideas, and for such an activity to be successful, a system that is understood by the receiver must be used. Mass communication requires that the system is used in a highly conventional and, to a large extent, highly predictable manner.

There are some who argue that if the typographer sticks rigidly to "the rules" that make up the convention, then he/she can remain an entirely neutral (e.g. impersonal, anonymous) influence in the communication process. The rules, however, are anything but rigid, being instead a range of often intentionally vague opinions passed on verbally or in written form by those who have the time and inclination, and the ego, to imagine that others might be interested.[1]

When readers engage in the various activities that constitute the reading of books, they make use of more information than is present in the literal content of the lines of graphic symbols. Signals are being communicated by every aspect of the typographic decisions that have been made by the typographer on behalf of the author. Then there are the myriad choices concerning the printing and finishing processes, the papers, the method of binding, the overall size, and the weight of the document, resulting in how it feels in the hand (or hands).

In other words, there is more to see on the printed page than a mere sequence of letters. In fact, it is the qualities that distinguish the document from a simple accumulation of letters which might finally be described as typography.

As Saussure explained, linguistic (typographic) symbols are abstract, their forms entirely arbitrary and "unmotivated." There is no necessary connection between the meaning of any word and its phonological structure. The necessity for interpretation by the reader is therefore unavoidable and the presence of semantics (to ensure an "effective" interpretation) and rhetoric (to ensure the "right" interpretation) is inevitable. On top of this, texts are designed by individual typographers with particular purposes in mind, so their work will bear the evidence of their intention, even when that intention is "purely functional."[2]

Analysis of the meanings and motivations of "banal" ephemera (government communications, timetables, etc.), the "neutral" or purely

"functional," has been the subject of semiotics (the all-inclusive study of structured human communication in all its variant forms—sound, sight, touch, smell, taste—and in all contexts—clothes, dance, film, music, typography etc.). This has provided the potential (at least) to identify the wherewithal of ideology and/or political dimensions.[3]

Semiotics is broader in its scope than any other method of analysis because it studies the significance of all signs within society. As a result, some theorists have maintained that semiotics is the "science" best qualified to determine "the logic of culture." Linguistics, rhetoric, semantics, and graphology all fall within its remit.

J. P. Gumbert described the significance of semiotic values as expressed in book form thus. "The giant choir book says 'We are a rich church'; the modest notebook of the friars says 'We have rejected all mundane pomp'. By being more expensive, or cheaper, more modern or more conservative, the book helps the owner to prove (to himself and to others) that he is more powerful, more virtuous, more intelligent, or more wise than others."[4]

If all signs relating to communication are intent, to some degree, to persuade, then the typographer must acknowledge the social and moral/political dimensions of all designing. It must also be accepted that there is no such thing as "pure" (i.e. neutral) information or that the typographer can possibly be an "innocent" and remain separate from the content of what is being conveyed.

Although there is value in exploring the potential of semiotics to typography, there are potential confusions about terminology due to different disciplines sharing words while giving them different meanings. For example, the words "signs," "signals," and "symbols," all

used in their semiotic mode, have other meanings in the world of typography. Although this can be disconcerting, if not confusing, the language of the various linked theoretical fields of study can be valuable by providing ways of thinking and discussing those aspects of typographic communication normally taken very much for granted in the practical world of design.

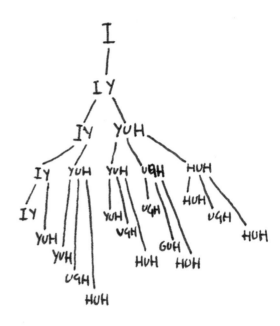

Communication aids
Left: The object of this student project was to communicate the concept of "two (or 2)." This solution uses forms inherent within the existing letterforms to describe both the word and how to say it.

Above: This diagram formed part of the introduction to a project concerned with "infinite phonetics." Such a diagram, presented (intentionally) as if scribbled onto the back of an envelope, still convinces us of its integrity. Both projects were produced by Alex Wright while a student at the Royal College of Art, London, 2005.

Linguistics

A history of language is, at the same time, a history of the cultures and civilizations from which language originated. Languages reflect and explain the cultures and histories of the communities to which they belong.

Of the (approximately) 7,000 language communities in the world today, more than half have fewer than 5,000 speakers, and 1,000 have fewer than a dozen. Clearly, many are likely to be extinct within a generation. The cause of this calamity is the universality of modern communication systems, or rather, the lack of effective hiding places in the world today.

There have been numerous attempts to invent an international language that would be easy to learn and equitable to all national languages. Although some have been ingenious, none have been accepted. The practical problem with artificial languages is simply that the amount of effort required can only be worthwhile if everyone else is prepared to put in the same amount of effort.

Each community develops a language system that is appropriate for its needs. The UK has approximately 40 words for rain[1] and as many again to describe its physical effects. (Inuits famously have a similar number of words to describe snow.)

Although the social and cultural conventions of language (which are reiterated almost every minute of the day) are in everyone's interests to master, we also appear to enjoy inventing new words (called neologisms) or new ways of using old words. Jargon serves to make a group cohesive and to establish group identity. In fact, as communication systems become truly international, jargon may ultimately replace the geographic diversity of language. New words constantly enrich our language and their creators are often highly regarded. These, of course, include authors and poets, but neologisms and other forms of play involving the conventions of language are also useful to editors and advertising copywriters.

It is argued that "typographic man" was a more rational, intellectual human being because he developed the means to record his thoughts by writing.[2] This notion is contested by those who subscribe to the view that oral cultures have alternative, though equally articulate, communication systems capable of describing and passing on complex ideas. What is not in doubt is that although language may not determine the way we think, it does condition the way we perceive the world.

Bliss Sementography
Charles Bliss (1897–1985) proposed an interlingual system of graphic discourse — Bliss Sementography. This relies on the principle of Japanese notation with a core set of ideographs designed to operate the grammar.
Courtesy of Clive Chizlett.

WIJ VREZEN DIE TEGENKANTING NIET, ALTHANS NIET, INDIEN DE PLATTELANDS-
BEVOLKING BEHOORLIJK WORDT VOORGELICHT. IN GROTE LIJNEN IS IMMERS
HET RESULTAAT DER VOORGESTELDE HERVORMING, DAT DE DAGSFEREN DER

BEVOLKINGSGROEPEN DE OP **ELFDE HOOFDSTUK** ERLOREN GEGAAN · VOOR DE
HOE DIT TE VERKLAREN? HOE TE VERKLAREN, DAT DEZE ARBEIDSREGELINGEN
AGRARISCHE **DE VOORGESTELDE HERVORMING EN HET PLATTELAND** MATERIËLE
ZO GEWORDEN ZIJN, DAT ZIJ ELKAAR IN ZOMER EN WINTER NAUWELIJKS MEER
SCHADE GEPAARD GAAN · **A. ALGEMEEN**
ONTLOPEN? VROEGER, ENKELE EEUWEN GELEDEN, TOEN HET KUNSTLICHT
NATUURLIJK ZULLEN ER — ALS ALTIJD — MENSEN ZIJN, DIE DE BEZWAREN TEGEN
SLECHT WAS (EN MEN OOK DAAROM MEER OP DAGLICHT WAS AANGEWEZEN),
DE VOORGESTELDE HERVORMING ONOVERKOMELIJK ACHTEN · ZIJ ZULLEN WAAR-
TOEN DE WISSELWERKING TUSSEN STAD EN LAND VEEL GERINGER WAS DAN
SCHIJNLIJK IN DE EERSTE PLAATS DENKEN AAN MOGELIJKE TEGENKANTING VAN
THANS, TOEN HET PLATTELAND NOG NIET GEDEELTELIJK WAS GEÏNDUSTRIALI-
DE ZIJDE DER AGRARISCHE BEVOLKING DOOR DE MOEILIJKHEDEN OPGEHEVEN ·
SEERD EN DAAR TE MIDDEN DER LANDARBEIDERS NOG GEEN INDUSTRIE-ARBEIDERS
WIJ VREZEN DIE TEGENKANTING NIET, ALTHANS NIET, INDIEN DE PLATTELANDS-
WOONDEN, TOEN DE ARBEIDSUREN DER BEIDE, NU DOOREENWONENDE, SOOR-
BEVOLKING BEHOORLIJK WORDT VOORGELICHT. IN GROTE LIJNEN IS IMMERS
TEN ARBEIDERS ELKAAR NOG NIET WEDERKERIG BEÏNVLOEDDEN, TOEN, KORTOM,
HET RESULTAAT DER VOORGESTELDE HERVORMING, DAT DE DAGSFEREN DER

Systems of writing

Above: Two texts, printed one over the other, but each can be distinguished using red or green reading glasses. *TypoGraphica* 16, 1959.

Left: There are two "empires" of writing, one derived from Phoenician scripts and based on the different sounds of the language. This was perfected by the Greeks and adopted throughout the Western world. The other, perfected by the Chinese, is based on ideographs. In China there are many dialects spoken, but people can communicate through a shared understanding of writing. This has made it a powerful and unifying factor in the east Asian cultural region. From *The Art of Writing*, designed by W. J. Sandberg for UNESCO, 1965.

Rhetoric

We can all lie and we all know it. We rely on the integrity of an organization or an individual to provide us with good—meaning true—information. It is often impossible to verify or prove that the information we are given is truthful and, if truthful, correct. Therefore, the value we apply to so much of the information we receive depends on the reputation—the integrity—of the presenter or the source of information, and we tend to judge integrity by the rhetoric used.

Rhetoric is concerned with those factors that attempt to ensure a predetermined interpretation of factual information. Language is regularly manipulated to achieve such a function and typography can, indeed should, reflect and reinforce the arguments within a given text. For this reason, there is a commonly held prejudice that pejoratively associates rhetoric specifically with deceit and seduction. However, if one believes that language is invariably about debate, upholding a point of view, or simply explaining the facts as one understands them, rhetoric must also be concerned with imagination, with form-giving, and with appropriate use of language to facilitate all forms of social interaction.[1]

In fact, it is difficult to imagine any information that does not involve some degree of interpretation. Our contemporary distinction in typography between information and persuasion reflects historic concerns about the merits of plain and ornamental styles of presentation. Because of this, many typographers believe that information can be presented without ever referring to modes of persuasion. Yet all communication, no matter how prosaic, has interpretable, stylistic qualities that go beyond the stated content of the message, and therefore become ornamental.

Even the choice of typeface, for instance, a decision that is unavoidable, must add *something* to the reader's perception and therefore could be described as ornamental. Consequently, the issue that typographers must face relates not to persuasion or the lack of it, but rather to the intentions behind it. So, typographers must question the purpose, the function of the given text, *before* any typographic decision is made.

Umberto Eco, Italian scholar and semiotician, describes New Rhetoric thus. "Almost all human reasoning about facts, decisions, opinions, beliefs, and values is no longer considered to be based on the authority of absolute Reason, but instead,

is seen to be intertwined with emotional elements, historical evaluations, and pragmatic motivations. In this sense, the new rhetoric considers the persuasive discourse not as a subtle, fraudulent procedure, but as a technique of 'reasonable' human interaction, controlled by doubt and explicitly subject to extra logical conditions."[2]

So, designing the appearance of any typographic layout involves a degree of rhetoric. The effectiveness of typography depends on the use of marks, symbols, or patterns that are familiar and pertinent for a given audience. A functioning message is one that succeeds in connecting with the habits and expectations of its audience. A conscious rhetorical approach to typography would be one which accedes that all design has social, moral, and political dimensions, that there is no sphere of "pure" information, and accepts the challenge to design typography that is functionally and conceptually appropriate for its purpose.[3]

Public records
Left: Military victories recorded on the Column of Trajan in Rome, AD 114. The detailed, carved narrative spirals up and around the column. Viewed from the ground, the end of the story can never be seen, suggesting that the power and influence of the Roman Empire goes on forever.
Right: The power of this message is due, in part, to the fact that it is painted on an otherwise typical house. The total absence of grandiosity or affectation makes for an undeniably emphatic statement.

Semantics

Semantics is concerned with the way we manipulate language so that it makes sense. Whenever we can, we try to structure and/or classify our information to make it more accessible. A typographer will use alignment, juxtaposition, hierarchic distinctions, and the recognized conventions of reading and typographic craft skills to ensure that the meaning of words is attainable.[1]

But there are many situations in which it would be inappropriate for the typographer to apply a system, where language, by its very nature, becomes a more freewheeling, less precise mode of communication. The linguist David Crystal cites this example. "In everyday life, we use such words as hill and mountain, stream and river, where the real world notions are quite indeterminate. When does a stream become a river, or a hill become a mountain?"[2] As words are, in themselves, often imprecise, this encourages the writer to be creative in the way word combinations, phrases, and sentences are composed. In other circumstances it might be the typographer's function to be creative in providing meaning to the text. However, regardless of subject or intent, every text requires that the typographer brings his/her craft skills to bear.

All of this only emphasizes the arbitrary relationship between words and things. Only onomatopoeic words such as crash and splash come close to this, and even these differ from language to language. Language is the result of an agreement between people to use words in a predetermined way. The problem is, as we have already seen, words themselves are imprecise. Interpretation of the meaning of any text is an essential part of the reading experience and it is the responsibility of the typographer to ensure that this is possible.

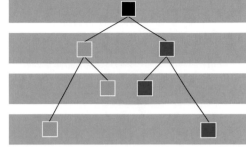

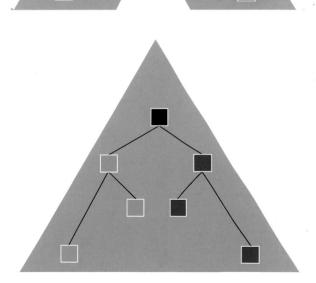

Providing clarity

Left: *Univers* was intended to have universal appeal and utility. It was certainly made universally available: hand composition, mechanical typesetting, and filmsetting were all included. The *Univers* family is arranged here according to width, weight, and posture. The rational nature of the typeface is reflected in this famous diagram. *Univers* was designed by Adrian Frutiger and distributed in 1957.

Above: From the *Nuremberg Chronicle*, printed in Germany by Anton Koberger in 1493. This is a book of monumental ambition. The text was intended to be a total world history: biblical, classical, and traditional interlinked by a complex, all-embracing range of illustrations often connected by decorated coiled vines. Illustrated is "The sanctification of the seventh day."

Right: Diagrams illustrating the personnel structure of a company in terms of hierarchic levels, geographic hierarchies, and the whole. From "Dynamic information display," *Visible Language*, XIX, No. 2, 1985.

Graphology

There are many ways of making typography function and although these share many typographic characteristics, they have developed separate traditions and disciplines of practice and study. Graphologists may provide the means of studying these interconnected areas afresh and bring new insights into their specialist expertise.

So, graphology is possibly the theoretical area of study closest to that which typographers might reasonably consider to be their territory. Principally, it involves the study of marks and/or symbols that have been devised to communicate language in a visual form, the means and resources of the linear writing system, including the methods and the rules that govern their use. (Its counterpart in the study of speech might be phonology.) However, as graphology has developed out of the study of language (for example, by people who are not practicing visual communicators), it has fostered an entirely independent terminology.

In graphology, each symbol is called a grapheme: the smallest units in a writing system capable of causing an alteration of meaning. Of course, the main graphemes of English are the 26 letters that make up the alphabet. Others include the various punctuation marks and special symbols. The form that a grapheme takes can vary. For example, the grapheme "a" can appear as A, a, *a*, and indeed, in many other forms depending on the typeface (or calligraphic, handwriting, sign-writing, stonecutting) style. Each of these possible forms is known as a graph and when graphs are studied as variants of a grapheme, they are called allographs.

The range of variation in graphic and hand-written practice is displayed in the representation of modern languages. Most notably, languages vary in the direction in which they are written,

left to right (e.g. English) and right to left (e.g. Arabic), top to bottom (e.g. Chinese), and bottom to top (e.g. some forms of Ancient Greek). More than one direction might be involved, as in the boustrophedon method of writing lines in alternate directions (see below). A language may use several different conventions simultaneously, such as the common use of a vertical arrangement on the spines of books, with a horizontal arrangement on the cover.

The tools and technology, the surface or substrate, all have an influence on the kind of communication systems that develop. In terms of graphic expression, hand tools have progressed from reeds, styluses, quills, brushes, steel points, fountain pens, ballpoint pens, and fiber-tipped pens. Mechanized or semimechanized methods have included printing from wood (woodcut and wood engraving), metal (etching, letterpress, lithography, and typewriters), and computers. Many surfaces have been used, such as bone, rock, wood, clay, wax, cloth, papyrus, parchment, paper, film, and electronic monitor screens.

Carved graphemes
Below: This stone inscription from the Forum in Rome is in Boustrophedon script, which is written in alternate directions, left to right and then right to left, etc. Carved around 600 BC, it is the oldest known Latin inscription.

Right: Graffiti in the soft red brickwork of a house, clearly carved when serif type was the norm.

Legibility

Legibility and readability are not the same. Legibility certainly influences readability and vice versa, but to understand how one influences the other it is necessary to consider them separately. The degree to which a typeface is legible is entirely dependent on the designer of the typeface, whereas readability is largely the province of the typographer.

Legibility is the degree to which individual letters can be distinguished from each other. Such letterforms are designed to present themselves in a clear and concise manner. This does not necessarily mean that a highly legible typeface cannot also have distinguishing characteristics—some of the most legible examples, such as Johnston's font for the London Underground, *Underground*, are also among our most distinctive faces—but it does mean that in the most demanding of environments, their individual forms remain highly visible, essential for those passengers for whom the station names are unfamiliar.

Generally, the most legible typefaces are those with larger, open or closed inner spaces. This inevitably means a generous x-height. However, if the x-height is large, then, as a consequence, the ascenders and descenders will be relatively short. This not only affects the legibility of individual characters (commonly causing, among other pairs, the h and n, and the i and l to be confused with each other), but also makes the recognition of word shapes more difficult.

Large counters (the enclosed and partly enclosed spaces within letters) are particularly important in helping to distinguish between some of the most commonly used characters—e, a, and s; and c and o. These lack distinguishing characteristics (they have no ascenders or descenders, and are all of a similar width and general shape) and contain similarly sized counters. There is little doubt that, owing to frequency of use, the most helpful aid to legibility in any given typeface is the provision of a generous "eye" for the e and enclosed a generous counter for the a.

The characters most commonly mistaken for each other are i, j, and l; and f and t. In many typefaces the l is also almost identical to the numeral 1, and the letter O to the zero 0. Relative legibility is also affected by the individual size of letters; for instance, m and w are intrinsically more legible than i or l simply because they have a larger presence.

Having considered legibility in terms of distinctive word shapes and definition of structural elements of letters (ascenders, descenders, counters, and serifs), there is a third aspect—that of type size. Using a small size of type, perhaps 6pt or less, will deny the text to a large proportion of the targeted audience. As discussed earlier, when a small size is unavoidable, then its deficiencies can be minimized by the use of a typeface with a large x-height.

Finally, another condition which governs legibility is tonal contrast, for example, between word and substrate. Naturally, where word and background tone are close, legibility will be affected. What is less obvious is that a text printed black will be more legible on a matte, off-white (cream) colored paper than a gloss high white. The mix of surface shine and high contrast can prove both irksome and tiring.

EAST FINCHLEY

Recognition and distinction
Left: *London Underground*, designed by Edward Johnston, is a distinctive face that can be recognized in the most demanding of environments. Its individual letterforms remain highly visible: essential for those passengers for whom the names are unfamiliar.
Below: Albatross was an English-language series begun in Hamburg with typography by Hans Mardersteig. Its appearence owed much to the Tauchnitz Editions (see page 39). Penguin books, launched in 1936, used the same format and a rather similar name. The design of the early Penguin Books, by Edward Young, was simple and striking. *Bliss* was published in 1935 and *A Safety Match* in 1938.

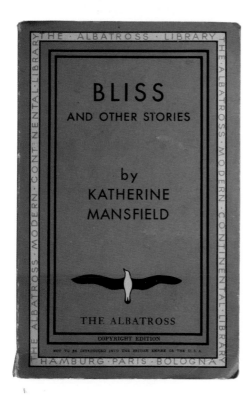

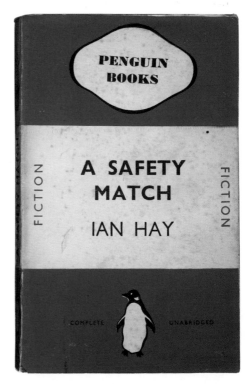

Readability

In the early years of a child's reading development, the attainment of mechanical skills is gained initially with the aid of a finger to help left to right progression and accurate return sweeps from the end of one line on to the beginning of the next. By reminding ourselves of what were the perfunctory difficulties of childhood reading, we give ourselves an insight into the fundamental mechanics and principles of setting text.

Alongside this is the recognition of words and the functions of spaces and accompanying punctuation. These essential skills are gained with great effort, but they must, as soon as possible, become automatic; eventually, the reader should not normally be aware of the activity of reading at all.

We also learn the various reading skills necessary for acquiring differing kinds of information. Documents such as directories, catalogs, indices, encyclopedias, flyers, forms, junk mail, etc. require an adjustment to learned reading skills. In effect, we learn how to find and select, and how to respond.

The ability to read quickly and to be able to select in order to use time efficiently depends very much on the order and arrangement of type being normal. Surprises are disruptive to the mechanics of reading.

Despite the thousands of typefaces available today, those typefaces most appropriate for textual setting fall into a narrow category and, on the whole, follow a traditional pattern. Fonts designed to incorporate old face characteristics are traditionally considered easiest to read (*Caslon*), transitional are less easy (*Baskerville*), and modern (*Bodoni*) are hardest to read (see opposite). Of course, all are normally perfectly legible, and with careful application all can be made readable (although some less efficiently than others).[1]

Today, sans serifs (type without serifs) vary so much in form that one cannot generalize about their readability. The rule was that sans-serif type was less efficient for reading, but better for legibility—initial character recognition—hence its use in early reading books and for signage. Notable efforts have been made to design sans-serif fonts with calligraphic characterisitics, providing a distinct left to right emphasis. *Foundry Form Sans*, the font used for the text you are reading now has such an emphasis.

Lowercase characters, unlike capitals, are designed to work in close proximity with each other, providing an uninterrupted visual flow, a dynamic left to right momentum, the idea being that the reader's eye is able to skim, without hesitation, along a line of type, recognizing the essential and distinctively unique shapes of each individual word. Consistency of style must be adhered to if the reader is to feel comfortable. It is not surprising then that the rule for good textual setting is that it should be so predictable, so normal, as to be invisible to the reader (while for display type the opposite must apply). The oft-repeated truism "a type which is read most is read easiest" only serves to emphasize that the appearance of textual setting, once established, must remain predictable.

Selecting a typeface
Choice of typeface will depend on several factors, including economic, color (the overall tone of gray when set as text), and which characteristics (visual, cultural, historic) best suit the subject matter. In the twentieth century, each change of technology has brought with it new typefaces and the adaptation of older typefaces, some more successful than others. The characteristics commonly

required of a readable typeface are openness of form, prominent ascenders and descenders, modeled serifs, and directional momentum.

Top: An example of a Modern-style newspaper typeface.
Middle: The same typeface as it appears under a microscope, printed on newsprint.
Bottom: *Excelsior* has open counters designed to avoid ink traps. (John E Allen, *Newspaper Makeup*, Harpers & Brothers, 1936.)

This is *Caslon*

This is *Baskerville*

This is *Bodoni*

Spelling

The Latin alphabet of 26 characters relates well to spoken Latin, but not so well to English. A match between spoken English would require an alphabet in excess of 40 characters. The disparity between English speech-sound and English notation has to be alleviated by a quirky use of spelling. The widely cited figure is that only 75% of English spelling is predictable. Unfortunately, a high proportion of the remaining 25% of words are among the most frequently used in everyday written and spoken language.

Portraying speech in a written or printed form requires ingenuity. When emphasis or hesitation, sadness or enthusiasm needs to be expressed, spelling can be altered, for example "what a byoo-ootiful song." This expression can be heightened considerably by the use of italics, "what a *byoo-ootiful* song" or, in circumstances outside a text, by the use of scale, color, and typographic form.

There are six or seven large dictionaries of the English language in daily use. They do not agree on the spelling of every word because spellings evolve as language evolves. There is also the question of national preferences—English dictionaries retain the u in, for example, honour and colour, and have a preference for s in words that North American dictionaries spell with a z, such as: authorise and harmonise. This book uses the American *Merriam Webster's Dictionary*. There are some words, such as theatre/theater, which appear in both forms in dictionaries on both sides of the Atlantic. Preference concerning compounds is also often different: co-ordinated/coordinated.

Program/programme is an example of a word that is currently changing because of the global influence of digital media and the dominance in that field by North American companies. In North America it is always program but in Britain, both spellings are currently in use: programme in conjunction with media such as television, radio, or to describe a plan of events, but program when referring to computers and computer software.

Similarly, fount was the word used to describe a complete set of typographic sorts: uppercase and lowercase, numerals, punctuation, etc. Font is

The Mock Turtle sighed deeply, and began, in a voice sometimes choked with sobs, to sing this:

" *Beautiful Soup, so rich and green,*
Waiting in a hot tureen!
Who for such dainties would not stoop?
Soup of the evening, beautiful Soup!
Soup of the evening, beautiful Soup!
Beau—ootiful Soo—oop!
Beau—ootiful Soo—oop!
Soo—oop of the e—e—evening,
Beautiful, beautiful Soup!

the North American spelling and it is this that has come to dominate, again due to North American origins of the computers that most people use.

Variations of British and American spelling and of compounded and separated words (rail road, rail-road, railroad) are of little importance to many readers. Toleration is conceded to national mannerisms that have been confirmed by their usage. Dictionaries, like typesetting manuals, follow rather than create or sustain convention.

How faithfully should a typographer follow the copy as presented? It might seem appropriate, indeed professional, to correct a client's text, but this is always done at risk. Unconventional punctuation and words that do not appear in any dictionary are common occurrences. Although the author is the expert in the subject of the text, the typographer is responsible for the presentation of the text in its printed form and so any doubts must be addressed as part of a fully structured strategy of proofreading and client checking agreed at the outset by all concerned.

In the 1960s through to the 1980s, the excellent typesetters (many being ex-compositors from the print trade) could be depended on to fix (or query, at least) such details as accents for foreign words and proper names, and oddly spelt geographical names. They would enter en or em dashes and, where appropriate, replace numerals in running text with words, and so on. Most typographers consider themselves capable of proofreading, but few (very few) have the appropriate knowledge, skills, and the very particular, tediously pedantic attitude required to do the job well. Proofreading is a skill quite separate from typography, although proofreaders who were previously employed in the printing industry are especially prized! Proofreading is equivalent to quality control in the manufacturing and service industries.

Portraying speech
Far left: Creative spelling and appropriate use of em dashes. Lewis Carroll, *Alice in Wonderland*, Hodder & Stoughton, London, 1982.
Below: A good proofreader and/or editor will do far more than simply correct spellings.

Variations of British and American spelling and of compounded and separated words (rail road, rail-road, railroad) are of little importance to many readers. Toleration is conceded to national mannerisms that have been confirmed by their usage. Dictionaries, like typesetting manuals, *follow* rather than ~~creating or even upholding~~ convention.

create or sustain

Alphabets

With the Latin alphabet, there is a direct correspondence between the marks written or printed on paper and the sounds in Latin which they represent. Instead of several thousand logograms, as required in Chinese writing, alphabetic systems need only a relatively small number of symbols which have been adapted to a wide range of languages.

Most alphabets contain somewhere between 24 and 40 characters/symbols, but the relative complexity or simplicity of individual sound systems will lead to varying numbers of symbols.

The evolution of the textual (lowercase) alphabet grew from the capital alphabet by way of a transitional uncial alphabet (used especially in Greek and Latin manuscripts). Attempting to write quickly using capitals only, uncials became an interim stage, a compromise.

Textuals as a full and true lowercase were eventually adopted possibly because the text was easier to write with haste by the scribe, and because the output gave a unique shape to every written word.

It is often stated that the Latin alphabet consists of just 26 (originally 24) characters, but if you include uppercase and lowercase, accented (diacritical) characters, continental consonants and vowels, the Latin alphabet grows to at least 260. If, to this, are added small caps; lining and nonlining numerals; punctuation; Hebrew and Greek characters; special technical and mathematical symbols; as well as the usual range of ligatures, then the number of "sorts" can easily exceed 400. If to this are added four weights (for example, light, book, medium, and bold), the number well exceeds 1,600.

**Alternative alphabets
Above:** Alphabets such as these were used as symbols for alchemical elements and as a code to conceal knowledge.

Right: Magic figures in a Thai inscription from Kiang-Mai, North Thailand, serving as protection for the city. *Etudes diverses*, Vol. 2. Paris, 1898.

In the eighteenth century, a hand-compositor had 152 compartments in the two (upper and lower) cases holding what was then considered to be the basic number of sorts in a given font. When more sorts were required additional cases would be used. In 1455, Gutenberg's cases held 290 sorts—all of a single typeface at one size (no accents) which he used to typeset his *42-Line Bible*.

Lowercase italic letters are traditionally narrower than lowercase roman letters and generally slope by varying degrees toward the right. Importantly, they also have certain details that are reminiscent of the cursive handwriting from which they are derived. Various sorts of sloping or quasi-cursive roman capitals have been designed in an attempt to match their lowercase equivalents. Although these might work reasonably well in combination with italic lowercase, italic caps generally do not work well when used exclusively together due to the necessary adjustments to the diagonals required in accommodating the slope of the letters.

As the industrial revolution took hold in the nineteenth century, large-scale manufacturers and service providers looked to the power of print to advertise, for example, products, transport, and entertainment. Bold, condensed, and expanded typefaces were designed and manufactured specifically for the purpose of attracting attention. Some of these "novelty" faces (see pages 122–127) were later adapted for use in textual setting and today we expect at least three, and sometimes five, weights.

There are several other systems of writing, usually devised for a purpose for which the normal alphabet is too complex or too time-consuming. Shorthand is a method of writing at speed using a mixture of symbols and abbreviations, and is best known for its use by journalists and secretaries. There is nothing new about such systems; Samuel Pepys famously wrote his diaries using a shorthand system devised in the early seventeenth century.[1]

Composing rooms
Woodcut of a Chinese composing room, 1777. The movable type was made of wood: metal was too expensive.

Punctuation

A normal font of type will usually include about 24 signs of punctuation. The punctuation we use today has its roots in rhetoric. The terms comma, colon, and period (also commonly called a full point or full stop) were used by Aristophanes to formulate a means of discourse for rhetoric where they were used to establish rhythmical units of speech.

As a source of rhetoric rather than grammatical cues, punctuation served to regulate pace and provide emphasis to particular phrases rather than just marking the logical structure of sentences. Punctuation, therefore, would be positioned wherever the speaker should make a momentary pause, and provide breathing cues.

However, after the invention of printing, grammarians began to base their punctuation marks on structure rather than the spoken word. For example, the comma became a mark of separation, the semicolon worked as a joint between independent clauses, the colon indicated grammatical discontinuity. Writing became separated from speech, and the proliferation of printing played an essential role in formalizing the rules about punctuation and every other aspect of grammar.

But although structure is the strongest rationale today, punctuation remains a largely intuitive part of writing. A writer can still choose several ways to punctuate, any of which will be correct, although each will provide a slightly different rhythm and expression. In this way, the rhetorical roots of punctuation still function. For example, in speech, a rising and falling speech pattern is widely interpreted as expressing a contrast between questioning (a rising inflection) and stating (a flat or falling inflection). In writing, such contrasts of inflection are attempted by means of punctuation (illustrated opposite).

Short and long pauses
In his *Authors' and Printers' Dictionary* (Oxford University Press, 1938), F. Howard Collins begins his entry concerning punctuation "The chief difficulty lies in the use of the comma, semicolon, colon and period. In general they correspond, in the order named, to shorter or longer pauses as heard in correct speech; but no absolute rules can be given." As a consequence, nine pages of concise explanation are required. (The cover of this book is reproduced on page 39.)

Oh really?
Oh, really?
Oh really!
Oh *really!*

Written inflections
A rising and falling speech pattern is widely interpreted as expressing a contrast between questioning (a rising inflection) and stating (a flat or falling inflection). In writing, such contrasts are suggested by means of punctuation. (The optional use of italic also helps.)

Punctuation 91

Numerals

Methods of recording numbers appeared in cultures long before attempts to formulate a record of spoken language. Numerical notation provides a profound visual statement about how cultures have attempted to depict order.

Although the formalistic nature of writing is generally considered secondary to the intuitive nature of the spoken word, early written representations of numbers show that the choice of numerical symbols helped to structure spoken language and give form to its written language.

In the general communication of numbers—bartering, counting, and sharing—it is common to use objects such as sticks, stones, beads, fingers, and other parts of the body, rather than graphic marks. The simplest form of recording a number of items is to make a mark for each one: a tally. A straight line, cut or drawn, is almost always the preferred mark presumably because of its distinct variance with the generally random characteristics of nature. It's *man*-made! However, larger numbers recorded this way cannot be read, in fact they have to be counted, which is time-consuming. To alleviate this, marks can be grouped into fives, tens, or twenties, etc. Linguists call this kind of activity indexical. Such marks are augmented by operational codes, for example: $+ - \times \div$ and $=$.

The reason most cultures use number sequences organized into groups of 5, 10, or 20 is simply the convenience of hands and feet, fingers and toes for counting. The word digit derives from digitus, Latin for "finger and toe."

Roman numerals were the dominant written numbers in Europe until the rise of the Hindu-Arabic system. The Roman system used the principle of ordering and grouping to the power of 10: I X C M; 1, 10, 100, 1,000. These are sub-divided by five: V L D; 5, 50, 500. The figure III represents three: one one one, whereas the figure CCC represents 300: 100 100 100.

The graphic symbols used by the Romans could be derived from tally marks. In this case, it is possible that the Roman alphabet is, at least in part, a development of the numerical system.

Arabic numerals entered the scribal tradition in Europe in the thirteenth century. Before that (and for many purposes afterwards) European

$$+ - \times \div = \# \wedge \approx \,^{\circ}$$

$$\Delta \Sigma \geq \infty \int \leq \mu \neq \Omega$$

$$^{a}\,^{o}\,\partial\,\%_{o}\,\Pi \pm / \sqrt{}$$

Augmentative symbols
Left: Mathematical and other symbols used with numerals: plus, minus, multiplied by, divided by, equal to, number (USA), to the power of, equivalent to, degrees, increment, summation, epsilon, greater than/equal to, infinity, integral, less than/equal to, prefix multiplier, not equal to, volume, ordinal a, ordinal o, partial difference, per thousand, product of, plus or minus, divided by (fraction bar), square root.

Roman numerals
Right: Roman numerals are commonly used where there is a need to differentiate between two sets of numbers. A contents page is a typical example because each chapter has a sequential number and a page number. H.E.V. Gillham, *Printing: a craft for schools*, Pitman Publishing Corporation, 1933.

scribes used roman numerals, written in capitals when they occur among capital letters and in lowercase when among lowercase letters.

When Arabic numerals became part of the Roman alphabet, they were also given lowercase and uppercase forms. Lowercase numerals are called nonlining numerals, text numerals, hanging numerals, lowercase numerals, and old-style numerals. Uppercase numerals are called lining numerals, titling numerals, and ranging numerals. In the twentieth century, lining numerals were also briefly called modern numerals (as opposed to old-style numerals).

Nonlining numerals were the norm in European typography between 1540 and 1800, but before the beginning of the nineteenth century, and coinciding with a period of rapid industrial and commercial growth, the British punchcutter Richard Austin had cut and successfully marketed a font of three-quarter-high lining numerals for the type founder John Bell. These single-height letters were preferred in documents where clear, clean, horizontal, and vertical lines of numbers were required, for example on price lists and transport timetables. Other founders quickly adjusted their own lining numerals to full cap-height. Lining numerals were further popularized by the manufacturers of typewriters, who presumably chose them over nonlining numerals because of the various forms of tabular work required for company accounts.

However, early in the twentieth century, there was a revival of the calligraphic-influenced letterforms of the Renaissance, and nonlining numerals found their way back into book typography. Since then, nonlining numerals have appeared irregularly, depending on the whim of the type designer and/or the foundry. Today the situation is much improved and the better digital foundries now regularly offer both lining and nonlining numerals with many fonts.

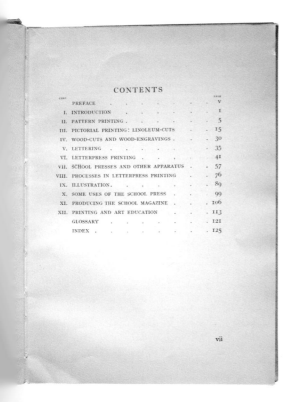

Spatial cues

So much of what might be termed the craft of typography is about the manipulation of space. Whereas the reader concentrates on the letterforms (or, more precisely, the words they construct), the typographer is constantly judging the spaces between the letterforms, words, lines of words, perhaps paragraphs, and the marginal spaces around the text.

Space, along with punctuation, is used to break a text into meaningful segments. Sometimes spatial and typographic cues are combined, for example, in the bold heading at the top of this page. A text that is clearly segmented or "opened up" is easier to comprehend, revise, and research. It is, therefore, common in texts of a technical nature for the paragraphs to be separated by a one-line space, whereas paragraphs in fictional texts are more discreet, generally indicated with a short indent at the beginning of all paragraphs (except the first).

The effect of a space within a page of text generally causes the reader to pause, and so, for the typographer, it can be a very effective way of providing emphasis, a sense of structure, and a control of rhythm. For the same reason, interword spaces must be closely monitored to ensure that where a smooth flow of uninterrupted information is required, spaces are as even as possible. The amount of space allocated between all character pairs is designed by the type designer as an integral part of a font. Nevertheless, "problem" character pairs, typically involving the T and W (for example, Ta, not Ta) should always be checked.

At textual sizes, it is rarely necessary to adjust the spaces between lowercase characters, but capitals of any size need to be carefully inspected (for example, LI LY not LILY).

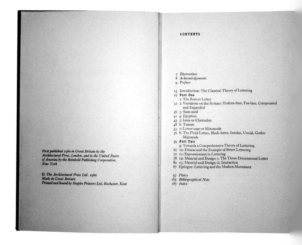

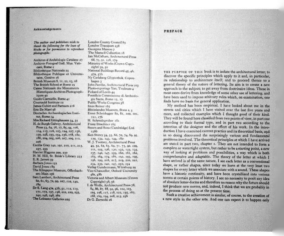

Space around text
The hierarchy of information is cued by space as much as by size or weight of type. Nicolette Gray, *Lettering on Buildings*, The Architectural Press, London, 1960.

The decision concerning word space depends on several factors, firstly the relative width of the typeface (the narrower, or more condensed the typeface, the less word space required) and the "fit" (the relative intercharacter space allocated by the type designer). The decision might also depend on the kind of text.

There has been a general tendency in new typefaces (including recuts of "classic" typefaces) for a slightly more condensed form (as well as a larger x-height) in an attempt to be more economical with space while maintaining readability. Along with this slightly more condensed form has come a slightly tighter fit. A result of this tighter appearance of textual material is that spaces following a full point and comma tend to appear too conspicuous because of the "additional" space contributed to the word

space by the area above the punctuation mark. Most typefaces look and read better for having these spaces slightly reduced.

Because of the inflectional power of the ! and the ? it is often good practice to add a little extra space between the previous word and the exclamation mark, and between the previous word and the question mark. After all, the inflectional power applies to the whole exclamation, the whole question, and not merely the last word! (Not word!)

Intercharacter spaces
Above: The space between characters and words depends on the amount of space *inside* characters which, in turn, depends on the character width. The counter of the *Baskerville* Q is far wider than that of the *Bodoni* Q. The "fit" (the amount of inter-character space) is allocated by the type designer.

Internal spaces
Right: Even when tracked at minus 5, these characters are still "close but not touching" and yet are clearly too close for comfortable reading. The spaces between the characters must balance with the spaces within the characters.

tight but not touching	+6
tight but not touching	+5
tight but not touching	+4
tight but not touching	+3
tight but not touching	+2
tight but not touching	+1
tight but not touching	0
tight but not touching	-1
tight but not touching	-2
tight but not touching	-3
tight but not touching	-4
tight but not touching	-5
tight but not touching	-6

Linear texts

The typographer's organization of a message should reflect the author's intent by determining the reading, searching, or looking strategy of the user. The wording linear text[1] is used here to describe those texts that generally consist of a continuous flow of words albeit with interruptions caused by line endings, paragraphs, chapters, sections or parts, and page turning. (Nonlinear texts, such as lists and matrices, as well as various uses of display type, are dealt with from page 110.)

The word text has a definite ring about it. Text has status; departing from a text means digressing, improvising, or embroidering. The lawmaking of governments and legislatures is based on the reading or interpretation of the text; the administration of justice and the regulation of institutional affairs turn on the interpretation of text. Apart from its use in religious sermons ("I take as my text …"), text is generally associated with sustained stretches of written language. Thus, the text of a book is referred to in contrast to anything that is not part of the continuous prose (i.e., nonlinear): folios, footnotes, captions, running heads, references, index, contents, etc.

When the effectiveness of the design of a text is assessed, the lack of empirical knowledge about what actually happens when a reader reads means that we tend to fall back on a mixture of personal esthetic and functional preferences.[2] It might be that esthetics are, in fact, an important element in ensuring that a text is readable. In fact, it is probable that the reader will find a text that is easiest to read is also, esthetically, the most pleasing. That both form and function should be based on "fit for purpose" is a long-held convention in typography.

A work of fiction generally consists of a continuous flow of words, with minimal pauses for paragraphs and broken only by each new

chapter. Textbooks, manuals, catalogs, and other non-fiction books, however, are generally broken down into many more parts, not only by chapters, but also with sections and subsections. Then there are captions, footnotes, block quotations, and, more likely than not, line spaces between paragraphs. To enable the reader to recognize the hierarchic structure, each "signpost" requires its own typographic identity, position, and form. Every layer must be consistently applied, distinct yet inexorably a part of the whole. Hierarchy articulates by providing such visual cues.

There are also visual cues in the shape of the text. Although a horizontal motion is predominant in handwriting and for early readers, a tall column of text suggests an expectation of reading fluency, and, therefore, a more sophisticated, more demanding content. A very narrow column, however, is associated with disposable information, perhaps lacking in substance or, even, credibility. (I suspect, largely owing to the impermanent nature of newspapers.)

The variety of media and guises in which text appears today has made the potential reader aware of the prevailing textual codes. This is, in

Visual cues
Below left: The *36-Line Bible*, printed by Fust and Schoeffer in Mainz in 1462. The text is based very much on the *Gutenberg* (or *42-Line*) *Bible*, printed circa 1455. Visual cues to help the reader through the largely unbroken text are provided by hand-applied highlights on the capitals at the beginning of sentences.

Annotated texts
Annotations were common in texts even before printing was introduced to Europe, but became particularly popular with the growth of universities during the Renaissance.
Below: Here both texts are justified. The original text, typically being the larger, requires a wider measure. The common problems of applying justified setting to such a narrow measure are clearly visible. In particular, the fractured appearance of the left-hand column and the holes in the right-hand column. Martin Gardner, *The Annotated Alice*, Penguin Books, 2001.

. It was characteristic of Carroll, ith his love of sharp contrast, to pen his sequel on an indoor, mid-inter scene. (The previous book ens out of doors on a warm May ernoon.) The wintry weather also rmonizes with the wintry symbols age and approaching death that er into its prefatory and terminal ems. The preparation for a bonfire d Alice's remark "Do you know at tomorrow is, Kitty?" suggest t the date was November 4, the y before Guy Fawkes Day. (The iday was annually celebrated at rist Church with a huge bonfire in kwater Quadrangle.) This is sup-ted by Alice's statement to the ite Queen (Chapter 5) that she is ctly seven and one half years old, Alice Liddell's birthday was May nd the previous trip to Wonder-l occurred on May 4, when Alice umably was exactly seven (see e 6, Chapter 7 of the previous k). As Robert Mitchell says in a r, May 4 and November 4, being months apart, are two dates that d not be further separated.

his leaves open the question of her the year is 1859 (when Alice ally was seven), 1860, 1861, or when Carroll told and wrote the story of Alice's first ad-re. November 4, 1859, was a y. In 1860 it was Sunday, in Monday, and in 1862 Tuesday. ast date seems the most plaus-a view of Alice's remark to the (in the next paragraph) that that she is saving up her punish-until a week from Wednesday. s. Mavis Baitey, in her booklet s *Adventures in Oxford* (A Pictorial Guide, 1980), argues e day was March 10, 1863, the ng day of the Prince of Wales. occasion was celebrated at d with bonfires and fireworks, his diary Carroll tells of taking

kiss to make it understand that it was in disgrace. "Really, Dinah ought to have taught you better manners! You *ought*, Dinah, you know you ought!" she added, looking reproachfully at the old cat, and speaking in as cross a voice as she could manage—and then she scrambled back into the arm-chair, taking the kitten and the worsted with her, and began winding up the ball again. But she didn't get on very fast, as she was talking all the time, sometimes to the kitten, and sometimes to herself. Kitty sat very demurely on her knee, pretending to watch the progress of the winding, and now and then putting out one paw and gently touching the ball, as if it would be glad to help if it might.

"Do you know what to-morrow is, Kitty?" Alice began. "You'd have guessed if you'd been up in the window with me—only Dinah was making you tidy, so you couldn't. I was watching the boys getting in sticks for the bonfire!—and it wants plenty of sticks, Kitty! Only it got so cold, and it snowed so, they had to leave off. Never mind, Kitty, we'll go and see the bonfire to-morrow." Here Alice wound two or three turns of the worsted round the kitten's neck, just to see how it would look: this led to a scramble, in which the ball rolled down upon the floor, and yards and yards of it got unwound again.

"Do you know, I was so angry, Kitty," Alice went on, as soon as they were comfortably set-tled again, "when I saw all the mischief you had been doing, I was very nearly opening the win-dow, and putting you out into the snow! And you'd have deserved it, you little mischievous darling! What have you got to say for yourself? Now don't interrupt me!" she went on, holding up one finger. "I'm going to tell you all your faults. Number one: you squeaked twice while Dinah was washing your face this morning. Now you ca'n't deny it, Kitty: I heard you! What's that you say?" (pretending that the kitten was speak-ing). "Her paw went into your eye? Well, that's *your* fault, for keeping your eyes open—if you'd shut them tight up, it wouldn't have happened. Now don't make any more excuses, but listen! Number two: you pulled Snowdrop[2] away by the tail just as I had put down the saucer of milk

Alice on an evening tour through the university: "It was delightful to see the thorough abandonment with which Alice enjoyed the whole thing." However, Carroll's diary for March 9 and 10 makes no mention of the snow Alice speaks of. However, Mrs. Baitey's conjecture is supported by the fact that in England snow is very rare in early November and quite common in March.

2. Snowdrop was the name of a kit-ten belonging to one of Carroll's early child-friends, Mary MacDonald. Mary was the daughter of Carroll's good friend George MacDonald, the Scottish poet and novelist, and author of such well-known children's fan-tasies as *The Princess and the Goblin* and *At the Back of the North Wind*. The MacDonald children were in part responsible for Carroll's decision to publish *Alice's Adventures in Wonderland*. To test the story's general appeal, he asked Mrs. Mac-Donald to read the manuscript to her children. The reception was enthusi-astic. Greville, age six (who later recalled the occasion in his book *George MacDonald and His Wife*), declared that there ought to be sixty thousand copies of it.

Kitty and Snowdrop, the black and white kittens, reflect the chess-board's black and white squares, and the red and white pieces of the book's chess game.

part, because "modern reading is faster reading,"[3] and the publishing industries recognize the importance of a potential reader/buyer being able to decide rapidly what a text has to offer. Typographic design is employed to make clear at a glance where the text stands among other texts. The fact that the appearance of the text alone has this communicative potential can be of great value.

The task of the typographer is often likened to that of a theater director, using actors with which to interpret a script, or the orchestra conductor, using musicians to interpret a score. I feel a little uncomfortable with such grandiose comparisons, probably because the typographer generally plays a quieter, more deferential role. There is, undeniably, the opportunity to use knowledge and technical skills creatively, but utilized to provide a text that is both coherent and pertinent above all else. The appearance of text establishes the care with which it is presented, its authenticity, and its persuasive power. It certainly represents the skill and creative sensitivity of the typographer who made the text visible. Even if the reader remains oblivious to the fact.

Linear arrangements
Catalog for an exhibition in which the introduction, made up of a series of linear texts, has been arranged so that it can be read in a number of interconnected ways. Printed in gray and black. Designed by Alan Robertson for the Whanganui Regional Museum, New Zealand, 2005.

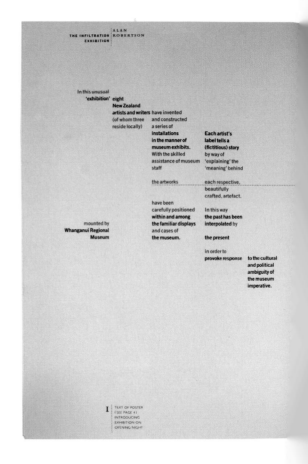

Text and image placement
This relentless text begins on the cover and flows over the black-and-white images that run throughout the book. The element of chance (for example, when and where the text happens to be readable) is an essential part of Rauschenberg's work. Andrew Forge, *Rauschenberg*, Harry Abrams, New York, 1969.

Out of Phase

Imagine a museum where the walkie-talkie art-appreciation gadgets some-how got the numbers of the pictures mixed: what would the pictures look like? Would it not be possible, in the absence of the familiar smooth agreement between the object and the idea, to find new spaces, new air to breathe, a new relationship with those objects?

When he was in London in 1964 with the Merce Cunningham Dance Com-pany, Rauschenberg visited the zoo. Afterward he gave an account of something that he had seen there. Two old people, a man and a woman, had been exploring the contents of a litter basket. When one found something he showed it or offered it to the other. The trouble was that by the time the old lady had straightened up and unwrapped and identified her find, the other was doubled up with his head in the basket, and by the time he was up to look, she was down again. Rauschenberg had been too far off to hear what they were saying, but he had watched it as an energetic though creaking performance, never quite in phase, of searching and showing and not looking, and crossing hands as if to cross hands but actually be-cause the one was not looking when the other was showing. Showing never com-municated, not that looking ever simply looking but was also turning away or being slow or gentle.

A gesture that I receive as a communicative sign has little value, at least not when I am looking at the message, but when it is to the pristine reality. This constant reality is simple folk all the way to the flick, to the pictorial mouthing of a man that recognize the sign, there, beyond us, and a kind of around the movement itself. Unharnessed, it seems to have room to breathe and stretch.

The more clearly I identify the cause for a person's behavior, the way he stands or walks his arms about or moves his eyes, the less room there is in my mind for whatever else needs to be bearing on him, or whatever else his demeanor might mean. This is most obvious when he is reacting spontaneously and single-mindedly; at a tender face or a boring subject I am hardly likely to speculate about the grimace that calls my neighbor's a gesture that flails the air. But split off from the indeterminate, it is the *prete* that turns the nichts of Giotto's anger, the caption that dignifies the statesman's bonhomie. Much is lost in this precise pinning of cause and effect and much is

Justified setting

There are several different kinds of reading tasks—verification, search, comprehension, and entertainment—and different layouts for different kinds of text.

The overall shape and form of text, as it is commonly presented today, has been influenced by several factors, and some of these originally had little to do with reading. Irregular right edges of columns were often used by medieval scribes. It was only in the latter part of the Middle Ages that the scribes of the Gothic book, whose love of decoration and regular patterns led them to manipulate texts, by any means possible, into solid, straight-edged (justified) rectangles.

To establish such a regular shape, the spaces between each word of a line will vary with those interword spaces on the next to ensure that the end of the last word on each line finishes at the same place. Studies into the psychological and physiological aspects of reading, as well as our own reading experience tells us that even spaces between words are a major aid to readability. If this is the case, why do so many publishers still justify texts?

Columns of text, in themselves, normally have no linguistic or semantic function. To achieve as even as possible interword spacing throughout a linear text, little attempt is made to match line breaks with linguistic or semantic boundaries. Consequently, when learning to read we quickly recognize that line endings are indiscriminate, interrupting sentences, clauses, phrases, and even words (which then have to be hyphenated) and therefore, are irrelevant to any meanings within the text.

The arbitrary nature of breaking linear text into lines is, in fact, helpful to the reader precisely because it is meaningless and can therefore be ignored. Justified setting confers neutrality on the appearance of text. The argument for justification is that the shape of the text varies so little from page to page, the reader has less to distract them from the act of reading.

Columns and grids
A two-column grid with very small margins. Throughout this book the text takes up just the right-hand column, leaving the left-hand column for headings, captions, reference material, diagrams, and illustrations.
John Lewis, *Typography: Basic Principles*, Studio Books, London, 1963.

Justifying justified setting
Top right: Justified setting designed to reflect the dark humor of the subject. *TypoGraphic* 63, HDR, 2005.
Right: As the author, John Cage, explains "The excessively small type is an attempt to emphasize the intentionally pontifical character of this lecture." John Cage, *Silence*, Calder and Boyars, London, 1968.

Olaf's extrovert behaviour and outspoken opinions continued throughout his career, garnering him some occasional critics as well as loyal supporters. Olaf hadn't heard of political correctness but if he had, it wouldn't make a lot of difference. His natural exuberance and humour drove him full tilt at whatever he was pursuing. During an annual gathering of German designers in the mid 60s in a southern mountain resort, Olaf was a principal organiser. I was one of four judges (alongside Wim Crouwel, Albert Hollenstein and Helmut Lortz) and we were working hard on selecting the awards for the best in the show. After a couple of days with Olaf noisily rousing everyone at 6.30am by banging on our doors with shouts of Raus–Raus–Frühstück! I was worn out. it was like all the films I had seen of Stalag 15 (except there was no way out). I figured that Olaf would slow down as he and many of his colleagues stayed up partying into the small hours, but no such luck. He continued unabated through five days, including the last night, when they somehow managed to burn down the old boathouse by the lake.

Still faltering in English, Olaf's typed letters to me are frequently hilarious and I have kept them all (he eschews the computer and prefers his treasured collection of old typewriters). A recent letter, received shortly after his final retirement last year, concluded: 'Typography was in my professional life very important, but I have always been a man between picture, copy and typography. The pure typography, for me is to[o] stupid. I like a claim, I like a headline, a subheadline – but I like more the general idea behind the job.' I have enormous respect and warmth for this go-getting, uncompromising, wickedly humorous, pipe-smoking designer, now a veteran typographer (Olaf's description), a doting grandfather and valued old friend. A very enduring benefit from a student travelling scholarship of fifty years ago.

Nonarbitrary line breaks

Implementing "meaningful" or "nonarbitrary" line breaks—in other words, lines that are broken for linguistic or semantic reasons—have been found to provide distinct advantages.

There are, of course, certain texts in which the line breaks are preordained by the author (called line-for-line setting). Verse, for example, certainly aims to clarify meaning through the signals provided by line breaks which, rather like a musical score, enable the reader to better interpret how the author intended the text to be read, especially when read aloud as a performance. (If a verse, for any reason, has to be printed as continuous text, the intended line breaks are normally indicated with oblique strokes.) However, clarity of meaning is gained at a cost to reading speed. But then, perhaps clarity of meaning is gained because the reader reads more slowly.

Nonarbitrary line breaks can also be implemented by the typographer to control the ragged right edge, when setting text ranged left. When the line length is shorter, selective hyphenation should be utilized. As mentioned above, one of the main reasons quoted for imposing ranged left setting is to avoid word

breaks. For this reason, some assume that nonhyphenation is synonymous with ranged left setting. However, because there are clear semantic reasons for the typographer to control line endings (and although astute maneuvers might be made, for example, dropping a short word down onto the following, shorter line, or, finally, by editing the copy), there will be occasions when the only sensible solution is to hyphenate.

Breaking a word at the end of a line of text is a last resort because it is considered to be the most disruptive of all the typographer's actions to the reading process. Efficient reading is normally the typographer's goal, who must decide, line by line, the means to be used to bring about the most satisfactory end to each and every one.

Most dictionaries will demonstrate where it is permissible to break a word, but there are semantic issues that will also be brought to bear on such decisions. The usual one is that no part of a word should comprise less than three letters.

As stated earlier, a short word—or part of a word—left at the end of a line does not, generally, look satisfactory or function well. So that the reading process is caused the least disruption, it

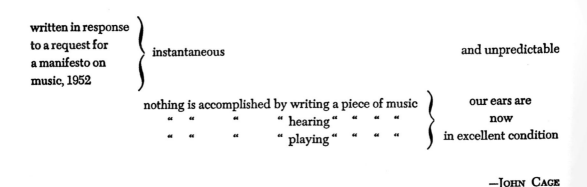

written in response
to a request for
a manifesto on
music, 1952

instantaneous

and unpredictable

nothing is accomplished by writing a piece of music
"   "   "   " hearing "   "   "   "
"   "   "   " playing "   "   "   "

our ears are
now
in excellent condition

—JOHN CAGE

is often suggested that the first part of the word should provide enough information for the reader (correctly) to surmise the rest of the word before the eye has traveled to the beginning of the next line. The worst scenario is when the reader is given an entirely erroneous clue by the first part of the word, so that when the eye does arrive at the second half, the reader is forced to reassess the previous assumption.

Meaningful line breaks
Below left: Linked ideas and trains of thought can be expressed visually through typography. Braces are put to good use here. From the foreword to John Cage's, *Silence*, Calder and Boyars, 1968.

Below: Verse aims to clarify meaning through the signals provided by line breaks which, rather like a musical score, determine how the text might be delivered if read aloud. Miguel González-Gerth, *The Infinite Absence*, printed by The Stone Wall Press, Iowa, circa 1964.

The Night Weavers

The darkness fastens
With its skillful touch
The circling skirt of the horizon

Surrounded by the gliding shadows
Fluid distances
And the wakes of pinions in descent

The movement of the night
Spins above the sleeping beach
And the moonbeams baste the tulle
That covers the meadows of the sea

A Dream

Something like a rain of glass
Fell over your image

I saw you as in a lagoon
Suspended by clear clouds
Surrounded by light and butterflies

And as you vanished
I wished to give my eyes to the voyage of your shape
Where the sky sailed
Through a thousand routes and among roses

19

Ranged-left setting

The reasons for setting texts ranged-left (also called ragged right or unjustified) might simply be to distinguish one text from another text on the same page or in the same document. Ranged-left is still associated with relatively ephemeral and informal kinds of texts.[1]

By contrast, justified setting is commonly assumed to be the norm for documents associated with formality and permanence, the perception being one of uniformity and control. If ranged-left is used in conjunction with justified setting (perhaps required for captions or footnotes), then the typographer will have to decide if ranged-left setting alone is sufficient or whether a change of size, weight, or typeface is also required.

When ranged-left setting is chosen for a main text the reason might be semantic: the typographer wants to ensure equal word spacing throughout and/or to avoid hyphenation (wherever practical) or rhetoric: the typographer wants to present a less formal tone. Both reasons apply to the typography of this book.

What is clear from the above is that the ragged edge is just a consequence of using a particular set of typographic preferences.[2] It is not the ragged edge that is required, but equal word spacing with minimum hyphenation. However, when line endings are conspicuous by extreme variation in length, the reader can find these apparently arbitrary events disconcerting. For example, when a short word at the end of a line is longer than those preceding and following it. Such a word, isolated and therefore given additional prominence, can appear out of keeping with a text of which it is an integral part. If the short, single word is also the first word of a new sentence its apparent isolation is intensified.

Such semantic criteria means that some typographers consider ranged-left to be more difficult and more time-consuming to do well than justified setting.[3] Certainly, to make ragged typesetting look good and function well means that the typographer must modify the results produced by the computer software. (Of course, the same must be said about any setting, but, as long as the line length is sufficient, justified setting will generally pose fewer problems.)

The term "look good" suggests a highly subjective judgment, and perhaps, finally, it is. There is the argument that a relatively smooth right-hand rag is likely to contribute to the saccadic movements of the eye. But if it is too smooth the right edge can give the appearance of a poorly set justified text. The conventional "good shape" is sometimes described as a series of D-shaped paragraphs.[4]

The reason for this is because such shapes provide visible clues to the reader about the status of text groupings, e.g., the beginning, middle, and ending of paragraphs. Others argue that any recognizable shape that can be perceived at the ragged edge of text is inappropriate and potentially disruptive to the reader. However, a series of fuzzy D-shapes will certainly be less disconcerting than a text that appears to have had steps or V-shaped lumps chiseled out of the right side of the column.

Consequently, when learning to read we quickly recognise that line-endings are arbitrary and therefore irrelevant to any meanings within the text. This arbitrariness of typesetting conventions.

The overall shape, texture and form of text as it is so often presented today has been influenced by number of factors, and some of these originally had little to do with reading. Justified setting provides a shape, usually a rectangular column. To re-establish such a regular shape, the spaces between each word of line will have vary with those inter-word spaces on the next to ensure that the end of the last word must end on each line finishes at the same place. Studies taken in the psychological and physiological aspects of reading, as well as our reading experience tells us that spaces between words are such a major aid to readability. Why do publishers still justify texts ?

Columns of text, in themselves, normally have no linguistic might semantic function. In order to achieve as even as possible inter-word spacing throughout a linear text, little attempt is normally made to match line breaks with linguistic or semantic boundaries. Consequently, we when learning read quickly recognise that line-endings are arbitrary and therefore irrelevant to any meanings within the text. This really arbitrariness of typesetting conventions for the breaking of text into lines is, in fact, helpful to the reader precisely because it is meaningless and can therefore be ignored. As Eric Spiekermann suggests, justified setting confers neutrality on the appearance of text. Since the shape of the text varies so little from page to page of reading.

However, implementing "meaningful" or "non-arbitrary" line breaks in other words, lines that are broken for linguistic or semantic reasons have been found to be advantageous to the reader, which, if it is put

Consequently, when learning to read we quickly recognise that line-endings are arbitrary and therefore irrelevant to any meanings within the text. This arbitrariness of typesetting conventions.

The overall shape, texture and form of text as it is often presented today has been influenced by a number of factors, and some of these originally had little to do with reading. Justified setting provides a shape, the spaces between each word of a line will have vary with those inter-word spaces on the next to ensure that the end of the last word must on each line finishes at the same place. Studies taken into the psychological and physiological aspects of reading, as well as our own reading experience tells us that even spaces between words are a major aid to readability. Why do so many publishers still justify texts?

Columns of text, in themselves, normally have no linguistic might semantic function. In order to achieve as even as possible inter-word spacing throughout a linear text, little attempt is normally made to match line breaks with linguistic or semantic boundaries. Consequently, when learning to read we quickly recognise that line-endings are arbitrary and therefore irrelevant to any meanings within the text. This arbitrariness of typesetting conventions for the breaking of linear text into lines is, in fact, helpful to the reader precisely because it is meaningless and so, therefore be ignored. And so Eric Spiekermann suggests, justified setting confers neutrality on the appearance of text. Since the shape of the text varies so little from page to page of reading.

However, implementing "meaningful" or "non-arbitrary" line breaks in other words, lines that are broken for linguistic or semantic reasons have been found to be advantageous to the reader, which, if it is put in certainly

Consequently, when learning to read we quickly recognise that line-endings are arbitrary and therefore irrelevant to any meanings within the text. This arbitrariness of typesetting conventions.

The overall shape, texture and form of text as it is often presented today has been influenced by a number of factors, and some of these originally had little to do with reading. Justified setting provides shape, usually a rectangular column. To re-establish such a regular shape, the spaces between each word of a line will have vary with those inter-word spaces on the next to ensure that the end of the last word must on each line finishes at the same place. Studies taken into the psycho-logical and physiological aspects of reading, as well as our own reading experience tells us that even spaces between words are a major aid to readability. Why do so many publishers still justify texts?

Columns of text, in themselves, normally have no linguistic might semantic function. In order to achieve as even as possible inter-word spacing throughout a linear text, little attempt is normally made to match line breaks with linguistic or semantic boundaries. Consequently, when learning to read we quickly recognise that line-endings are arbitrary and therefore irrelevant to any meanings within the text. This arbitrariness of typesetting conventions for the breaking of linear text into lines is, in fact, helpful to the reader precisely because it is meaningless and can therefore be ignored. As Eric Spiekermann suggests, justified setting confers neutrality on the appearance of text. Since the shape of the text varies so little from page to page of reading.

However, implementing "meaningful" or "non-arbitrary" line breaks in other words, lines that are broken for linguistic or semantic reasons have been found to be advantageous to the reader, which, if it is put

Paragraph shapes
Left: Line endings that combine to create recognizable shapes create distracting, "negative" paragraphs (far left). Classic D-shaped paragraphs (middle). A right-hand edge that looks natural and entirely unaffected remains "invisible." It is often necessary for the typographer to intervene to obtain a natural appearance.
Below: First and last lines of paragraphs generally look more comfortable if they are not conspicuously longer than those following or preceding. This example also illustrates the importance of ensuring that short words are not left hanging and thus effectively isolated from the text of which it is part.

The idea is to ensure that *no* individual word stands separated or appears to stray from its proper place.

The idea is to ensure that *no* individual word stands separated or appears to stray from its proper place.

Dividing words

Word breaks are among the most disruptive acts imposed by the typographer on the reader and should be avoided wherever possible. However, the occasional, well-considered word break is still preferable to the holes and cracks that appear in a justified page of text or the distracting line endings when set ranged-left, ragged right.

Some maintain that a word should be divided on syllables according to its structure. For example, geography would be divided at the second syllable, on the letter o, geo-graphy. But in its pronunciation, this word divides more naturally on the g, geog-raphy. Breaking on the g also provides the reader with a far better clue as to what the complete word will be before the eye arrives at the beginning of the next line. Happi-ness rather than hap-piness is often quoted as a good example of this.[1] For the same reason, it is also best to avoid dividing the name of a person (or a place), or dividing a name from its title Mr., Mrs., The Right Honourable, etc. Wherever possible, even the first and surname should also be on the same line.

Related to this is the convention of not dividing a word if the first or second half of a word is less than three characters, for example, re-lated or relat-ed. Headings and subheadings should not contain word breaks at all, particularly when the second line is shorter than the first.

Some long words are of one syllable and therefore cannot be divided; for example, through. There are many others of two distinct syllables but which are pronounced as words with one syllable (the last e being almost silent), crooked, fasten, given, heaven, listen, moisten, often, soften, voices, verses, etc.

Words are also brought together to form a compound word, for example, on-screen. This practice varies greatly, with British English often using the hyphen where American English would probably omit them.

Never split a word at the end of a heading, part-
icularly if the second line is shorter.

Setting headlines
Avoid hyphenation at the end of headlines. Even compound words should not be split in a heading if it is possible to avoid it.

beau–
beauti–
beautiful

No smoking section
No-smoking section

six-year-old children
six year-old children

Reading flow
Above: Recommended word breaks to optimize reading flow and meaning.

Meaning and readability
Left: These examples illustrate the difference a hyphen can make to the flow of reading, and the meaning of a statement.

Type on screen

Many people assume that, despite obvious differences between screen and print, some existing knowledge may be transferable. Certainly, general design principles, such as consistency, hierarchy, and structure in graphic presentation, and, of course, accuracy, legibility, and readability, still apply.

But issues such as readability and legibility, and whether the performance of type on paper is, in any way, equivalent to its performance on screen are, so far, largely subject to differing views.

Basic ergonomic factors of screens have been investigated to attempt to explain reading speed differences between print and screen. But whereas such reports—written, for example, by cognitive scientists—might confirm that differences in reading efficiency exist, they are not written with any typographic knowledge, and to those with such knowledge, the outcome might be considered to be common sense!

For example (and based entirely on my own, unscientific observations), text to be read from a monitor should, perhaps, be succinct, contain a clear hierarchy, shorter sentences, and plenty of visual breaks to compensate for less than perfect ergonomic factors. When black type is presented on a white-light screen, the glare tends to modify the shape and, in effect, shrink the letters and lose crispness of definition. These problems are not difficult to minimize, and many Web sites place text on backgrounds other than white and use more robust fonts for textual material.

Scientists and typographers have different aims. Psychologists or vision researchers are generally interested in identifying the individual variant(s) that account for changes in, for example, reading speed. However, the typographer knows that changing one variant (for example, size of type) will need to be accompanied by other changes to compensate (for example, a longer or shorter measure, more or less interline spacing). But although such results might not further the typographer's knowledge, they may confirm the foundation on which sound practice might be based.

Since the 1950s, the nature of type—influenced by photographic, electronic, and digital technologies—has changed quite dramatically. As the technology has evolved, so have our own esthetic standards. Our typical experience of type on a daily basis is undeniably broader, in both style and layout, and also in the way it is received: paper, fax, e-mail, and World Wide Web.

Screen-based type
Right: ASCII code has a similar appearance and limitations to those of the early standard typewriter, and, in the same way, offers only basic choices: uppercase, lowercase, underlining, indenting, lining numerals, etc.
Far right: The Web site of Vince Frost makes good use of the technology while retaining the physical character of his typography.

```
Your order #026-3730869-2234865 (received 21 September 2000 19:03 BST)
--------------------------------------------------------------------------
Ordered  Title                                Price   Dispatched  Subtotal
--------------------------------------------------------------------------
1        The Internet Bubble : Inside t 17.24 GBP     1           17.24 GBP
1        Cyberselfish                   11.24 GBP     1           11.24 GBP
1        The Fifth Discipline           11.99 GBP     1           11.99 GBP
1        The Innovator's Dilemma: When  19.99 GBP     1           19.99 GBP
1        Blown to Bits                  13.29 GBP     1           13.29 GBP
1        Information Appliances and Bey 23.16 GBP     1           23.16 GBP
1        The Cathedral & the Bazaar     10.36 GBP     1           10.36 GBP
1        A Brief History of the Future  19.13 GBP     1           19.13 GBP
--------------------------------------------------------------------------
                                              Subtotal:   126.40 GBP
                                       Delivery Charge:     6.88 GBP
                                                 Total:   133.28 GBP
```

Surprisingly, no significant research into the effects of new technologies on readability has yet been attempted. One of the reasons for the loss of interest in legibility and readability (explained by Wim Crouwel[1]) is possibly the passing of its apparent relevance. If similar research were carried out today, the odds are that no differences would appear in the perception of legibility and readability any more, as our reading habits have changed so dramatically.

Certainly, the pervasive use of on-screen information and the growing use of abbreviated language, of contractions, and other space-saving devices formulated on an ad hoc basis suggest a plethora of potential research material. Ironically, it is probably the speed of technological change and the diversity of media currently used to receive texts that discourages research into the effects of the use of electronic and digital technologies on readability.

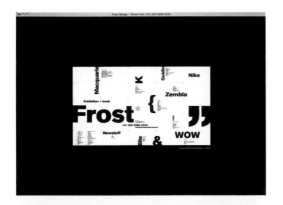

Nonlinear texts

Pictures predate typographic interpretation of verbal language as a means of communicating information. Although continuous text dominated during the first epoch of printing, maps, tables, diagrams, and drawings describing, for example, scientific information had been in use long before the invention of printing in Europe.

However, it was not until the eighteenth century that nonlinear typography became widely used as a means of clarifying or providing a more efficient method of communication in fields such as, for example, history and economics. The movement toward tabular or schematic methods of presenting information gained momentum in the nineteenth century: the Victorian epoch was a golden age for encyclopedias, illustrated dictionaries, guidebooks, route maps, etc. Mechanized transport transformed landscapes, economies, and the imagination. New-found methods of controlling power also revolutionized the printing industry. Powered first with steam, then electricity, huge, mechanized printing presses enabled newspapers to become a mass-print medium from which emerged the advertising industry.

During the interwar years of the twentieth century, Otto Neurath, a Viennese philosopher and social scientist, pioneered the use of pictographic symbols. This system of graphic communication, specifically intended as a means of cross-cultural education, was known as Isotype and was used to transform data and statistics into clear and understandable information. This was achieved by dramatic editing of the information, and the presentation of statistics with pictorial elements. These charts not only aimed to display information so that it would be accessible to the widest possible readership, they also intended to illustrate the information as

graphic representation. The symbols developed by Neurath were reinvented in the second half of the century and frequently adapted to the ubiquitous wayfinding systems found at airports, museums, hospitals, etc.

Transport systems (road, rail, and in particular air) took another huge step forward after 1945, and many aspects of commerce and industry endeavored to take on global proportions.

The kind of design overhaul undertaken by the Container Corporation of America, beginning in 1934, became the benchmark for any company with international aspirations after World War II.

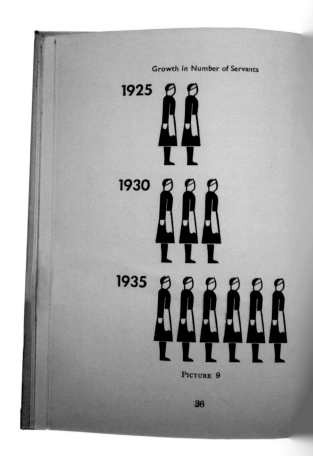

Growth in Number of Servants

1925

1930

1935

PICTURE 9

36

London Office: 12 Bedford Square, w.c.1
Telephone: Museum 7676
Telegrams: Lund Museum 7676 London

Bradford: Telephone 3408 (two lines)
Telegrams: Typography Bradford

Graphic clarification
Below, far left: Otto Neurath's system of graphic communication, known as Isotype, was used to transform data and statistics into pictorial elements. Otto Neurath, *International Picture Language*, 1936.
Left: Mundane information beautifully arranged. Herbert Spencer.
Below: The new Church of England Prayer Book, *Common Worship*, designed by Derek Birdsall and John Morgan. Integrity through clear, but distinctive design.

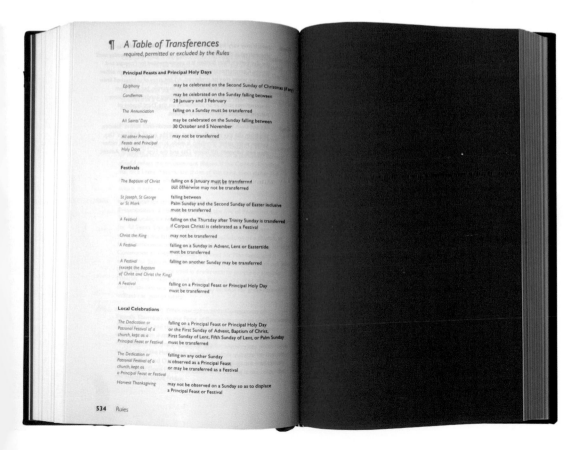

¶ *A Table of Transferences*
required, permitted or excluded by the Rules

Principal Feasts and Principal Holy Days

Epiphany	may be celebrated on the Second Sunday of Christmas (if any)
Candlemas	may be celebrated on the Sunday falling between 28 January and 3 February
The Annunciation	falling on a Sunday must be transferred
All Saints' Day	may be celebrated on the Sunday falling between 30 October and 5 November
All other Principal Feasts and Principal Holy Days	may not be transferred

Festivals

The Baptism of Christ	falling on 6 January must be transferred but otherwise may not be transferred
St Joseph, St George or St Mark	falling between Palm Sunday and the Second Sunday of Easter inclusive must be transferred
A Festival	falling on the Thursday after Trinity Sunday is transferred if Corpus Christi is celebrated as a Festival
Christ the King	may not be transferred
A Festival	falling on a Sunday in Advent, Lent or Eastertide must be transferred
A Festival (except the Baptism of Christ and Christ the King)	falling on another Sunday may be transferred
A Festival	falling on a Principal Feast or Principal Holy Day must be transferred

Local Celebrations

The Dedication or Patronal Festival of a church, kept as a Principal Feast or Festival	falling on a Principal Feast or Principal Holy Day or the First Sunday of Advent, Baptism of Christ, First Sunday of Lent, Fifth Sunday of Lent, or Palm Sunday must be transferred
The Dedication or Patronal Festival of a church, kept as a Principal Feast or Festival	falling on any other Sunday is observed as a Principal Feast or may be transferred as a Festival
Harvest Thanksgiving	may not be observed on a Sunday so as to displace a Principal Feast or Festival

534 Rules

The CCA commissioned Egbert Jacobson to redesign everything the company owned or handled: buildings, offices, uniforms, vehicles, stationery, advertising, etc. Similarly, Knoll International commissioned Herbert Matter in the 1940s, and IBM commissioned Paul Rand and Eliot Noyes in the 1950s. This kind of corporate "packaging" came to be known as corporate identity.

Advertising was already a well-established, highly sophisticated marketing and communication process, its influence aided substantially by the advent of television. These developments carried with them a huge growth in nonlinear typography: advertising, corporate identities, signage systems, manuals, directories, etc. It was the phenomenal growth in these areas of communication that created the new profession that would, in the second half of the twentieth century, come to be known as graphic design.

By the mid-1960s there was much talk of an "information explosion" and "information overload". It was at this time that a method of presenting data and information was developed called information mapping,[1] which required an author to organize and display his/her text in a way that made the structure and content immediately apparent. This was achieved by the use of rules that broke the information down into a series of linked, titled boxes. (See below.)

The argument for information mapping was that it made the retrieval of information significantly more efficient because the system allowed the reader to skim the texts and locate the answers more easily than one can with conventional, continuous text. The main criticism (which, thankfully, prevailed) was that "complex information can only be made to appear easy and approachable by overlooking the exceptions and the special cases [for example] 'No dogs' is semantically less complex than 'No dogs except guide dogs for the blind'"[2] but, clearly, a good deal less informative.

Again, it was the typewriter that, for many years, determined the initial configuration of tabulated graphic communication. A manuscript that included graphs, tables, charts, etc. would inevitably be presented to the compositor in

Information mapping
A typical training document and, next to it, the "information mapping" version. Looking at these examples, it is clear that information retrieval is made easier in the second, "mapped" version. Mapping procedures have found their way into textbooks and certain forms of administrative records, but, on the whole, such presentation is unacceptable because it makes all information, regardless of subject or context, appear the same. James Hartley, "Information mapping: a critique," *Information Design Journal*, 8/1.

typed form. Only more complex, more subject-specific material would be recognized as requiring a specialist (draughtsman, cartographer, or, perhaps, typographer).

A large proportion of nonlinear material produced by such specialists has few parallels in oral language, making the term visual language suddenly more acute. The range of such work often utilizes a particularly visual mode of communication that often has less to do with reading and more to do with the viewer searching out, comparing, and selecting just the information —or parts of information—considered situationally relevant to the viewer.

Dynamic mapping
Vibrant information that describes not only the location of the studio, but also the reason for going there in the first place. Alan Kitching, *Prospectus for the Typography Workshop*, printed letterpress, London, 1992.

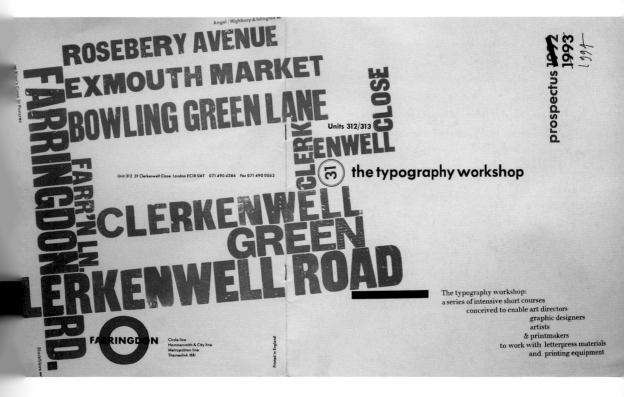

Information

Visual information is normally presented to enable the reader to discover, reason about, communicate, document, and preserve knowledge. Charts, diagrams, graphs, tables, guides, instructions, directories, and maps, together and individually, comprise an enormous amount of information. This material provides an essential service and yet, despite the efficiency and consummate elegance of the best work, design of information has engaged very little critical or esthetic notice.[1]

The indifference might arise from the fact that schematic information (as distinct from verbal and pictorial information) tends to be logico-mathematical in form and substance so that sentiment and inclination are generally excluded. For example, an accurate pie chart is "merely" an accomplished fact.

The operating moral premise of information design should be that the reader is alert and interested; they may be busy and in a hurry, but they are not stupid. Good design generally means clarity and simplicity, but there are also circumstances where more complex information can, while providing a clear and eloquent visual solution, maintain something of the richness and integrity of a multifarious subject. In other words, there are certain situations and subjects for which it is realistic to expect the reader to enjoy deciphering a rich and visually complex piece of information about a rich and complex subject.

Maps are a good example of this. The design of a motoring map and the information it contains will reflect the fact that the driver is likely to be traveling at speed. Such a map does not need to give information that wanders too far from the road, so its content is generally restricted to the classification of roads and roadside services that a driver (and vehicle) might require. A walking map, however, functions at a much slower pace,

enabling far more detail, and, with time to study it (perhaps, with the landscape in front of the reader) a remarkable amount of information is both necessary and appropriate. It is here, in large-scale maps, that the craft and invention of the cartographer can be fully appreciated.

Exactly the same design strategy applies to road signage. On motorways, the information and the way it is presented is usually standardized throughout a given country. Designed to be read at speed, the signs are edited to be as succinct as possible. Local signs are less stringently monitored so that a sign on a country lane might be old and rich in local character. Such vernacular qualities will not be lost on the traveler and, on the whole, it will not matter that such signs take a little more time to read because, presumably, the motorist or cyclist is traveling at a slower pace. Signs indicating footpaths will be least visible of all (with very little consistency in size, materials used, position, or style), but because these signs are often in the depths of the countryside, the lack of any rule-governed, systematic application is generally preferred (see page 60).

Other means of travel—bus, rail, and air, for example—require the use of timetables. The first means of transport to aspire to punctuality were

Schematic information
Rail travel was the first means of transport to aspire to punctuality, with timetables being printed as newspaper advertisements from the 1840s. Today, key information including departure times and platforms, are displayed overhead where hundreds of people can see it at the same time. More detailed information inevitably means *more* information, so this is still provided in printed, pocket-sized form.

the railways. Their timetables appeared from the 1840s, initially published as newspaper advertisements and later as handbills. The multiplicity of services and interconnections between increasing numbers of company lines brought tremendous typographic problems, so much so that many travelers confessed their inability to read timetables.

Timetables, like all visual information, require detailed editing of the data to be conveyed and detailed editing of the visual means of conveying the information. For example, the 1985 version of the New Jersey Transit Northeastern Corridor Timetable (below) employs rules, both vertically and horizontally, to separate the trains and their arrival/departure times. The redesigned version uses space alone to separate the trains whereas a series of broad, pale-tinted horizontal bands help the reader scan across the timetable. The newer version takes up a little more space, but is infinitely easier to read, more inviting, and importantly, gives the reader the impression of a smooth, uninterrupted journey.

Towns and cities that have maintained some of their older architecture will have inherited lettering on buildings, their physical presence remaining even though the building itself might have changed owners and function several times. This hardly matters when words have been chosen and cut with care; they become an integral part of the building which is itself integral to the street.

Street signs remain stubbornly local, their character created not only by the type of letter chosen, but also by the materials used, the size, position, use of color, and borders. Even when the quality varies (as it will), it is generally preferred that towns and cities maintain a degree of individuality—if not eccentricity. Such qualities are the reason for traveling in the first place.

Editing information
Left: New Jersey Transit, *North-eastern Corridor Timetable*, 1986 and its redesign. Railway timetables are renowned for their complexity and many people find them impossible to decipher. More recent designs have attempted to reduce the visual presence of the grid, cut down the amount of information, and de-emphasize the less important data. The new timetable (bottom) focuses on the information whereas the colored bars enable the eye to pass from left to right to find the appropriate time.

Vernacular vs. systematic
Above and right: The way information is presented says a great deal about the organization providing the information. These two examples show similar information conveyed in contrasting ways. Auckland, New Zealand (Alan Robertson), and Colchester, UK.

Ephemera

In the context of typography, the definition of ephemera that has gained widest currency is "minor transient documents of everyday life,"[1] although not every item of ephemera can be regarded as minor or even transient.

While including items with a very short life span—tickets for public events or for transport, for example —ephemera also include items designed to be saved (such as cigarette cards), and celebratory, informational, and legal documents that are of considerable importance (at least to the individual concerned). The scope of its subject is clearly endless.

Until the 1800s, there was little scope or opportunity for the printer to design. And when the opportunity did arise, with the sudden growth of the industrial and commercial sector, there were many printers who considered such work— promoting theater productions or the advantages of a new cleaning product—demeaning.

Between 1801 and 1875, in both Europe and the United States, those jobbing printers who took up the challenge[2] had a highly productive time making brilliant use of an ever-increasing range of novelty or "fancy" display letters on printed ephemera of, apparently, no significance whatsoever. The content and appearance of ephemeral material, because of its immediate and specific purpose, often provides the social historian with a particularly candid, more veritable kind of information, and, by its design, an understanding of intent, manners, opinions, and a view of the general social perspective, not of the period, but often of the day. Printed ephemera are second only to recorded oral history in providing "first-hand" information of times past.

Ephemeral material might be designed to function for a specific time span, but this does not necessarily mean that it is conceived and printed

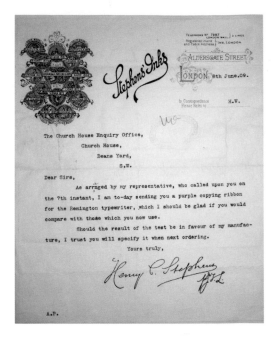

The faces of business
Above: A letter (dated June 8, 1909) from the company Stephens' Inks, extolling the benefits of purple copying ribbon for the Remington typewriter "… which I should be glad if you would compare with those which you now use," and signed by Henry Stephens. Scale of turnover is one of the key factors in commercial operations of all kinds today and this has an effect on the appearance of all the products we purchase.
Right: Food and household products waiting to be put out on the shelves of a large foodstore chain. This packaging is largely utilitarian and will be quickly discarded and recycled.

RAMON ALLONES
25 - Allones Specially Selected
Made by Hand
REY DEL MUNDO
25 CHOIX SUPREME
MONTECRISTO
PARTAGAS
HABANA

without great skill and imagination. (Much of this material is what an advertising agency in the twenty-first century might call "below the line" material.) In fact, the nature of such work—the fact that it is so often the means of both attracting attention and describing an event, service, or object considered to be unique—suggests that the printed item itself must also embody uniqueness by utilizing the very latest, innovative technology and the full resourcefulness of both typographer and printer.

For example, chromolithography, a print process closely associated in the United States with Louis Prang, was developed in the latter part of the nineteenth century. It is essentially the lithographic print process, but Prang made innovative use of colors and varnishes (12 or 13 printings were not uncommon, although an example requiring 52 printings has been recorded), often designed in collaboration with embossing, debossing, and elaborate die-cutting processes. Chromolithography was very widely used in advertising and promotion; trade cards, calendars, posters, showcards, and packaging were chromolithographically printed in prodigious numbers and, arguably, their quality has never been surpassed.

In contrast, the Belgian telecommunications network RTT, in response to repeated vandalism in coin-operated phone booths and the increasing demand for long-distance calls, was prompted to commission the technology consultants Landis & Gyr to develop and introduce a plastic telephone card as an alternative method of paying. These were introduced in 1979 and proved to be a huge and instant success.[3] The technology incorporated was, and remains, impressive; magnetic strips, silicon chips, and reactive optical devices ensure a secure and generally efficient operation. Telephone cards are now issued (often in collectible sets) for Christmas and commemorative events, promotional campaigns, or any other special local or national occasion and are thus an excellent source of ephemera for those wishing to collect a concise and compact image of an era.

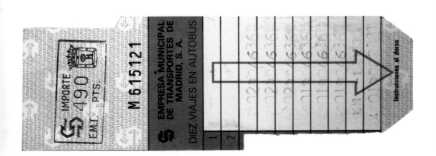

Novelty and invisibility
Far left: These Cuban cigar box labels show a fantastic range of display faces, all of which can still be bought today. The type foundries that spanned most of the nineteenth century (such as Figgins, Thoroughgood, Caslon and Catherwood, Stephenson Blake, Wilson, Austin Wood, Harrild, and others) have clearly been plundered in the creation of these designs, most of which originated circa 1900.
Left: The most insignificant of printed material, the bus ticket. This multiple-ride version is from Madrid.

Novelty

During the eighteenth century, a major cultural movement toward neoclassicism had been developing and, by 1800, this dominated all aspects of art and design. The cool, grandiose typefaces of the Italian Giambattista Bodoni epitomized the *beau idéal* of neoclassicism. His typefaces also erased, finally and completely, any lingering suggestion of handwriting. It has been said and written (by those claiming the importance of a calligraphic form in type design) that Bodoni's books were designed to be looked at rather than read.

These radical designs of typeface (below) and the way they were being used, brought into question for the first time (for the layman

The cultural movement toward Neoclassicism
Below: The title page of Pierre Simon Fournier's *Manuel Typographique*, Paris, 1764, and the title page of Giambattista Bodoni's *Manuale Tipografico*, Parma, 1828.
Right: Large wood type required for posters was selected from type specimen books such as this. Vincent Figgins, London, 1832 (St Bride Print Library.)

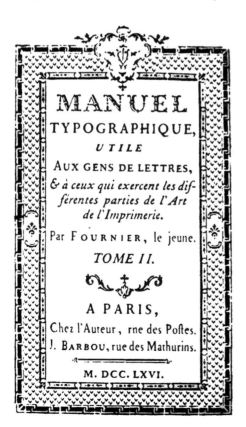

HERN

TWENTY LINE PICA, SANS-SERIF.

V. FIGGINS.

at least) the entire nature and purpose of typography as well as the function of the printer/typographer. This was the first time that the appearance of type had been consciously designed to reflect esthetic taste or fashion, placing appearance above readability. Bodoni was lauded as a great typographer/printer, and moreover, a great artist. During his lifetime his books were collected throughout the world, but appraisals of his work since his death are generally critical.

Not surprisingly, these new types, and their creators, were perceived to have a brashness about them that went against the tradition of type design as being essentially neutral—a self-effacing means by which the author could communicate directly to his/her reader. In short, the new school of typographers was getting in the way.

The distracting qualities of Bodoni's types (still formally classified in the Modern sub-category of typeface designs) are sometimes described as

★ **BASUTO**
THE
COMPELLING FORCE
FOR YOUR
ADVERTISING

★

★

★

AN ATTRACTIVE TYPE FACE
YOU CANNOT IGNORE

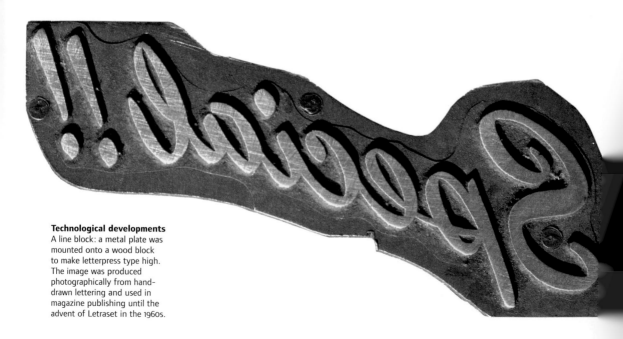

Technological developments
A line block: a metal plate was mounted onto a wood block to make letterpress type high. The image was produced photographically from hand-drawn lettering and used in magazine publishing until the advent of Letraset in the 1960s.

the precursors of the novelty or ornamented typefaces that flooded the market during the nineteenth century. But although Bodoni's work distracted by its austere, self-conscious majesty, these new "freak" types[1] attracted simply by being bigger, bolder, fatter, thinner, more simple, or more complex than any other type in the vicinity. The reason, the need for this entirely new breed of types, was advertising. Suddenly, type had an entirely new purpose — to attract. Only if it caught the attention of the reader would its message be read, and novelty was the answer. As advertising became ever more pervasive, so the novelty had to become more pronounced.

At about the same time as Bodoni's innovations in the design of letterforms, there was the discovery (circa 1835) and rapid development of the lithographic principle of printing. The letter-forms, hand-drawn onto a prepared, flat, porous stone by the lithographer, were regularly based on the works of sign letterers rather than type founders. The introduction of large and/or decorated wood letters was a response to the impact of lithography.

Historians of typography usually ignore novelty types and limit themselves to the study of book types, but it is generally agreed that although the Victorians lost the idea of good type to read this does not necessarily mean that they lost the idea "of good lettering."[2] Letters that aimed to attract attention were, by no means, unique to the Victorian period. Before the technical/cost limitations of printing reduced books to black and white, manuscripts were often illuminated with extravagantly complex and distorted letters. Lavishly complex and obtuse design reflected the time it took to complete, which, in turn, reflected the high status of the owner. "The Anglo-Saxon scribes were all working with the same idea. They

Commercial imperatives
Above left: Typefoundries encouraged printers to purchase "novelty" fonts for advertising purposes. *Printing types*, Stephenson Blake & Company, 1924.

Above: Letraset encouraged studio-based display typography. Letters photographed through patterned glass is typical of this period. Henning Boehike, 1967.

all seem to seek to make a static, self-contained beauty; a beauty independent of any connection with the sense of what is written…"3

In North America, the burgeoning print industry had an appetite for all things modern, but what is more surprising is how the famously conservative British printer began to use his highly regulated, sophisticated medium in a way entirely alien to its rule-governed culture, and use it with ingenuity and discernment. These raw and quite revolutionary typefaces were usually designed anonymously by employees of commercial foundries supplying commercial printers. The aim of both was to provide the public with novelty types and decorative elements that would attract and amuse. Because their intentions were purely commercial, considerations of historical precedence, or of typographic principle, did not influence their design. The results are a strange mix of naivety and exuberance, remarkable craftsmanship unhindered by convention. An alternative view, and one surely shared by the many who despaired of typographic standards, considered this to be a period in which "the businessman defeated and annihilated the philosopher and poet."4

Demand stimulated technological innovation. The introduction of the combined pantograph and router in 1834 revolutionized type manufacture by allowing different sizes and styles of a font to be generated from a single drawing.

Size was suddenly important (encouraging the use of wood for their manufacture), as posters and public notices became the prevalent and popular form of communication on the street.

This dramatic change in scale altered the nature of typography. At once, the perception of type was one of a more flexible medium, one which could be compressed, expanded, made fatter or thinner, given outlines and shadows. As attraction was a prime motivator, the relationship between letters within a font became more important than the identity of the individual characters. In other words, legibility was not the prime concern any more; letters were being turned into images, something to be seen and recognized rather than (and even preferable to) being read. Typography had found a new purpose for which, to be successful, all previous rules (of book typography) had to be turned on their head.

"Fancy" display fonts continue to have an important function in the general milieu of visual communication, but their requirement to attract means that their effectiveness is short-lived: novelty must remain different in order to succeed.

In the past, the nature of letterpress technology meant that novelty types could only be used for display setting, while the integrity of text type remained intact. With digital technology there are no such restrictions, and flexibility really does mean that all letterforms—including classic book fonts—can be stretched as easily as an elastic band.

Although the early novelty types had to "attract, amuse, and please," they were, in the main, designed with a knowledge of how type works. Some may have been exuberant, but the balance and weight of the characters were adjusted to ensure that each character functioned to its full potential. It is common today to see typefaces such as *Times* and *Helvetica* (both default fonts on many computers) condensed— squeezed—like sponges, and with as much visual impact.

Standout
When novelty is a prerequisite, there is no point in being subtle and repetition remains the major tactic.

Lists

Lists are a method of organization common in numerous forms to all aspects of graphic communication. In books, for example, there will be a list of contents, illustrations, bibliographies, references, and indexes. For most of us, lists are memory aids of things to do or to buy. For others, collectors of plane or train numbers, for example, a list can be a record of things seen.

Because of this, lists are sometimes scorned because their use suggests a lack of mental acumen or interest in alternative, more spontaneous behavior. Typographers have a reputation for being obsessively controlling, and when I find myself writing that "… for the typographer, a list offers not only the opportunity to show discipline and discernment, but also the ability to utilize the full range of punctuation," this is difficult to deny.

The conventions of the index have developed away from the normal rules of sentence construction. The systematic deployment of space, punctuation, and typographic variants enable the abbreviated and compressed language to function while taking up a minimum amount of space. Typically, each new entry starts on a new line, sometimes augmented by a series of incremental indents. Indexes are complex, and aim to provide a great deal of information succinctly. Such information is, therefore, already compressed and highly systematic. In such circumstances, the careful deployment of space, as well as punctuation and typographic variants (for example, small caps, italics, parentheses, and brackets) need to be absolutely consistent.

Each space, mark, and typographic variant signals a meaning and those meanings must be unambiguous. To make so many different typographic elements appear comfortable in such close proximity takes time and skill. Learning how to read an index also takes effort, but like reading itself, it is not something the reader wishes to be aware of while looking for a particular reference.

Typically, the reader of an index (or a dictionary or telephone directory) scans down the left edge of the column for a key word or name, noting the appropriate information, where it was found, and then resumes scanning. This stop-start activity is in sharp contrast with the smooth flow of normal reading. However, the stop-start nature of any list should be presented in such a way as to provide the reader with a tangible and rhythmic pattern. Patterns, though sometimes complex, are always predictable and this is an essential factor of any list.

Typographers can provide a great deal of help in clarifying these patterns by the judicious use of typographic variants, commonly, a bold face to denote each new entry with, perhaps, subsequent lines indented, the use of italic for book, magazine, or journal titles, and quote marks to denote the title of an article that appears in a journal. There are standard, academic procedures, but, as always, consistency of application is the key.

The characteristics of a list is that each item is of a different length and each must start on a new line. Even when some lines are likely to occupy a full measure, the last line of each item will, invariably, fall short. For these reasons, justified setting for lists is normally inappropriate because it can so rarely achieve its aim—to present the text as a rectangular area.

Subjects and names   **INDEX**

199

Grids

To ensure that the position of text was the same on every page, it was common practice for the scribe to push a pin (presumably through a *master* sheet) into several sheets of parchment or vellum placed underneath to provide a guide for the beginning and end of each baseline.

The importance of every line of text being directly beneath that on all the following pages is the visually disruptive effect of "see-through." If the lines on the following pages are allowed to move about, their gray, ghostly forms will stray into what should be the clear, white spaces between each line of text. The master sheet, providing the baselines and the position of the text on the sheet (forming margins above, below, and to each side), is what is generically called the grid today.

The grid provides a rational basis on which a set of recognizable arrangements can be repeated, enabling the reader to navigate a document and its individual pages. It also enables any number of individuals to collaborate on a longer or more complex project or series of projects, such as, for example, a daily newspaper or a weekly magazine. The grid increases efficiency. These highly practical functions are also the cause of the grid's reputation for inhibiting the freedom of the typographer to make choices. However, such complaints usually come from typographers having to work within a grid system that is not of their making. As a device, the grid is as simple or as complex, confining, or liberating as the originator requires it to be.

The grid structure of any spine-bound document is always devised as a double-page spread (a typical pair of facing pages). Traditionally, the grid structure of a book was based on the principles of Greek esthetics incorporating the series of "golden ratios,"

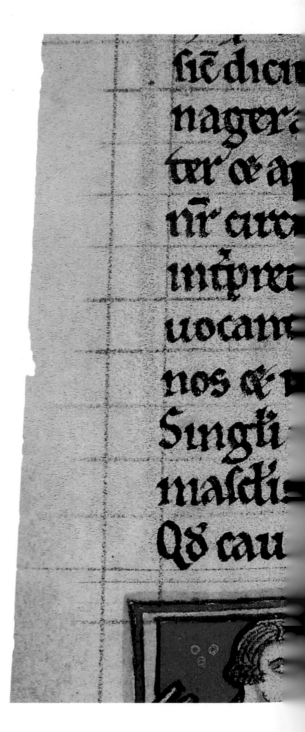

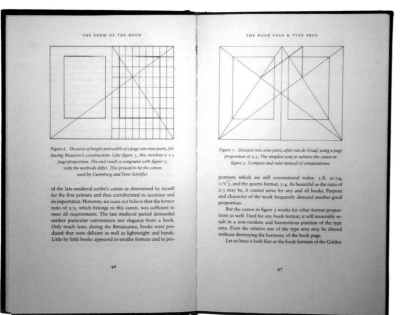

Figure 6. *Division of height and width of a page into nine parts, following Rosarivo's construction. Like figure 5, this involves a 2:3 page proportion. The end result is congruent with figure 5; only the methods differ. This proved to be the canon used by Gutenberg and Peter Schöffer.*

Figure 7. *Division into nine parts, after van de Graaf, using a page proportion of 2:3. The simplest way to achieve the canon in figure 5. Compass and ruler instead of computations.*

of the late-medieval scribe's canon as determined by myself for the first printers and thus corroborated its accuracy and its importance. However, we must not believe that the format ratio of 2:3, which belongs to this canon, was sufficient to meet all requirements. The late medieval period demanded neither particular convenience nor elegance from a book. Only much later, during the Renaissance, books were produced that were delicate as well as lightweight and handy. Little by little books appeared in smaller formats and in pro-

portions which are still conventional today: 5:8, 21:34, 1:√3, and the quarto format, 3:4. As beautiful as the ratio of 2:3 may be, it cannot serve for any and all books. Purpose and character of the work frequently demand another good proportion.

But the canon in figure 5 works for other format proportions as well. Used for any book format, it will invariably result in a non-random and harmonious position of the type area. Even the relative size of the type area may be altered without destroying the harmony of the book page.

Let us have a look first at the book formats of the Golden

46

47

Page structure
Far left: Detail of a manuscript, circa 1200, showing the drawn lines used by the scribe as a guide to ensure that the lines of text are in the same place on every page.
Above: Medieval scriptorium. The scribe is writing onto a large parchment, copying text from the book above his bench. Around him can be seen huge leatherbound books requiring heavy straps to keep them closed.
Left: Research into the structure and proportion of text to page in medieval manuscripts by Jan Tschichold explained how such arrangements could be achieved without recourse to measuring tools, regardless of the shape or size of the page. Jan Tschichold, *The Form of the Book*, Lund Humphries, London, 1991.

principles that were rediscovered during the renaissance. The ratio 1:1.618 helped establish the facing pairs of text areas plus margins at the head, foot, spine, and opening. The geometrically constructed grid structure has the advantage of requiring no calculations, the text areas being derived solely from the shape of the pages themselves. It also means that the proportion of text area to page area remains constant regardless of page size or shape.

The results derived from this method of applying a structure to the page are still much in evidence in contemporary book publishing, particularly where a single, continuous text (fiction, for instance) is the subject. Margins today are smaller but, remarkably, the spatial proportions remain much the same.

The influence and popularity of magazines, both in appearance and in the way they are used, can be seen in the growing market for random access books designed and published to be looked at and dipped into, rather than read serially from beginning to end. Digital technology has made it so much easier (and cheaper) to present more complex and varied material on the page. In such documents, the preference is often to have supporting material accessible simultaneously with the main text. Therefore, a grid structure that can accommodate far more flexibility is often required. Certainly, each document requires a grid structure that is specific to its purpose.

A modern, basic grid structure, typically arranged in conjunction with the dimensions of the outer margins, subdivides the page into

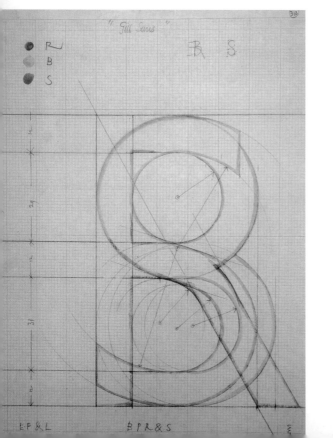

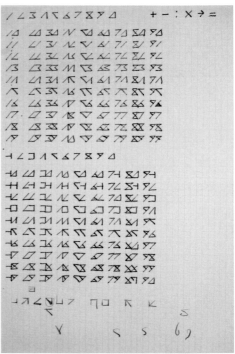

several smaller modules (or fields) that are separated by vertical intervals. The number of modules and their size will be determined by the nature of the text and images. If the document carries text only, the structure might be simpler, with the modules predominantly in the shape of columns. The requirements of the text (choice of typeface, size, weight, kerning, and tracking) need to be addressed in conjunction with the grid design. Neither can be planned in isolation from the other. If the content is a more complicated mixture, including photographs, illustrations, diagrams, etc., then the grid might need to be broken into many more, smaller, modules.

The grid provides the underlying structure on which the various aspects of the document can be presented in a coherent and consistent manner. It is not necessary (or even desirable) to use all of the modules all of the time, but a consequence of the consistent application of textual and other material is that the effects of see-through, in fact, reinforce the coherence of the document as a whole. The grid was an essential component of all documents, long before the invention of printing. Its existence has nothing to do with technology and everything to do with reading.

Letter structure
Far left: Eric Gill often used graph paper on which to draw letterforms. Pencil sketch for *Gill Sans*, circa 1932.
Center: Much of Wim Crouwel's work has been concerned with the design of letterforms that make best use of crude technologies. Sketches for the *New Alphabet*, 1964.

Letter placement
Left: This design was printed onto the envelope containing a brochure for the engineering company Sulzer Brothers. The grid that governs the position and arrangement of the type is derived from the composition of the photograph. Designed by Bernhard Lüthi, Basel, circa 1960.

Kerning, tracking, and ligatures

Kerning is the selective expansion and compression of the individual spaces between characters and words. These spaces have been provisionally kerned by the font designer, but there are many circumstances that require the typographer to intervene. When kerning a line of type, the typographer is simply trying to achieve what an infant teacher encourages in a young child's handwriting: fluidity, a sense of rhythm, and clarity.

When the setting is a little looser, it will be noticed that the reading experience tends to be slower. Alternatively, when the text is set tighter, the reading experience tends to speed up, until the point is reached where the characters begin to merge.

Old Style fonts, with their strong calligraphic left to right emphasis, and flowing lines that suggest a fluent link between one letter and the next, generally need to be "close but not touching." However, typefaces that are more upright (for example, the nineteenth-century *Fournier* and *Bodoni*, and the many sans-serif faces of the twentieth century) benefit from a little extra intercharacter space, especially at smaller sizes. A bold sans serif needs most intercharacter spacing. When all of the spaces between the characters in a word, a line, or a whole page of text are expanded or compressed, this procedure is called tracking. The reader should always remain unaware of such discreet adjustments.

As the size of a typeface increases, so do the spatial areas between the characters, thus loosening the necessary grip required by each character to ensure a distinctive word shape. Type used at a larger size generally needs space to be reduced between characters and words, whereas smaller size type normally needs additional space.

There is no discernible word shape when caps are used, so the reader has to be more aware of the individual characters, and to achieve this caps require more space. This happens quite naturally if the inner spaces of caps are used to judge kerning values. Reading a line of capitals is an unavoidably slower process, an inherent characteristic that should be used by the typographer to the author's advantage. A line of capitals should always be kerned selectively: standard tracking will not suffice.

Certain character pairs, such as LA, tend to require the slimmest kerning value, whereas H I (not HI) or any other character pairing that offers adjacent verticals require the widest kerning value. Space between characters and words set entirely in uppercase or small caps will generally need to be wider than those set in lowercase.

Numerals exist to convey numbers. Numerals frequently need kerning when set within a linear text because until they are selectively kerned they have all been assigned the same set width to enable them to align vertically when used in tabular work. The effect is that, for example, the

Tracking
Top right: Varying degrees of tracking. At small sizes some typefaces might require additional space between characters and words; at larger sizes some will need less. When letters are reversed out, the necessity of these spatial considerations is generally exaggerated.

Kerning
Right: The purpose of kerning is to change an awkward-looking row of letters or numerals into an integrated pair of series.

The spaces between characters have, effectively, already been kerned by the fount designer, but there are many circumstances that require the typographer intervenes. *Old Style* founts, with their strong left to right emphasis and whose structure suggests a linkage between one letter and the next, generally need no extra inter-character space. As typefaces become more upright instance, Bodoni and the Modern sans serif faces benefit from a little extra space, especially at smaller sizes.

Akzidenz Grotesk, 5 point with zero tracking

The spaces between characters have, effectively, already been kerned by the fount designer, but there are many circumstances that require the typographer intervenes. *Old Style* founts, with their strong left to right emphasis and whose structure suggests a linkage between one letter and the next, generally need no extra inter-character space. As typefaces become more uprightinstance, Bodoni and the Modern sans serif faces benefit from a little extra space, especially at smaller sizes.

Akzidenz Grotesk, 5 point type with +3 tracking

The spaces between characters have, effectively, already been kerned by the fount designer, but there are many circumstances that require the typographer intervenes. *Old Style* founts, with their strong left to right emphasis and whose structure suggests a linkage between one letter and the next, generally need no extra inter-character space. As typefaces become more uprightinstance, Bodoni and the Modern sans serif faces benefit from a little extra space, especially at smaller sizes.

Akzidenz Grotesk, 5 point with +6 tracking

The spaces between characters have, effectively, already been kerned by the fount designer, but there are many circumstances that require the typographer intervenes. Old Style founts, with their strong left to right emphasis and whose structure suggests a linkage between one letter and the next, generally need no extra inter-character space. As typefaces become more upright instance, Bodoni and the Modern sans serif faces benefit from a little extra space, especially at smaller sizes.

Akzidenz Grotesk bold, 5 point with 0 tracking

The spaces between characters have, effectively, already been kerned by the fount designer, but there are many circumstances that require the typographer intervenes. Old Style founts, with their strong left to right emphasis and whose structure suggests a linkage between one letter and the next, generally need no extra inter-character space. As typefaces become more upright instance, Bodoni and the Modern sans serif faces benefit from a little extra space, especially at smaller sizes.

Akzidenz Grotesk bold, 5 point with +3 tracking

The spaces between characters have, effectively, already been kerned by the fount designer, but there are many circumstances that require the typographer intervenes. Old Style founts, with their strong left to right emphasis and whose structure suggests a linkage between one letter and the next, generally need no extra inter-character space. As typefaces become more upright instance, Bodoni and the Modern sans serif faces benefit from a little extra space, especially at smaller sizes.

Akzidenz Grotesk bold, 5 point with +6 tracking

1900–1970

−16   +5   +10   +30   −16   −3 kerning values

1900–1970

numeral 1 (one) will normally need space reduced from both sides, whereas space on both sides of a zero might have to be increased. In other words, any sequence of numerals set within text will require kerning.

Depending on the fit of a typeface, spaces next to punctuation and parentheses often need to be kerned. The spaces immediately following a full point or comma can appear too large because the inherent area above those two punctuation marks visually increases the area of the standard word space that immediately follows. The colon and semicolon need to be separated from the preceding word by the addition of a little extra space. Depending on the typeface, the space following a semicolon or a colon and the beginning of the following word can often be reduced. The question mark and the exclamation mark also need to be separated from the previous word and, depending on the typeface, this space might need a little more than that provided before a colon or semicolon.

Full points and commas will sometimes need to be pulled closer to certain preceding characters, particularly r, v, w, and y. But with letterspaced caps, it is important also not to position full points and commas too closely, particularly with F, P, T, and V. Not F, P, T, and V. The lowercase italic *f* when used with roman punctuation: *f' f! f)* and *f]* and the lowercase italic: *j, j' j! j)* and *j]* will often need kerning (as do these). Here are the same character pairs kerned: *f' f! f) f]* and *j' j! j) j]*.

One of the most common errors, (and seen every day in even the best-designed newspapers), is caused by a failure to use the fi and ffi ligatures. The arm of the f in most typefaces invariably invades the space of the character in front of it, resulting in the two characters overlapping. The

consequences of this can be seen easily at normal text size, so to see it every day in newspaper headlines is truly bleak.

To avoid this happening, there are normally five standard ligatures provided with most fonts in both roman and italic, for example: fi fl ff ffl ffi.

By using ligatures, not only are unsightly character overlaps avoided, but the intercharacter spaces remain consistent. However, if the text is to be tracked, it must be remembered that the spaces within each ligatured character will remain fixed.

After World War II, there was a move to design fonts that have a universal aspect (i.e., do not have national associations), *Univers* being a prime example. This "new world" approach recognized the growing polylingual demands on alphabets by designing characters that were more robust, less prone to regional conventions, and, in so doing, eliminated the need for ligatures.

Decorative, or quasi-calligraphic ligatures, for example, ſt and ɛt from the *Caslon* font, are becoming popular because of a resurgence of interest in humanistic typefaces, but should be used with caution. A good ligature is designed to correct textual, spatial inconsistencies. Decorative ligatures do not have this function and their idiosyncratic appearance, though undoubtedly elegant, can be too conspicuous in text, and, eventually, a tedious distraction for the reader.

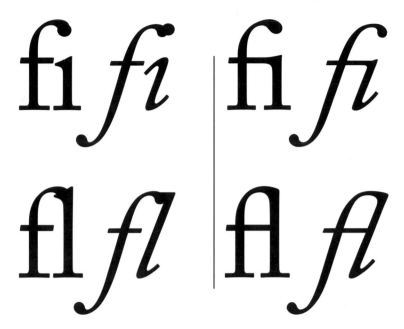

Ligatures

Ligature means "laced together." Ligatures are specially designed pairs or trios of characters linked to form a single character. For example, in most typefaces the arm of the f reaches into the space of the following character. When this happens, the result is ungainly. A diphthong is a ligature that represents a single sound, for example, æ. (Typeface: *Caslon*.) *Below*: A decorative (unnecessary) ligature. (Typeface: *Caslon Expert*.)

Default character-pairs

Ligatures

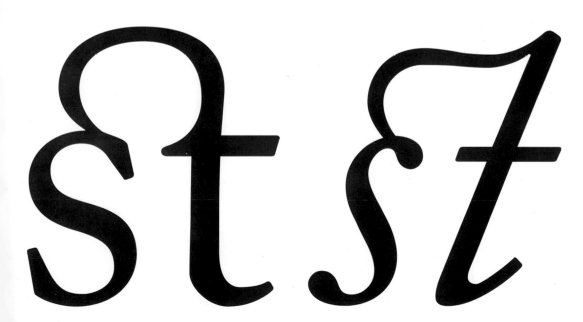

Space between words

The reading experience will be impaired if the setting of the type cannot keep the reader's eye on the line, and tight spacing between words will greatly help. There should be a clear, perceptible division between the line of text and the interline spaces, allowing each to provide strength and support to the other.

As a guide, the appropriate amount of space between words is said to be roughly the same as the space between the uprights of the letter n. (See right.) But, in making all interword spacing *appear* even, the spaces will not, in fact, be the same width. Allowance has to be made for the irregular shapes of different letterforms. When a word ends with the letter d, and the next word begins with the letter b (or h or k), the default space between them will appear smaller than that between e and o, for example, "the old hat."

Set ranged left (as here), this will not normally be a concern, but if the setting is justified (thus enforcing interword spacing that might be less than ideal), such irregular letterforms offer the typographer the opportunity to choose *where* to reduce or enlarge interword spaces. The aim in all textual setting is to provide visually even spaces between words, an ideal that should also be aimed for in justified text.

It is easier to achieve this visually rhythmic evenness of interword spacing when justifying text if the line length is longer rather than shorter. The accepted rule for the number of words per line for comfortable reading is between 10 and 12.[1] A longer line (of the same size type) contains more words and therefore more spaces, which makes it easier to add and retrieve space without drawing the reader's attention. The other essential aid to even, justified setting is a willingness to occasionally divide words, when helpful, at the end of a line. The narrower the column of text, the greater the necessity (and regularity) of word breaks.

Lines of text can be tracked only to the extent that the reader cannot perceive that such adjustments have taken place. The tracking tool needs to be used with great caution.

In justified setting, when word spacing becomes excessively loose, the en or em dash can appear to be joining words together (like a hyphen) rather than providing the pause as intended. If this visual fault occurs, it can be assumed that the interword spacing is far too wide.

A dense, darker, closely textured page of text will provide a challenging prospect for the reader, and, depending on the subject, this might be appropriate. There are no "optimum" values for letter or word spacing. Judgment concerning the final tonal value of the text will depend on the subject, the intended audience, and, occasionally, the conditions in which the text will be used. Achieving an appropriate tonal value depends on five factors: the typeface, the space within words, the space between words, the space between lines, and the space around text. Such combined considerations (in relation to size and weight of type; and color, surface, and weight of paper) are, in essence, what typography *is*.

■ A guide to the appropriate amount of
■ space between words is said to be
▪ roughly the same as the space between the
■ uprights of the letter n.

PART ONE

The Setting
of Text Matter

By far the greater volume of type composition today is of matter for continuous reading, i.e. text. And so it has been since the day when printing
from movable types was invented. For this reason the first part of this
book has been devoted to an explanation of some of the fundamentals
involved in the proper setting of body matter, viz. spacing between the
words, the determination of the measure, or length of line, and the leading or spacing between the lines. Indications are then given showing how
the principles which govern these vital factors are translated into day to
day practice.

In beginning with text settings we are simply putting first things first.
The setting of displayed matter forms a relatively small part—though, of
course, it is a most important part—of the total volume of all composition. Displayed setting grew out of the treatment of the text page, and of
the various needs of publisher, printer, and reader—and thus naturally
follows the treatment of text setting. That the bulk of the latter is now produced mechanically is a further cogent reason for giving first place to it in
this primer.

THE SPACING BETWEEN WORDS

From the time of the invention of printing from movable types in Europe,
that is, *circa* 1440, up to the present day, one of the hall-marks of good

1   B

Justified setting
Above: Justified setting
inevitably means that the
spaces between words will
vary. Only the last line of
the paragraph will have
the "correct" word spacing,
similar to the space between
the uprights of a letter n.
Left: Justified setting is
difficult to do well (and very
easy to do badly on the
computer). An excellent
example of justified setting
and a lucid book on the
subject of spacing in typography is Geoffrey Dowding's
*Finer Points in the Spacing
and Arrangement of Words*,
Wace & Company, 1954.

Space between lines

One of the most critical actions repeatedly made by the reader is the return, from the end of one line to the beginning of the next. It is an elementary typographic service to ensure that this fundamental activity is achieved by the reader without notice.

The space between the lines of text (called leading) aids the focused vision of the reader to sweep back, right to left at an acute angle, from the end of a line to the beginning of the next. If there is insufficient interline spacing (and particularly if the interword spacing is too wide or uneven), the text will not have the horizontal emphasis essential for efficient reading. If a text is evenly set with less leading, it will appear darker and more dense.

If the length of line is longer than normal then the eye has further to travel, and at a severely acute angle, to find its way back to the beginning of the next line. To help cancel the disruptive effect of longer lines, wider interline spacing can be used. A stronger, white horizontal space will help prevent inadvertent skipping or missing of lines or rereading of lines just completed.

The space between lines will appear wider (with or without leading) if the typeface used has a smaller x-height, and narrower if the typeface has a larger x-height (see page opposite).

This fact will, of course, influence the decision concerning the use of leading. A typeface such as *Bembo* or *Caslon*—which have relatively small x-heights—will look and be extremely readable with considerably less leading than a typeface such as *Times* or *Univers*, which have a relatively large x-height. The style of the face will also influence leading. The serifs on a face such as *Caslon* provide a horizontal emphasis, predominantly along the baseline and the top

ZEHN
JAHRE
NEUES
OPERN
HAUS

Novelty spacing
Left: This poster, designed by Gert Wunderlich, uses negative interline spacing. Leipzig, Germany, 1970.

Influences on spacing
Right, top: Ascenders and descenders affect the perceived amount of space between lines of type.
Right: Because the size of the x-height (the height of a lowercase x) differs from typeface to typeface, leading (interline spacing) needs to be adjusted from the computer default setting of 20%.

of the x-height, an emphasis that is missing from a sans serif face. In fact, many sans serif faces have a distinctively upright stature that, to be made readable, should be more generously leaded. Sans serifs with a more calligraphic structure, such as *Syntax*, do not suffer to the same extent.

With these, and most other typefaces, heavier, bolder versions require more leading than the light versions. The Modern typeface, *Bodoni Heavy*, for example, will comfortably carry leading equal to its body height.

The computer default setting for leading is normally 20% of the body height regardless of the size, weight, or style of typeface used. This should always be overridden with an appropriate amount of leading to be decided by the designer.

Where lines of uppercase are being used, there is the option of drawing the line together (called negative leading) because there are no ascenders or descenders to crash into each other. However, care should be taken to ensure that horizontal reading action is maintained by making the interline space larger than the interword spaces.

Where display setting includes a mixture of uppercase lines and lowercase lines, or all lowercase, the interline spaces will need adjustments if they are required to be optically the same.

the
spaces
between
lines

the
spaces
between
lines

The space between lines will appear wider if the typeface used has a smaller x-height, and narrower if the type-face has a larger x-height.

Space around text

The spaces around text are called margins. There are, of course, pragmatic reasons for margins. There is an optimum size of type that needs to be set in lines averaging 10 to 12 words per line. There is a minimum size of document that can be held comfortably in the hand (and standard paper sizes to work with). The difference between the two—the area of text and the edges of the document—are the margins.

Margins do not have a direct influence on readability and therefore, because margins are not essential (from the point of view of readability), it is clear they can only be justified in terms of esthetics.[1] Esthetic considerations (of balance, proportion, and support in relation to the textual area) are important, as are concerns about establishing a framework that isolates the text area from the environment beyond the book or magazine. But margins also have a semiotic function in conveying the nature of the text and should, therefore, be considered (together with the shape and texture of the text) as much an agent of communication to the prospective purchaser as the design of the cover.

In books, the proportion of text area to margin area on a paired spread of pages is roughly half and half. That any page might consist of 50% white space is, perhaps, surprising, but should alert the typographer to the attention these areas should be afforded. Magazines often use tighter margins, but rarely utilize the whole text area and follow a judicious placement of images—factors that are used to vary the pace of each article and the publication as a whole.[2]

Generally, the rule is that the varied height of the head margin should be half that of the foot (or tail), whereas the paired back margin across the spine should equal the width of each fore-edge margin. These proportions are designed to draw the facing two pages together and also to lift the text into a visually comfortable location. The paired narrow back margins optically combine to form a channel between the two pages of the same width as, or a little less than, each of the fore-edge margins.

A generously leaded text will look quite comfortable with smaller margins whereas a text with less leading will look better with more generous margins. Similarly, the use of a lighter typeface will look comfortable with smaller margins whereas a heavier typeface will require wider margins. In other words, generous space *within* the text area appears to compensate for minimal space *outside* the text area—in the margins—and vice versa.

Margins contribute greatly to the comfort and pleasure of reading, providing a calm environment in which the text can function to the full. But they are rarely *just* space. Chapter headings, subheadings, running heads, folios, illustrations and captions, footnotes, and reference material are often positioned in the margins, and, for this reason, a portion of the margin area is often represented in the grid specifically to carry supporting material.

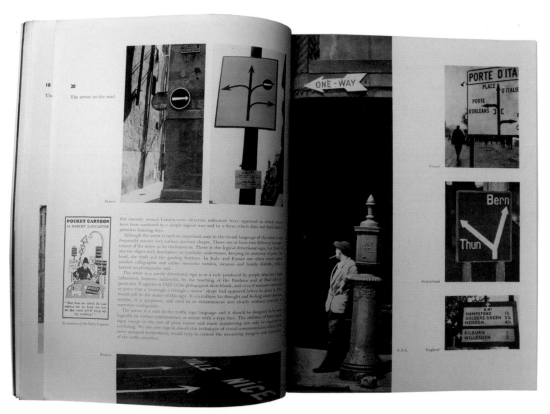

Space in books

Left: Here, the proportions of text to page are closely based on those utilized by the subject of the book. G. P. Winship, *Gutenberg to Plantin*, Cambridge University Press, 1926.

Space in magazines

Below: The margins of the magazine *Typographica* are active areas, utilized as and when necessary. As with many magazines, the margins are often invaded by graphic material giving the reader the impression that there is less white space on the page. In fact, there is generally far more space than in books, but carefully distributed in and around the pictorial and textual matter. *Typographica* 13, edited and designed by Herbert Spencer, London, 1957.

Italic and sloped letterforms

It was the French scholar/printer Robert Estienne who methodically introduced italics in the sixteenth century, in particular to clarify texts, to allow the reader to differentiate between different kinds of information, for example, in a dictionary.

In the nineteenth and twentieth centuries, italic has been used within text, again to clarify meaning, but also to provide emphasis. The reason for using italic for emphasis within text, rather than, for instance, a bold weight of type, is that the reader receives the emphasis at the appropriate moment, not before. Used in this way italic remains an integral part of the text itself. Wayfinding devices such as a heading or sub-heading, which need to be seen from the outset, are better candidates for the use of bold weight of type.

Unusual words or phrases, including those in a foreign language, are often set in italic as a way of alerting the reader. Similarly, it is common for an author to use italics for the names of processes and/or objects that the reader meets in the text for the first time.

In this book, I have used italics for the names of typefaces to differentiate between its designer/punchcutter/printer and the name of the typeface, Caslon's *Caslon*, for instance. Perhaps for the same reason, it is common for the titles of books, plays, songs, magazines and newspapers, buildings, and ships to be set in italic. An alternative, although less satisfactory solution, is to use quotation marks. These tend to clutter the text and, even with judicious kerning, they create holes. It is better to reserve quote marks for the titles of articles published within books, magazines, or newspapers.

Roman letterforms are upright whereas italic letterforms slope to the right. But a true italic is different from its roman counterpart in a more fundamental way. It is calligraphic or quasi-calligraphic. In other words, italic letterforms are closely based on handwriting, with an emphasis very much on the flow of the pen, with the beginnings and endings of each stroke curving into, and away from, each character. The extent of the calligraphic influence in an italic varies from face to face, but an italic will always be a more calligraphic version of its roman counterpart.

Computer software is capable of visually modifying letters in innumerable ways, but, for instance, the measurement tool bar or type style menu in QuarkXPress does not "automatically" provide a true italic. If you do not have the true italic typeface in the font you are using on your computer, the software will mechanically slope the roman version it does have. And do not be misled by output from laser writers. If you send a job to an image setter to output film or plates, you will be disappointed when a font "italicized" in this way reverts to its roman style. Always ensure you use the correct PostScript font. Even if the font being used has an oblique (or slanted) version rather than an italic, the true oblique version must be used because the distribution of weight, especially in the curved lines, is crucial to its appearance and function.

ABCDEFGHIJKLMNOPQRSTUVWXYZ

a b c d e f g h i j k l m n o p q r s t u v w x y z

a b c d e f g h i j k l m n o p q r s t u v w x y z

ABCDEFGHIJKLMNOPQRSTUVWXYZ

a b c d e f g h i j k l m n o p q r s t u v w x y z

a b c d e f g h i j k l m n o p q r s t u v w x y z

ABCDEFGHIJKLMNOPQRSTUVWXYZ

a b c d e f g h i j k l m n o p q r s t u v w x y z

a b c d e f g h i j k l m n o p q r s t u v w x y z

ABCDEFGHIJKLMNOPQRSTUVWXYZ

a b c d e f g h i j k l m n o p q r s t u v w x y z

a b c d e f g h i j k l m n o p q r s t u v w x y z

Italic vs. roman
Top to bottom: *Caslon Regular*: roman uppercase and lowercase and italic lowercase. *Bodoni Book*: roman uppercase and lowercase and italic lowercase. *Gill Sans Light*: roman uppercase and lowercase and italic lowercase.
Univers Light: roman uppercase and lowercase and oblique. The red highlights characters that retain their essential form in roman uppercase and lowercase, and italic/oblique lowercase. If the four italics are compared, the *Caslon Regular* example is the one that differs most from its roman version. This can be seen most clearly in the f, v, and w. *Bodoni Book* italic retains many of the calligraphic forms seen in *Caslon*, but in all cases, they are less pronounced. *Gill Sans Light* italic maintains a calligraphic aspect, but is far more subdued in character. Certainly the v and w have lost their rotund form and look almost identical in form to the uppercase and lowercase characters. Only the p maintains a distinctive (if refined) calligraphic quality; the extended upright of the f provides a hint of earlier versions. The *Univers Light* "italic" makes no pretence at a calligraphic style and is, in fact, designed as an oblique rather than an italic version of the roman lowercase. Note that the oblique "a" is exactly the same as the roman "a," but set at an angle. In all the other fonts shown here, the italic "a" is different from its roman counterpart.

Numerals and small caps

There are two kinds of Arabic numerals, essentially the equivalents to uppercase and lowercase, lining and nonlining numerals 1234567890 (lowercase). Not all typefaces have both, although such omissions are most noticeable in typefaces designed in the first half of the twentieth century, when lining numerals were called *Modern* and nonlining were called *Old Style*.

At that time the typewriter was perceived as a modern, efficient, "visible writing" machine whose manufacturers/designers, faced with a limited number of keyboard options, chose lining (Modern) numerals. Type designers, for whatever reason, followed suit.

Roman numerals also have been given the equivalents of uppercase and lowercase, as in XVIII and xviii.

If numerals are required in a text made up of uppercase and lowercase, nonlining (or lowercase) numerals should be used. Because lining numerals have the general appearance of capitals, they tend to be too conspicuous, distracting the eye in the same way as a word in capital letters does in the midst of lowercase. Perhaps it is for this reason that lining numerals are, sometimes, slightly shorter in height than the caps of the same font. The result of this, however, is that some lining numerals can look too small when set within a line of caps. If necessary, it should not be detrimental (meaning noticeable) to scale the numerals up to the same height as the capitals. A general rule is not to enlarge (or reduce) by more than 5%.

In tabular work, such as timetables and financial reports, the fact that all lining numerals are all the same height is helpful to the reader who has to scan both horizontally and vertically to gain information. It can be speculated that the choice to use lining numerals on typewriters was because it was foreseen that tabular work would be predominant in commercial administration and that lining numerals were best suited to this task.

Numerals (both lining and nonlining) often need a little extra space between them because, like capitals, they tend to be read digit by digit. To help the reader to "read" a number, it is also common to position a comma after every third digit from the right, for example, 1,234 and 1,234,567. For the same reason, telephone numbers are generally divided into shorter groups, such as 123 4567 8910, though the preference for grouping varies from country to country.

The preference for small caps (used predominantly for abbreviations and acronyms) over standard caps within text is similar to that of nonlining numerals, namely to present textual material as an even texture, rather than a texture with dark patches caused by clusters of capitals and holes caused by uneven interword spacing and em dashes.

Abbreviations and acronyms can appear as HMS Victory, NATO, 270 BC, but acronyms that stand for personal names should appear as W. S. Churchill PM. Small caps should be used alongside nonlining numerals: CO15 8LX, and standard-sized caps with lining numerals: CO15 8LX. Of course, small caps have to be used with standard-sized caps and their over enthusiastic use can lead to complications, and worse, misinterpretations. For example, a PhD cannot be a PHD.

Small caps, however, have inherent difficulties that, it seems to me, can only be overcome by editorial intervention. Although it is often cited that the typographer is the servant of the text, it is equally true that preparation of the text for publication should include consideration of the typographic style under which it will be set.

So, if it were the typographer's intention to use small caps for acronyms, it would be wise to request that the author avoids starting a sentence with an acronym. BBC looks ridiculous and is quite wrong. BBC, however, does not provide the expected signal for the beginning of a sentence (despite the full point and space in front of it).

Acronyms in the plural can, and should, also be avoided because s is one of those lowercase letters taken directly from its uppercase counterpart (see previous page). It is common for small caps to be slightly taller than lowercase characters, as you can see from this example, MPS' salaries. The difference is discreet, but sufficient.

Small caps are not small versions of standard-sized capitals (see below). They are drawn to have the same weight of line, fit, and internal proportions as the rest of the font at any given size. Italic or sloped versions of small caps are rare, although italic or sloped nonlining numerals will be available with most text fonts.

Desbois G

DESBOIS G, 68 New Kiln Rd,Colchester ... (01206) 540439
S.L, 6 Easterford Rd,Kelvedon............ (01376) 570942
DESBOROUGH D.J,
    51 Drury Rd,Colchester .... (01206) 542270
J, Albert,Thorrington Rd,Ltl Clacton....... (01255) 860273
J.M, 18 Gosbecks Rd,Colchester.......... (01206) 561447
K.S, 188 Point Clear Rd,St. Osyth........ (01255) 820845
M.R, 23 Oatfield Clo,Stanway .... (01206) 541656
P, 35 Humber Rd,Witham................ (01376) 520174
DESCOMBES C, 36 North Rd,Clacton-o-S . (01255) 427326
DESCUBES A,
    14 Laburnum Gro,Colchester .... (01206) 501614
DESHMUKH D,
    1 Hereford Road,Colchester .... (01206) 866900

DIAMOND
    Little
DIAPER A
C, 22 Que
C.F, 22 Q
D.A.W, 2
L, 21 Holr
P, 5 Cross
Rev T.C,
DIAS P, Br
    Lexde
P.G.S, Sa
    Fingri
R, Saresta

Lining numerals
Above: Wherever lists of numbers are required, it is almost inevitable that lining numerals will be preferred because their uniformity of height makes for a tidier horizontal line. British Telecom telephone directory, 2005.

Small caps
Below: Small caps are designed to be the same weight as the other characters within a font and, usually, only a little taller than the x-height of the lower case characters. Reducing the size of upper-case characters to use as small caps will result in them looking considerably lighter in weight.

Gill Sans was made available in 1928, the same year as *Perpetua*
Gill Sans was made available in 1928, the same year as *Perpetua*

GILL SANS WAS MADE AVAILABLE IN 1928, THE SAME YEAR AS PERPETUA
GILL SANS WAS MADE AVAILABLE IN 1928, THE SAME YEAR AS PERPETUA

GILL SANS WAS MADE AVAILABLE IN 1928, THE SAME YEAR AS *PERPETUA*
GILL SANS WAS MADE AVAILABLE IN 1928, THE SAME YEAR AS *PERPETUA*
GILL SANS WAS MADE AVAILABLE IN 1928, THE SAME YEAR AS *PERPETUA*

Small caps with numerals
Above: (Top two lines) The use of lining numerals with upper and lowercase characters is too conspicuous and overbearing. Nonlining numerals (line two) with their ascenders and descenders blend with the rest of the text. (Middle two lines) Lining

numerals look too conspicuous when used with small caps. Nonlining numerals look far more comfortable. There are no small cap italics in this version of *Caslon*. (Bottom three lines) This time it is the turn of nonlining numerals to look conspicuous. Lining numerals blend well with caps.

With some fonts, lining numerals are a little shorter than their uppercase counterparts which can look odd. Here, in the second line, the numerals have been slightly enlarged, from 8·5 point to 8·9 point.

Dashes and virgules

The standard typewriter has only one short dash, effectively a hyphen. But a standard font includes at least three: a hyphen, an en dash, and an em dash. (- – —)

In a typewritten document, a double hyphen (--) will be used where an en dash should be used and, perhaps, three or four hyphens where an em dash should be used, depending on the context or personal style. The rules of the typing manual (although entirely redundant) and a prevailing lack of typographic knowledge mean that the hyphen is, today, commonly used for all dashes, just as it was when this was due to the technical limitations of the typewriter.

The em dash was universally popular in the nineteenth century and remains so in North America where it is used with no space between the words that precede and follow it.

The size of the em dash makes it conspicuous in any column of text. There are situations in which the em dash, or even the double em dash, is useful, for example, when a meaningful pause is required ("What the — ?" or "What the ——?"), although ellipses do a similar job less conspicuously ("What the…?"). Indeed, not all fonts include an em dash. When necessary, two en dashes can be easily kerned to make one em dash (unkerned ––, kerned —).

In most fonts, dashes and virgules (and some parentheses) are traditionally designed with no attempt to provide stress or variation to the weight of the line. Because of this it is possible to substitute dashes from other fonts if prefered. For example, the *Univers* en dash happens to sit slightly lower than the *Akzidenz Grotesk* en dash (– –). The lower position of the *Univers* is a distinct improvement over *Akzidenz Grotesk* if it is to be used with lowercase because the dashes are positioned closer to the centre of the x-height of the lowercase characters: "What the ——?". This, of course, makes it a little too low when set with caps: "WHAT THE ——?".

There are a small number of typefaces in which the hyphen and other dashes have serifs (of a sort) and/or are drawn at an angle. *Arrighi*, designed by Frederic Warde, and many of Frederic Goudy's faces are canted and tapered; *Kennerley*, for example.

Where a hyphen appears at the end of a justified column of text, it is good practice to "hang" it in the right margin. This will help maintain the strong, clean, vertical edge to the column of text.

As well as suggesting a pause, the en dash is also used as an alternative for the words to or until, for example,1880 –1980. But when such information is presented in linear texts, it is generally preferable, both editorially and typographically, to use the word to, for example, 1880 to 1980.

The virgule (or slash) functions in much the same way as a full point, for instance, in the arrangement of dates 15/03/49, 15.03.49. It has had a sudden reemergence since the establishment of e-mail where it is commonly described as a forward or backward slash (/ \ ).

Dashes
Right: Dashes, in most cases, appear much the same regardless of the typeface to which they belong. Some, such as this version of *Caslon*, don't even have an italic version. Shown here are the hyphen, en dash, and em dash in *Caslon* and *Univers*.

The virgule is similar to the fraction bar (solidus), which has a less acute angle, and is generally a little lighter in weight (/ /) to enable it to function in close proximity to small and therefore lightweight numerals. However, if level fractions are to be set, then the virgule should be used, for example, virgule 1/2, solidus ½. I have used the "preconstructed" fraction available with *Caslon* for this example. Self-constructed fractions, built using the solidus and raised and lowered numerals, rarely look as good. (When constructing fractions always use lining numerals.)

In the general communication of numbers it was common to employ objects such as sticks/stones/beads.

Poor typesetting
Typographic misuse of punctuation can make the text setting look untidy and cause ambiguity for readers. *(Top)* When setting text justified the variations of interword spacing can cause the function of the en or em dash to become ambiguous.

Here the en dash appears to take on the appearence of a hyphen and so, instead of causing the reader to pause it creates the opposite affect. *(Above)* Words connected by virgules should be broken at the end of a line: sticks/ stones/beads.

In the general communication of numbers –bartering, counting, sharing– it is common to employ objects such as sticks, stones and beads.

Caslon

Univers

Parentheses and brackets

Parentheses are rule-governed in their application to written and printed texts (to indicate that the contained words or numbers or phrases have been included by the author for purposes of clarification from the author's viewpoint; rather like the aside to the audience or stage-whisper in a playscript). Brackets are also rule-governed in their application to printed texts [to indicate a necessary or desirable intervention by the editor of the text].

Parentheses ( ) traditionally had no variation to the weight of the line (like the virgule / and en- and em-dashes – —). They were set with ample space between each one of the pair and the words or phrases they enclosed to ensure that neither of the pair appears to be attached to the first and the last letter or numeral which they enclose. Today, parentheses tend to be narrower (see right and opposite).

Parentheses first began to appear with a varied thickness of line in the early Baroque period and whilst the original single-thickness line has been revived from time to time: (the Monotype Corporation's *Bembo* for example) the modulated version, based on the natural form created by a flex-nibbed pen, has, on the whole, persisted. The parentheses of this typeface (*Foundry Form Sans*) have a varied thickness of line: thicker in the middle and tapering toward each end.

Italic parentheses are a relatively new phenomenon. Upright (or "roman") parentheses, brackets [ ] and braces { } were once used even in the context of a text set all in italics. Today, text set in italic would generally contain italic (or sloping) parentheses. However, in a text set in roman, parentheses containing a word set in italic will be set in roman: (*like this*). Whenever roman and italic characters are used together the characters will often require kerning.

Italic characters within italic parentheses. No kerning required. Typeface: *Caslon*.

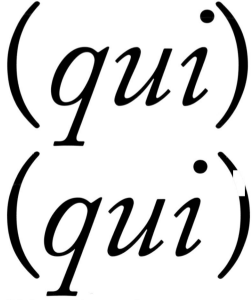

Italic characters within roman parentheses.
Above: unkerned **Below:** kerned

Hæc est Præfatio(ostendens) quemadmodum Sanctus Gregorius hunc librum fecit, quem homines Pastorale nuncupant.

Elfredi regis amplissimi (qui olim toti ferè Britanniæ præfuit) histori-am, tibi (humanissime lector) exhibemus : à Io-

Modern parentheses
Modern parentheses tend to be shallower and have a considerable amount of variation in the width of line. When italic characters must be set inside roman parentheses, kerning will be necessary to make them fit appropriately.

Traditional parentheses
Parentheses originally had little or no variation in the weight of the line. The generous amount of space between each parenthesis and the following or preceding character was, in part, due to the physical nature of letterpress. Both examples printed by John Day in London, early sixteenth century.

Portfolios

The "work of others" has always been an important resource for the designer. For those seeking typography it might, at first, appear that the task would be an easy one since, as this book has attempted to illustrate, typography is everywhere, functioning on many levels and in many ways. But here in the Portfolios section a clear distinction has been drawn by presenting the work of those typographers in "professional practice." In other words, who earn their living by typography.

I resisted using the work of contemporary typographers wherever possible in the previous sections of this book because I think it is easier to look at typography objectively when it does not carry the gloss (or otherwise) of contemporaneity. The Portfolios section, however, being concerned with current practice, will inevitably reflect passing whims and I am quite content that they should do so. Much talk is made of good design being timeless, but when we look back at the work of previous years and previous centuries, it is the differences that cause us to thrill in wonderment at the phenomenal skills or the audacity of design. Such difference is often caused by technological changes, developments in the tools and processes used, and/or by socioeconomic changes. Graphic design is, and always has been, a malleable practice. It may not quite be fashion, but it certainly does, often of necessity, reflect social fads and fancies. It is often by these fancies that graphic design is defined.

Of course, typography is *different*! Or so many would like to believe. But while there certainly are parameters (set by the activity of reading) which keep the typographer in check, there are also, as recorded on the following pages, so many other opportunities, so many other functions, in which typography today must operate. It is this diversity of requirements to which typographers must respond and which dictates that typography will continue to change. Books and other continuous-text material follows in the wake of these changes. A *long* way behind.

The work displayed in the Portfolios section of this book is intended to provide an indication of the breadth of such projects and the creative endeavor brought to bear by practising typographers. These examples will, inevitably, also provide ample evidence of the technical, political, marketing, social, and budgetary issues which (usually, but not always) are imposed by the client, and the genuine function of creative and expedient typographic applications brought to the solution.

The work illustrated here has been produced by individuals, by teams within large multidisciplinary design consultancies, and, the majority, by studios whose size is somewhere between the two. It is often said that standards are easier to control in smaller studios but "standards" are what every individual typographer makes them and the work of the larger studios illustrated here is testament to the dedication and sheer energy of the art directors and typographers within these busy studios. They continually find the inspiration to maintain the highest standards.

Walking into a small studio is a very different experience. There may be a pet dog named Caslon, and the radio might be playing. I enjoy visiting typographers' studios of all sizes. So much of what a typographer does is, of necessity, prescriptive, and yet solutions so often have the undeniable stamp of their designer. Such occurrences are often difficult to define and, even to another typographer, can remain elusive until you walk up the same steps the typographer walks up each day and see the name on the studio door. Once inside, the studio provides a myriad of clues: the windows and what is beyond, the tools, the computers and peripherals, the scored (or pristine) tabletops, job bags, files, schedules, reference material, drawers of paper, shelves of books, and piles of CDs. You might come across huge pieces of old railway signage "rescued" from rubbish dumps and casually leaning against the wall, or, rare archive travel posters from the beginning of the twentieth century, presented in elegant steel frames on immaculate white walls. To go in search of these places and to meet these individuals is tremendous fun because it is always so enlightening. I hope the following pages provide something of this experience.

A2-Graphics/SW/HK

In 1998 Scott Williams (Liverpool, England) and Henrik Kubel (Copenhagen, Denmark) entered the Royal College of Art, School of Communication Art and Design in London. Shortly after arriving the duo started to collaborate on a variety of projects and while still at college, formed the studio A2-Graphics/SW/HK.

The team has a conceptual approach to problem solving across various disciplines, including design for print, screen, and environment. Williams is interested in and motivated by lateral approaches to design production and Kubel is fascinated by drawing bespoke type for all projects—both methodologies inform their work.

A2-Graphics/SW/HK has been recognized nationally and internationally with awards from the British Design & Art Directors Club (D&AD), *Design Week*, the Art Directors Club of New York, the Type Directors Club of New York, the Danish Design Center, and The International Society of Typographic Designers (ISTD).

Scott Williams studied Design Communication at the University of Salford (1996–1998) and Communication Art & Design at the Royal College of Art, London (1998–2000). He lectured in Graphic Design at the Chelsea College of Art and Design, London from 2001–2004. He was a judge for the Cream Design and Advertising Awards 2001.

Henrik Kubel studied Graphic Design at Denmark's Design School (1992–1997) and Communication Art & Design at the Royal College of Art, London (1998–2000). He lectured in Typography and Design at Buckinghamshire Chilterns University College (2000–2003). He was a judge at the British D&AD Awards 2001, Denmark's Design Prize 2003, and Consort Royal Awards 2005.

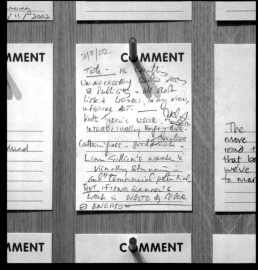

Turner Prize reading room
A2-Graphics/SW/HK were commissioned by Tate Britain to design the exhibition graphics and "interpretation space" for the Turner Prize. The project included the design of all exhibition graphics, a 16-page broadsheet, and the design of the reading room. The reading room accommodates a plasma screen, a fixed seating area, movable stools, bookcases, information panels, a Web point, and a public comments board furnished with pencils and cards for visitors to post a comment or message.

Christine Borla
Cai Guo-Qiang
Charles Crumb
Marlene Dumas
Susan Hiller
William Kentri
Paul McCarthy
Elizabeth Manch
Daniela Steinfel
Jon Thompson

Christine Borla
Cai Guo-Qiang
Charles Crumb
Marlene Duma
Susan Hiller
William Kentri
Paul McCarthy
Elizabeth Manc
Daniela Steinfe
Jon Thompson

Christine Borland
Cai Guo-Qiang
Charles Crumb
Marlene Dumas
Susan Hiller
William Kentridge
Paul McCarthy
Elizabeth Manchester
Daniela Steinfeld
Jon Thompson

Exhibition catalog
Apparition: the Action of
Appearing, was a group
exhibition curated by Roger
Malbert with Lucy Steeds,
and featuring the work of
10 international artists.
The exhibition catalog
is divided into two distinct
sections, one printed on
uncoated and the other on
coated paper. All page designs
adhere to a grid based on the
golden section, a device that
accommodates extensive

footnotes, supporting
illustrations, and a flexible
arrangement of images.
A typeface, *FY-Monday*,
specially designed by A2-
Graphics/SW/HK, has been
employed throughout and
appears in both regular
and italic versions.

Cai Guo-Qiang

The making of *Money Net* 2002, Japanese paper and gunpowder
Overleaf: gunpowder event at The Royal Academy of Arts, London, 7pm, 12 September 2002

52

Harry Shunk, *Yves Klein Saut dans le Vide*, Paris, 1960
Photograph
Unframed 44 x 11" (33.8 x 27.9 cm)
Albright Knox Art Gallery, Buffalo, New York, gift of Seymour H. Knox, Jr. 1976
© ADAGP, Paris and DACS, London, 2002

Robert Doisneau, *La ligne de chance*, Picasso in Vallauris 1952
© Robert DOISNEAU/RAPHO

42

resemble a Robert Doisneau photograph of Picasso, when
a boyish (if balding) 71-year old. In *La ligne de chance* (1952)
Picasso is seen through a window, his hands pressed flat
against the glass, palms either side of his head, eyes troubled.
Needless to say, there are alternative interpretations of this
image and the initial impression of the artist imprisoned
by the picture plane is jokily undermined by the resemblance
to Marcel Marceau, miming his invisible wall.

Picasso himself used body-prints in his work[17] but since
it may be possible to trace such imagery in all cultures,
of all periods, including ancient European cave art and
that of Native American cliff dwellings, it is perhaps best
not to search for precedents. Consider instead Vito Acconci's
video *Trademarks* (1970), in which the artist bites himself on
every reachable part of his body, not only leaving teeth-prints
but breaking skin. The marks act as an authenticating signature but they also represent an attack on the artist, which
brings to mind Johns's *Painting Bitten by a Man* (1961),
in which we see the remnants of a literal bite into encaustic
on canvas, which looks waxily like skin.[18]

There are many recent examples that may also be compared;
for instance, last year Mike Stubbs, video artist, returned
to his home town of Bedford to film his attempts to perfect
the hand-brake turn, and more specifically the resulting tyre
marks, which brand the road with a circle of black rubber
residue.[19] An artist's attempt to draw the perfect, free-hand
circle; an anarchist's pursuit of the perfect, wild-style graffiti
tag. Is this a flourished signature or an existential yelp?
This question, which is pertinent to all graffiti, may also
be asked of Picasso's photographed hands, Acconci's bitten
limbs and the Johns drawing and prints.

43

17 For instance, a hand print appears in Picasso's aquatint illustrations for Paul Eluard's
    'Le Barre d'Appui', 1936
18 For further analysis see Christine Poggi *Following Acconci: Targeting Vision*, *Performing
    the Body, Performing the Text*, ed. Amelia Jones and Andrew Stephenson, London and
    New York: Routledge, 1999, pp.264 –265
19 'Doughnut' by Mike Stubbs, 2001, made in collaboration with Gins Cwrnechi, Scanner
    and Bedford Community Arts, presented as twin DVD projection and 3 monitor installation
    at Image Gallery Bedford, 2001, and CCA Glasgow, 2002

Exhibition signage
A2-Graphics/SW/HK designed the exhibition graphics and two bespoke typefaces for Eyes, Lies & Illusions, held at the Hayward Gallery in London. The exhibition presented over 1,000 pre-cinematic optical devices drawn from the collection of experimental filmmaker Werner Nekes, alongside the work of eight contemporary artists. In developing the graphic identity for this exhibition, A2-Graphics devised a typographic solution that reflects some of the themes of the show.

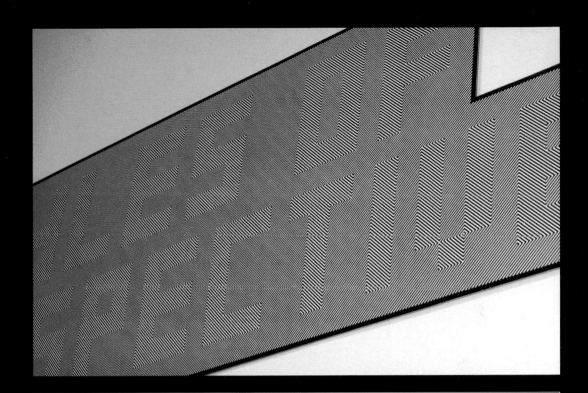

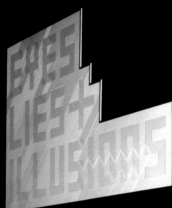

The exhibition includes works by eight contemporary artists, each of whom is differently inspired by the imaginative power of visual illusion. The historical works are from the Werner Nekes Collection unless otherwise stated.

The show begins with Shadowplay, which leads on to Tricks of the Light and Riddles of Perspective. They in turn lead to further sections in a spiralling route through The World Revealed, Enhancing the Eye, Deceiving the Mind and Persistence of Vision. The exhibition ends with Moving in Time, which explores the beginnings of motion pictures and cinema.

The objects in this exhibition are antique original

CONTEMPORARY ARTISTS

CHRISTIAN BOLTANSKI
CARSTEN HÖLLER
ANN VERONICA JANSSENS
ANTHONY MCCALL
TONY OURSLER
MARKUS RAETZ
ALFONS SCHILLING
LUDWIG WILDING

Paul Belford

Paul Belford is an art director and creative director who has worked at some of London's top advertising agencies. The process of producing advertisements for magazines, posters, and television can be long and complicated, with many people (art directors, copywriters, account managers, planners, clients, typographers, photographers, producers, film directors, and yet more clients) involved at each production stage.

The ideas behind ads are usually created by an art director working with a copywriter. Most advertising agencies also employ typographers or designers, who work in the production studio. Art directors spend much of their time coming up with ideas for ads and many art directors do not have the time or inclination to get too involved with typography and design.

Paul, however, designs most of the ads he creates with his writing partner, Nigel Roberts. He also occasionally collaborates with graphic designers to try to achieve a new and distinctive graphic look for their campaigns. This often involves interesting typography. Current trends in print advertising tend to result in simple visual layouts that are dominated by photography or illustration with very little innovative use of type, but this results in very similar-looking ads. Typography can be one way of making the work stand out more.

Promotional material for Le Creuset
Woodtype, printed using letterpress, is used here to create type pictures that complement the copy lines and evoke a sense of tradition and craftsmanship.

INVITE THE BOSS AROUND FOR DINNER

SHOW HOW AMBITIOUS YOU ARE

LE CREUSET® ADVENTURE EQUIPMENT

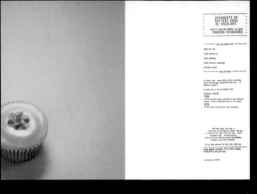

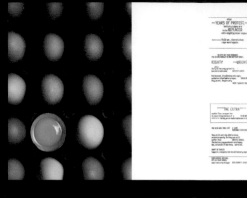

RSPCA: Free-range eggs campaign

As the aim of this campaign was to appeal to food lovers, and the copy talks about the decisions consumers make when buying food, the type was set like a supermarket cash register receipt.

RSPCA: Broiler chickens campaign

The animal welfare charity wanted to highlight the plight of broiler chickens raised in appalling conditions on an industrial scale. To this end, the typography references the graphic language of industrial packaging.

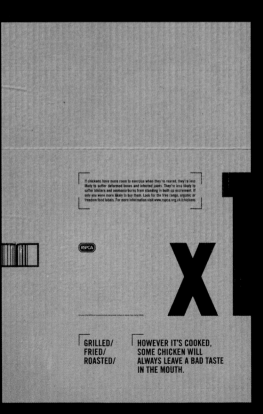

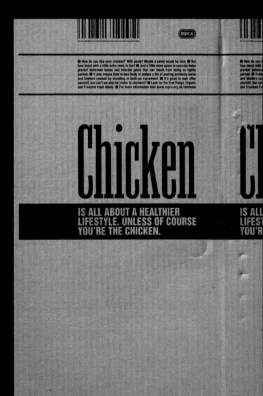

ICKEN

THE MORE YOU
SAVE, THE MORE THE
CHICKEN PAYS.

● Instead of saving money, you could save suffering. ● Just a little more money means chickens
have more room to move, helping to prevent deformed bones and infected joints due to lack of
exercise. ● A little more money means birds are more likely to avoid searing ammonia burns and
blisters caused by standing in built-up excrement. ● A little more money might not make much
difference to you, but it can reduce suffering for the chicken. ● Look out for the Free Range,
Organic and Freedom Food labels. ● Or for more information visit us at www.rspca.org/chickens

48
PORTIONS

The aims of the RSPCA are to prevent cruelty and promote kindness to animals. Reg. charity 219099.

ADOLF HITLER
POL POT &
MAO TSE-TUNG

were right about one thing

THE POWER OF BOOKS

WATERSTONE'S

Waterstone's campaign
A brand campaign from the UK bookseller, with the message "we love books." Each ad is designed like a book jacket and photographed wrapped around a book on a white background. The type is as diverse as it would be in a bookshop, and tailored to the title of each ad.

Al Mohtaraf

Al Mohtaraf is a pan-Arab graphic design house with more than two decades of activity in the field of corporate design and communications. They have offices in four different cities: Khobar, Riyadh, and Jeddah in Saudi Arabia, and Beirut in Lebanon. With a team of 40 people including graphic designers, calligraphers, type designers, illustrators, photographers, journalists, and copywriters, Al Mohtaraf is renowned for its Arabic typographic work, editorial design, and bilingual corporate identities.

Among the studio's most recent activities is Arabic type design. As the current typographic scene in the Arab world demands more attention and higher input, both in the quantity of Arabic typefaces available for use and in the quality of their execution for digital application, Al Mohtaraf tries to breach this gap by designing its own typefaces for display and body text. Drawing from its long experience in the disciplines of Arabic calligraphy, the studio is developing a multitude of Arabic typefaces for various usages.

Al Mohtaraf believes that the spontaneous handwriting movement is at the heart of the type design process. Above all, Al Mohtaraf focuses on liberating Arabic typefaces from the residues of classical calligraphy. Keeping in mind the important influence of this heritage, Al Mohtaraf's primary concern is to preserve high standards of legibility, simplicity, fluidity, and balance. It takes meticulous care in designing avant-garde Arabic typefaces with new forms of esthetics and a high quality of production. Over time, it has developed a collection of diverse typefaces for different uses, such as display, television, corporate, text, etc. To date it has supplied two major Saudi newspapers with two families of fonts, and a major bank with a family of four fonts.

In fact, Al Mohtaraf was recently recognized with an award of excellence from the International Society of Typographic Design for the design of a three-volume book set. This set has also been selected by the judges at D&AD as a historic record of great creativity for 2004.

Masthead design
Proposal for the masthead of *Arab Dialogue*, a cultural magazine published by the Arab Thought Foundation. The continuity in calligraphic strokes is intended to resemble the continuity of Arab dialog.

Calligraphic drawing
A calligraphic drawing of the name Princess AlBandari.

Newspaper font set

Al Mohtaraf was commissioned to design an exclusive set of five fonts for the daily newspaper *Al Yawm* in an effort to revamp the whole identity of the paper and increase its readership. The fonts (two headline and three text fonts) are designed to follow a smooth handwriting movement with an emphasis on legibility, simplicity, clarity, and balance.

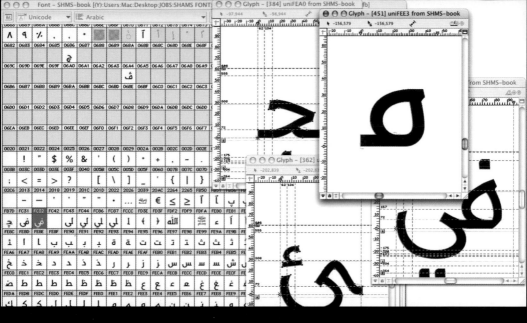

صباح اليوم الوطني وشمس جديدة
صباح اليوم الوطني وشمس جديدة
صباح اليوم الوطني وشمس جديدة

Tabloid font set
Al Mohtaraf designed an exclusive family of four fonts—two text and two headline fonts—for a new daily tabloid, geared toward the youth in Saudi Arabia. It is designed with prominent slabs—reminiscent of sports leagues—and a slight inclination toward the right to create a fast, bold, and energetic feel.

الأغـــاني

المجلد الثاني

أمّ كلثوم

د . فكتـور سـحَاب

موسيقى الشرق
Musica al Sharq

**Oum Kolthoum:
Life and Songs**

This three-volume set records
and analyzes Oum Kolthoum's
life and all her documented
songs. Special motifs, inspired
by the singer's typical dentelle
dresses and Islamic miniature
art, were designed (with
atelier Himmelbraun,
Germany) to complement
the typography and conclude
each chapter in the book. This
set was intended to establish
a house style for the newly
founded publishing house,
Musica Al Sharq, by designing
a flexible template that can be
adapted for all future books.

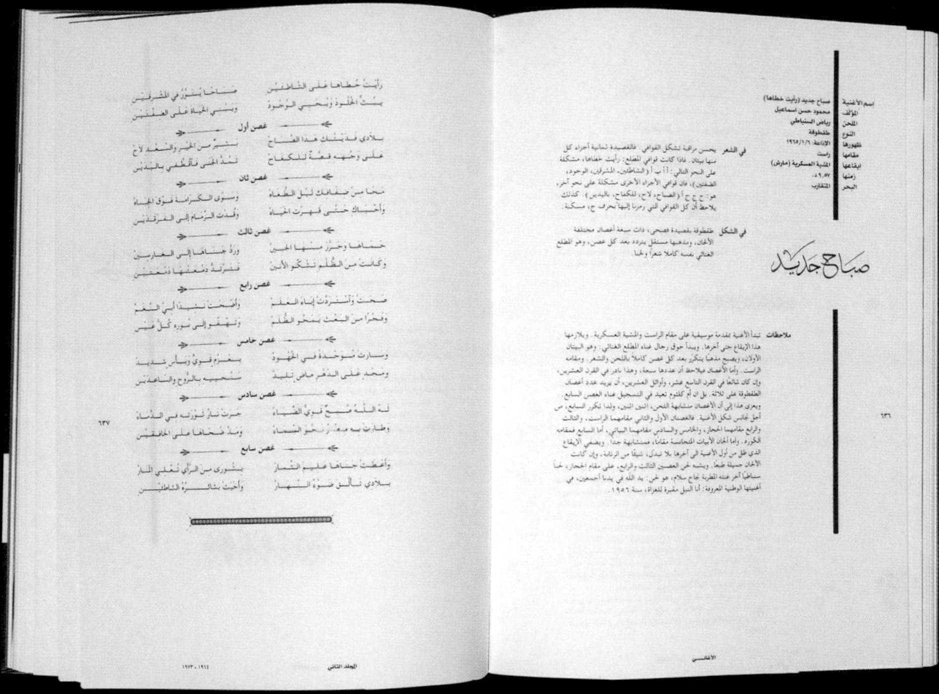
صباح جديد

اسم الأغنية صباح جديد (رأيت خطاها)
المؤلف محمود حسن اسماعيل
الملحن رياض السنباطي
النوع طقطوقة
ظهورها الإذاعة: ١٩٦٥/١/٦
مقامها راست
إيقاعها المشية العسكرية (مارش)
زمنها ٩,٥٧ د.
البحر المتقارب

في الشعر يحسن مراقبة تشكل القوافي. فالقصيدة ثمانية أجزاء كل منها بيتان. فاذا كانت قوافي المطلع: رأيت خطاها، مشكلة على النحو التالي: أأب أ (الشاطئين، المشرقين، الوجود، الضفتين)، فان قوافي الأجزاء الأخرى مشكلة على نحو آخر، هو: ح ح ح أ (الصباح، لاح، للكفاح، باليدين). كذلك يلاحظ أن كل القوافي التي رمزنا إليها بحرف ح، مسكّنة.

في الشكل طقطوقة بقصيدة فصحى، ذات سبعة أغصان مختلفة الألحان، ومذهبها مستقل يتردد بعد كل غصن، وهو المطلع الغنائي نفسه كاملا شعراً ولحنا.

ملاحظات تبدأ الأغنية بمقدمة موسيقية على مقام الراست والمشية العسكرية. ويلازمها هذا الإيقاع حتى آخرها. ويبدأ جوق رجال غناء المطلع الغنائي: وهو البيتان الأولان، ويصبح مذهبا يتكرر بعد كل غصن كاملاً باللحن والشعر. ومقامه الراست. وأما الأغصان فيلاحظ أن عددها سبعة، وهذا نادر في القرن العشرين، وإن كان شائعًا في القرن التاسع عشر، وأوائل العشرين، أن يزيد عدد أغصان الطقطوقة على ثلاثة. بل ان أم كلثوم تعيد في التسجيل غناء الغصن السابع. ويعزى هذا إلى أن الأغصان متشابهة اللحن، البين البين، ولذا تكرر السابع، من أجل تجانس شكل الأغنية. فالغصنان الأول والثاني مقامهما الراست. والثالث والرابع مقامهما الحجاز، والخامس والسادس مقامهما البياتي، أما السابع فمقامه الكورد. وأما ألحان الأبيات المتجانسة مقامًا، فمتشابهة جدا. ويضفي الإيقاع الذي ظل من أول الأغنية الى آخرها بلا تبدل، شيئًا من الرتابة، وإن كانت الألحان جميلة طبعًا. ويشبه لحن الغصنين الثالث والرابع، على مقام الحجاز، لحناً سنباطيًا آخر غنته المطربة نجاح سلام، هو لحن: يد الله في يدنا أجمعين، في أغنيتها الوطنية المعروفة: أنا النيل مقبرة للغزاة، سنة ١٩٥٦.

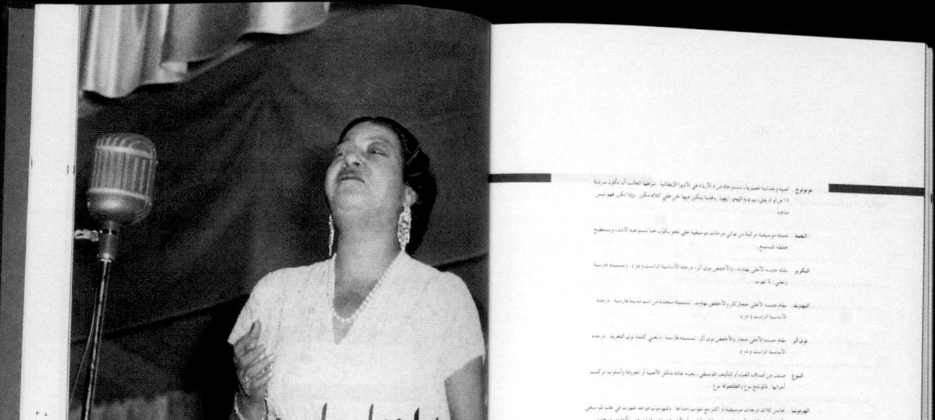

Atelier is the studio practice of Irish designer David Smith. He is a graduate of the design program at Dun Laoghaire College of Art and Design. He continued his studies at L'Atelier National de Recherche Typographique, which at the time was based in Paris. There, he studied typography and type design under the direction of Peter Keller and Jean Widmer.

On graduating, he worked briefly as a freelance graphic designer in Paris and Dublin before moving to the Netherlands to work with UNA (Amsterdam) designers. There he had the privilege of working on a series of high-profile projects including the millennium stamps for the PTT and the Asko and Schönberg Ensembles visual identity, which won the Netherlands Huisstijl Prize and an ISTD Premier Award in 2001.

Returning to Dublin, he established Atelier in February 2000. He continues to combine project work for selected clients with his teaching commitments—he is currently course coordinator of the BA (Hons) Visual Communications program at the Institute of Art, Design and Technology, Dunlaoghaire (IADT).

Although based in Dublin, the studio practice is clearly informed by the combined experience of studying and working in Paris and Amsterdam. Starting with objective analysis, the work is characterized by a methodical approach to typography, bold use of color, and an inventive use of ordinary production techniques. Working almost exclusively with public- and cultural-sector clients, the studio has established an excellent reputation for the caliber of its publishing and visual identity projects. This reputation has been enhanced by consistent national and international recognition.

Currently the practice consists of two designers, David and colleague Oran Day, with regular contributions from associates and design interns. Despite their small output, national awards include commendations from the Institute of Designers in Ireland and most recently bronze, silver, and gold awards from the Institute of Creative Advertising and Design, Ireland. Atelier projects have been published/exhibited in Ireland, France, Spain, Italy, Japan, Slovakia, the UK, the Netherlands, and the USA.

of that which is conscious and thinks

Exhibition poster
This poster was designed for the Emerging Designers exhibition at the first Graphic Europe Design Conference, held in Barcelona in 2003. Ten designers/design groups were nominated for inclusion by the conference advisory panel and asked to submit a poster design for exhibition. The poster was originally digitally printed on HP plotters in various formats, and subsequently published in a limited edition of 100.

Program identity
The design used for this program identity was also applied to brochures, advertising material, and posters.

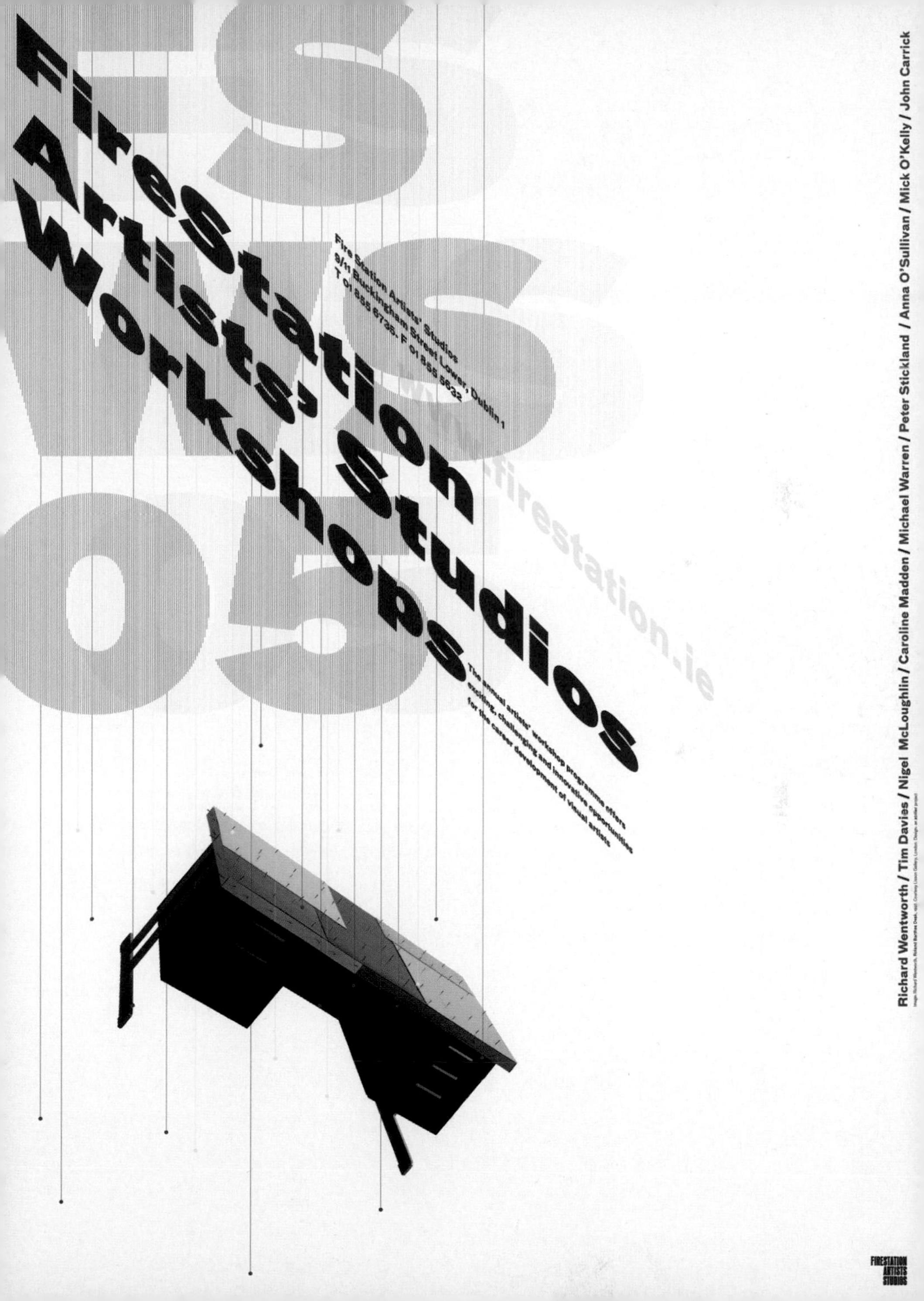

FireStation Artists' Studios Workshops

05

Fire Station Artists' Studios
9/11 Buckingham Street Lower, Dublin 1
T 01 855 6735, F 01 855 5632

www.firestation.ie

The annual artist workshop programme offers exciting, challenging and innovative opportunities for the career development of visual artists

Richard Wentworth / Tim Davies / Nigel McLoughlin / Caroline Madden / Michael Warren / Peter Stickland / Anna O'Sullivan / Mick O'Kelly / John Carrick

Festival posters and brochures

Originally devised for the 2002 Dublin Fringe Festival, the "typographic comb" was adopted by the Festival as their main identity due to the high level of recognition it achieved. The comb device continued to feature during subsequent years even though visual and typographic treatments changed.

September 23 –

ESB DUBLIN FRINGE FESTIVAL

October 12 **2002**

esb dublin

FRINGE

www.fringefest.com

festival

Book online at www.fringefest.com.
Book by phone 1850 374 643
The ESB Dublin Fringe Festival operates a fully electronic
Information and Box Office at the Project, 39 East Essex St.,
Temple Bar, Dublin 2. Open 11am – 6 pm, Monday – Saturday

ESB + arts Dublin City Baile Átha Cliath   the arts council ealaíon

WHW lecture papers
The publication of the WHW lecture papers celebrated the first in a series of annual Institute of Designers in Ireland (IDI) design lectures. The inaugural lecture was in commemoration of William H. Walsh, the founder of the Kilkenny Design Workshops.

Exhibition catalog with CD, invitation, and poster
The structure found on reflective road signs provided the basis for the typographic system devised for TRANSIT 2004, the Visual Arts program of the Dublin Fringe Festival. A hexagonal matrix features throughout, and directional arrows of various sizes are extracted and emphasized on each application.

"On the whole, the marriage of pictures and text is often unsuccessful, in fact, almost always unsuccessful," says Atelier partner Quentin Newark. "Many designers rely on a small number of conventions, such as placing a caption under a picture, or embedding a picture into text. They slavishly follow these limited means without specific adaptation to the material in hand."

So the ephemeral use of type (i.e. to "sprinkle" it across a surface) is not something the Atelier team consider. Ian Chilvers, another Atelier partner, explains why. "Every word has graphic potential so the marriage of the right word with the right typeface is where we expend our effort. Examining our subconscious relationship with words and interpreting this by drawing upon five centuries of evolving letterforms defines us as a profession. Without that serious backbone, we are merely 'designers' in the same way that everything is labeled as 'designer' nowadays."

Hugh Pearman wrote of Atelier "They know what they're about, these people. They think a lot about who they are and what they are doing." This is certainly true. Unlike many design studios that doggedly cling to a style of design, it is the words and their meaning that influence Atelier's esthetic. "Words are very important to us," concludes the third and last Atelier partner, John Powner. "Often a single word will trigger a design direction—take Sheffield for instance. The name has a double f and an i. We immediately spotted the lack of a ligature

on their letterhead when the brief was sent to us. Sheffield was home to Stephenson Blake, in its time one of the greatest typefounders in Britain and an exemplar of typographic exactitude. The thought of Sheffield without a ligature so appalled us that we dug deep into the Stephenson Blake archives to find a Sheffield typeface that we could revive. The result was a new typeface based on their original—*Granby*—complete with a proper ligature set and the ffi ligature restored to its proper home."

For Atelier then, typography should not bow to contemporary style, but to the timeless power of the word itself.

City signage typeface
As part of a citywide signing scheme for Sheffield, Atelier worked with Jeremy Tankard to develop a new typeface, *Sheffield Sans*, based on *Granby*, one of the original typefaces produced in the city in 1930.

A	X	Ï	i	œ	š	¤	6	/\	√
B	Y	Ñ	j	æ	ù	€	7	|¦	µ
C	Z	Ò	k	à	ú	£	8	–	∏
D	Þ	Ó	l	á	û	$	9	—	π
E	Ð	Ô	m	â	ü	¢	¼	•	∑
F	Ł	Õ	n	ã	ý	¥	½	·	Ω
G	Ø	Ö	o	ä	ÿ	ff	¾	({[	+×
H	Œ	Š	p	å	ž	0	%	)}]	–
I	Æ	Ù	q	ç	?	1	‰	*	÷
J	À	Ú	r	è	?	2	&	†‡	=≠
K	Á	Û	s	é	ff	3	,	§	±
L	Â	Ü	t	ê	?	4	;	¶	≤≥
M	Ã	Ý	u	ë	?	5	:	_	~≈
N	Ä	Ÿ	v	ì	fi	6	.	' "	<>
O	Å	Ž	w	í	ffi	7	...	@	^◊
P	Ç	a	x	î	?	8	-	©	¬
Q	É	b	y	ï	?	9	!¡	®	°
R	É	c	z	ñ	?	0	?¿	™	ffi
S	Ê	d	ß	ò	?	1	' "	#	e
T	Ë	e	þ	ó	fl	2	' "	ℓ	
U	Ì	f	ð	ô	ffl	3	„ "	№	
V	Í	g	ŧ	õ	ª	4	‹ «	∫	
W	Î	h	ø	ö	º	5	› »		

Sheffield

Sheffield

Sheffield

SLADE GARDEN
ADVENTURE PLAYGROUND

CHATTING
JOKING
MEETING
BUILDING
SMILING
LAUGHING
CHILLING
MUNCHING
MAKING

Term opening times
Tuesday – Friday   3.30pm – 6.30pm
Saturday   11.00am – 4.00pm

Holiday opening times
Monday – Friday   10.00pm – 6.00pm

Open to 5 – 16 year olds
All children must be registered

Important notice for parents
Slade Gardens is an adventure playground not
a childcare facility. This means that we are open
for children and young people aged 5–16 years
who are free to come and go as they please.
Some adventure playground activities have
a controlled element of risk, the children are
supervised by trained staff who ensure that
they can play safely and have fun without
being bullied while they are in the playground.

For more details please contact a staff member
T 0207 737 3829

Slade Gardens Community Play Association registered charity number 1083670

No adults unless accompanied by a child

LEARNING
READING
DESIGNING
EXERCISING
PLAYING
COOKING
RUNNING
JUMPING
THINKING
SLIDING
DIGGING
CLIMBING
DISCOVERING
PAINTING
CRAFTING

**Slade Gardens adventure
playground**
The structures in this local
community playground
inspired Atelier's typographic
solution for its regeneration
project. They even wrote
the copy for the children to
clamber over. This is type as
image, instantly understood
by the youngsters.

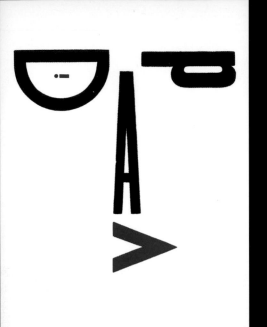

Typographic self-portraits
It's not all rigor at Atelier.
Rather than spend lots of
money on a Christmas party
they spent it on a day in a
letterpress print shop. Here,
everyone had fun creating a
self-portrait and discovering
letterforms that had remained
hidden for decades.

Boag Associates

Helping its clients to communicate clearly, Boag Associates is a creative graphic information design and strategy company. It helps companies to develop their business or organization by making information easy for people to understand, and good to look at. Boag Associates makes information clear through the use of plain language and accessible design. When information is clear in forms, bills, manuals, and Web sites, organizations can expect fewer calls to their helplines, for example. On this kind of basis, Boag can measure the impact of its designs and strategies. Organizations need to communicate clearly in everything they produce—from their advertising and marketing materials right through to their forms, customer letters, and e-mails. Information design is therefore central to brand strategy.

Boag's design process involves researching user and client needs and objectives, observing existing communications, developing strategies in response to this research, developing content and designs based on these strategies, evaluating the designs through user testing, agreeing final designs, implementing them, and monitoring their success.

Bills for Northern Ireland Electricity
For utility and telecom companies, bills provide the core, regular communications channel with their customers. It is vital that consumer bills are accurate and clear, but also that they are excellent manifestations of the company's brand. These designs for Northern Ireland Electricity respond to this need by clearly signaling the total amount due and the helpline number, and giving the bill a clear title. The period that the bill covers, and when it must be paid by, is also emphasized. The design allows for a summary of the customer's account, and detail on how the bill's charges have been calculated.

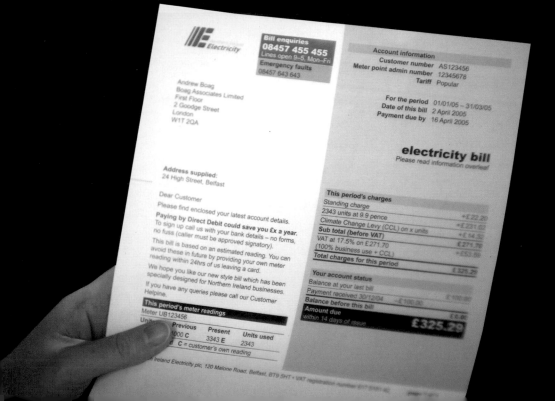

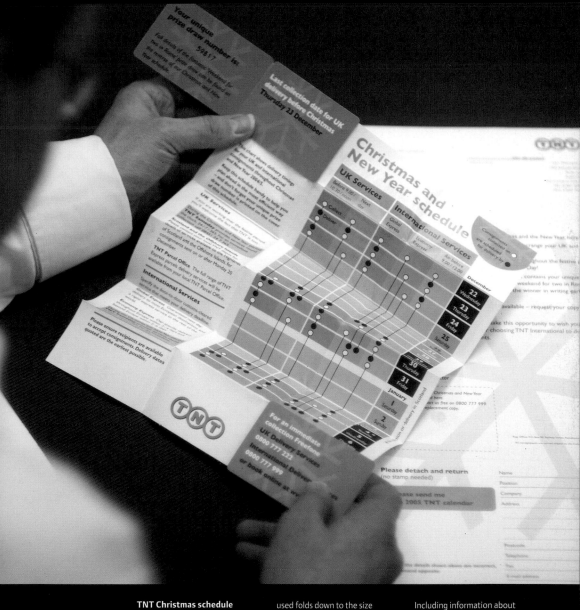

TNT Christmas schedule
Boag developed a leaflet for TNT, in a Z-card format that accommodated the Christmas TNT delivery schedules for both UK and International services. The one A4 sheet

used folds down to the size of a credit card. The mailing letters were economically printed and produced, with the Z-cards attached. The cards were individualized for a prize draw.

Including information about all services on one leaflet reduces print complexity, and presents one coordinated suite of services to TNT's customers in each part of the business.

New dictionary design
The fresh editorial approach and entry structure of *The New Oxford Dictionary of English* is mirrored in its sympathetic design. Entries are stacked so that each new meaning starts a new line, with the result that sense numbering (in *Arial Black*) is

less obtrusive than in other dictionaries. Many definitions are followed by an explanatory section of additional meaning statements and examples of usage. These take on the same typestyling as the definitions, and are differentiated by their smaller typesize. Word origins, derivatives, and phrase sections

start new lines and are introduced by stylish, letterspaced, small-cap headings. Encyclopedic, technical, and usage information is set in *Arial* to clearly distinguish it from definition text and examples, which are set in the space-efficient *Swift* typeface.

The design maintains graphic elegance while meeting the conflicting demands of character and page counts.

and enamels. See also **BORACIC**.
● Chem. formula: $B(OH)_3$.

boride /ˈbɔːrʌɪd/ ▶ **noun** a binary compound of boron with a metallic element.

boring ▶ **adjective** not interesting; tedious: *I've got a boring job in an office.*
– DERIVATIVES **boringly** adverb [as submodifier] *my boringly respectable uncle.* **boringness** noun.

Boris Godunov /ˈbɒrɪs/ see **GODUNOV**.

bork ▶ **verb** [with obj.] US informal obstruct (someone, especially a candidate for public office) by systematically defaming or vilifying them.
– ORIGIN 1980s: from the name of Robert *Bork* (born 1927), an American judge whose nomination to the Supreme Court (1987) was rejected following unfavourable publicity for his allegedly extreme views.

Borlaug /ˈbɔːlɔːɡ/, Norman Ernest (b.1914), American scientist, a central figure in the green revolution. He has worked for many years on the improvement of wheat crops and the adaptation of new strains of wheat to parts of the world where it has not previously been grown.

borlotti bean /bɔːˈlɒti/ ▶ **noun** a type of kidney bean with a pink speckled skin that turns brown when cooked.
– ORIGIN Italian *borlotti*, plural of *borlotto* 'kidney bean'.

Bormann /ˈbɔːmən, German ˈbɔːɐman/, Martin (1900–c.1945), German Nazi politician. Considered to be Hitler's closest collaborator, he disappeared at the end of the Second World War; his skeleton, exhumed in Berlin, was identified in 1973.

Born /bɔːn, German bɔrn/, Max (1882–1970), German theoretical physicist, a founder of quantum mechanics. Nobel Prize for Physics (1954).

born ▶ **adjective** existing as a result of birth: *she was born in Aberdeen* | *I was* **born with** *a sense of curiosity* | *a newly born baby.*
■ [in combination] having a specific nationality: *a German-born philosopher.* ■ [attrib.] having a natural ability to do a particular job: *he's a born engineer.* ■ [predic., with infinitive] perfectly suited or trained to do a particular job: *men born to rule.* ■ (of an organization, movement, or idea) brought into existence: *on 1 January 1992, the new company was born.* ■ (**born of**) existing as a result of (a particular situation or feeling): *his work is born of despair.*
– PHRASES **born and bred** by birth and upbringing, especially with reference to someone considered a typical product of a place: *he was a Cambridge man born and bred.* **born on the wrong side of the blanket** see **BLANKET**. **be born with a silver spoon in one's mouth** see **SILVER**. **in all one's born days** used to express surprise at something one has not encountered before: *in all my born days I've never seen the like of it.* **not know one is born** Brit. used to convey that someone has an easy life without realizing how easy it is. **there's one** (or **a sucker**) **born every minute** informal there are many gullible people. **I** (or **he**, **she**, etc.) **wasn't born yesterday** used to indicate that one (or another person) is not foolish or gullible.
– ORIGIN Old English *boren*, past participle of *beran* 'to bear' (see **BEAR**[1]).

USAGE On the difference between **born** and **borne**, see usage at **BEAR**[1].

Borna disease ▶ **noun** [mass noun] an infectious neurological disease affecting horses and other mammal and bird species, caused by an RNA virus (**Borna disease virus**).
– ORIGIN 1920s: from *Borna*, the name of a town and district near Leipzig in Germany where an outbreak occurred.

born-again ▶ **adjective** relating to or denoting a person who has converted to a personal faith in Christ (with reference to John 3:3): *a born-again Christian.*
■ figurative newly converted to and very enthusiastic about an idea or cause: *born-again environmentalists.*
▶ **noun** chiefly N. Amer. a born-again Christian.

borne past participle of **BEAR**[1]. ▶ **adjective** [in combination] carried or transported by the thing specified: *waterborne bacteria.*

Borneo /ˈbɔːnɪəʊ/ a large island of the Malay Archipelago, comprising Kalimantan (a region of Indonesia), Sabah and Sarawak (states of Malaysia), and Brunei.
– DERIVATIVES **Bornean** adjective & noun.

Bornholm /ˈbɔːnhəʊm/ a Danish island in the Baltic Sea, south-east of Sweden.

Bornholm disease ▶ **noun** [mass noun] a viral infection with fever and pain in the muscles of the ribs.
– ORIGIN 1930s: named after the island of **BORNHOLM**, where it was first described.

bornite /ˈbɔːnʌɪt/ ▶ **noun** [mass noun] a brittle red-dish-brown crystalline mineral with an iridescent purple tarnish, consisting of a sulphide of copper and iron.
– ORIGIN early 19th cent.: from the name of Ignatius von *Born* (1742–91), Austrian mineralogist, + **-ITE**[1].

boro- /ˈbɔːrəʊ/ ▶ **combining form** Chemistry representing **BORON**.

Borobudur /ˌbɒrəʊbʊˈdʊə/ a Buddhist monument in central Java, built c.800.

Borodin /ˈbɒrədɪn/, Aleksandr (Porfirevich) (1833–87), Russian composer. He is best known for the epic opera *Prince Igor* (completed after his death by Rimsky-Korsakov and Glazunov).

Borodino, Battle of /ˌbɒrəˈdiːnəʊ/ a battle in 1812 at Borodino, a village about 110 km (70 miles) west of Moscow, at which Napoleon's forces defeated the Russian army.

boron /ˈbɔːrɒn/ ▶ **noun** [mass noun] the chemical element of atomic number 5, a non-metallic solid. (Symbol: **B**)

Boron is usually prepared as an amorphous brown powder, but when very pure it forms hard, shiny, black crystals with semiconducting properties. The element has some specialized uses, such as in alloy steels and in nuclear control rods.

– ORIGIN early 19th cent.: from **BORAX**, on the pattern of *carbon* (which it resembles in some respects).

boronia /bəˈrəʊnɪə/ ▶ **noun** a sweet-scented Australian shrub which is cultivated for its perfume and for the cut-flower trade.
● Genus *Boronia*, family Rutaceae.
– ORIGIN modern Latin, named after Francesco *Borone* (1769–94), Italian botanist.

borosilicate /ˌbɔːrəʊˈsɪlɪkeɪt/ ▶ **noun** [usu. as modifier] a low-melting glass made from a mixture of silica and boric oxide (B_2O_3).

borough /ˈbʌrə/ ▶ **noun** a town or district which is an administrative unit, in particular:
■ Brit. a town (as distinct from a city) with a corporation and privileges granted by a royal charter. ■ Brit. historical a town sending representatives to Parliament. ■ an administrative division of London. ■ a municipal corporation in certain US states. ■ each of five divisions of New York City. ■ (in Alaska) a district corresponding to a county elsewhere in the US.
– ORIGIN Old English *burg*, *burh* 'fortress, citadel', later 'fortified town', of Germanic origin; related to Dutch *burg* and German *Burg*. Compare with **BURGH**.

Borromini /ˌbɒrəˈmiːni/, Francesco (1599–1667), Italian architect, a leading figure of the Italian baroque.

Borrow, George (Henry) (1803–81), English writer. His travels with Gypsies provided material for the picaresque narrative *Lavengro* (1851) and its sequel *The Romany Rye* (1857).

borrow ▶ **verb** [with obj.] **1** take and use (something belonging to someone else) with the intention of returning it: *he had* **borrowed** *a car* **from** *one of his colleagues.*
■ take and use (money) from a person or bank under an agreement to pay it back later. ■ take and use (a book) from a library for a fixed period of time. ■ take (a word or idea) from another language, person, or source and use it in one's own language or work: *the term is* **borrowed from** *Greek.*
2 Golf allow (a certain distance) when playing a shot to compensate for sideways motion of the ball due to a slope or other irregularity.
▶ **noun** Golf a slope or other irregularity on a golf course which must be compensated for when playing a shot.
– PHRASES **be (living) on borrowed time** used to convey that someone has survived against expectations, with the implication that they will not do so for much longer. **borrow trouble** N. Amer. take needless action that may have detrimental effects.
– DERIVATIVES **borrower** noun.
– ORIGIN Old English *borgian* 'borrow against security', of Germanic origin; related to Dutch and German *borgen*.

USAGE Some people confuse the two words **lend** and **borrow**, which have reciprocal but different meanings: see usage at **LEND**.

borrowing ▶ **noun** [mass noun] the action of borrowing something: *a curb on government borrowing* | [count noun] *the group had total borrowings of $570 million.*
■ [count noun] a word or idea taken from another language, person, or source and used in one's own language or work: *the majority of designs were* **borrowings from** *the continent.*

borrow pit ▶ **noun** a pit resulting from the excavation of material for use in embankments.

Borsalino /ˌbɔːsəˈliːnəʊ/ ▶ **noun** (pl. **Borsalinos**) trademark a man's wide-brimmed felt hat.
– ORIGIN early 20th cent.: from the name of the manufacturer.

borscht /bɔːʃt/ (also **borsch** /bɔːʃ/) ▶ **noun** [mass noun] a Russian or Polish soup made with beetroot and usually served with sour cream.
– ORIGIN from Russian *borshch*.

Borscht Belt /bɔːʃt/ ▶ **noun** N. Amer. humorous a resort area in the Catskill Mountains frequented chiefly by Jewish people of eastern European origin.

borstal /ˈbɔːst(ə)l/ ▶ **noun** Brit. historical a custodial institution for young offenders.
– ORIGIN early 20th cent.: named after the village of *Borstal* in southern England, where the first of these was established.

bort /bɔːt/ (also **boart**) ▶ **noun** [mass noun] small, granular, opaque diamonds, used as an abrasive in cutting tools.
– ORIGIN early 17th cent.: from Dutch *boort*.

borzoi /ˈbɔːzɔɪ/ ▶ **noun** (pl. **borzois**) a large Russian wolfhound of a breed with a narrow head and silky, typically white, coat.
– ORIGIN late 19th cent.: from Russian *borzoi* (adjective), *borzaya* (noun), from *borzyi* 'swift'.

boscage /ˈbɒskɪdʒ/ (also **boskage**) ▶ **noun** [mass noun] a mass of trees or shrubs.
– ORIGIN late Middle English: from Old French; ultimately of Germanic origin and related to **BUSH**[1]. Compare with **BOCAGE**.

Bosch /bɒʃ/, Hieronymus (c.1450–1516), Dutch painter. Bosch's highly detailed works are typically crowded with half-human, half-animal creatures and grotesque demons in settings symbolic of sin and folly. His individual style prefigures that of the surrealists.

Bose /bəʊs/, Satyendra Nath (1894–1974), Indian physicist. With Einstein he described fundamental particles which later came to be known as *bosons*.

bosh ▶ **noun** [mass noun] informal nonsense; rubbish: *that's a load of bosh.*
– ORIGIN mid 19th cent.: from Turkish *boş* 'empty, worthless'.

bosie /ˈbəʊzi/ (also **bosey**) ▶ **noun** Cricket Australian term for **GOOGLY**.
– ORIGIN early 20th cent.: from the name of Bernard J. T. *Bosanquet* (1877–1936), English all-round cricketer, + **-IE**.

boskage ▶ **noun** variant spelling of **BOSCAGE**.

bosky /ˈbɒski/ ▶ **adjective** literary covered by trees or bushes; wooded: *a slow-moving river meandering between bosky banks.*
– ORIGIN late 16th cent.: from Middle English *bosk*, variant of **BUSH**[1].

Bosman /ˈbɒzmən/ ▶ **noun** [usu. as modifier] used with reference to a European Court ruling which obliges professional football or other sports clubs to allow players over the age of 25 to move freely between clubs once their contracts have expired.
– ORIGIN 1990s: named after Jean-Marc *Bosman*, a Belgian footballer who brought a legal case which resulted in the ruling.

Bosnia /ˈbɒznɪə/ short for **BOSNIA–HERZEGOVINA**.
■ a region in the Balkans forming the larger, northern part of Bosnia–Herzegovina.
– DERIVATIVES **Bosnian** adjective & noun.

Bosnia–Herzegovina (also **Bosnia and Herzegovina**) a country in the Balkans, formerly a constituent republic of Yugoslavia; pop. 3,964,388 (est. 2002); capital, Sarajevo.

Bosnia and Herzegovina were conquered by the Turks in 1463. The province of Bosnia–Herzegovina was annexed by Austria in 1908, an event which contributed towards the outbreak of the First World War. In 1918 it became part of the Kingdom of Serbs, Croats, and Slovenes, which changed its name to Yugoslavia in 1929. In 1992 Bosnia–Herzegovina followed Slovenia and Croatia in declaring independence, but ethnic conflict among Muslims, Serbs, and Croats quickly reduced the republic to a state of civil war. An accord signed in December 1995 formally brought the conflict to an end.

bosom ▶ **noun** a woman's chest or breasts: *her ample bosom* | [mass noun] *the dress offered a fair display of bosom.*
■ a part of a dress covering the chest. ■ literary the space between a person's clothing and their chest

Baumann & Baumann

In and through their Baumann & Baumann office, Barbara and Gerd Baumann develop comprehensive design and communication concepts for businesses, institutions, and communities; for exhibitions and representations at trade fairs; and for orientation and information systems. They also design books and posters.

Their work for the German Bundestag Bonn, for the Great Court of the British Museum, London, and for international companies such as DaimlerChrysler and Siemens are well known. Yet they have also put their design mark on numerous smaller initiatives and cultural or social institutions.

In addition to various guest professorships, the designer couple has also held lectures at home and abroad, can look back on extensive publications in journals and books, and has continuously been awarded national and international prizes for numerous works.

Quite independently of any fashionable zeitgeist trends in visual communication, Baumann & Baumann may look back on 25 years of inventing and developing a visual grammar and language referring to the subjects they represent.

Theirs is an idiom that results from a certain notion, an attitude, geared toward an idea, both helping to determine and to initiate its subject matter. They relate and link form and content, subject matter and expression, experimental programs, and programmed experiments.

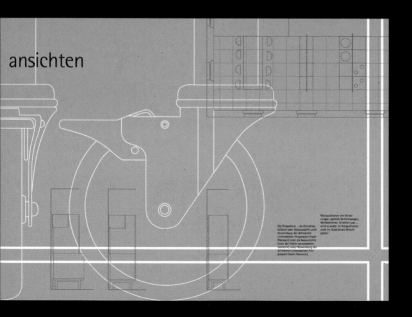

ansichten

Style guide and design manual for Corporate Design Bulthaup
This manual explains the range of styles and treatments to be used in the presentation of the company's product range. It covers the application of typography along with the use of illustrative drawings, linear folders, and color.

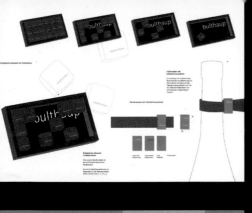

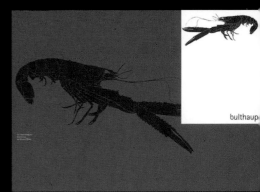

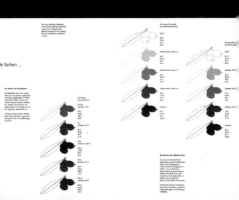

logo vertikal

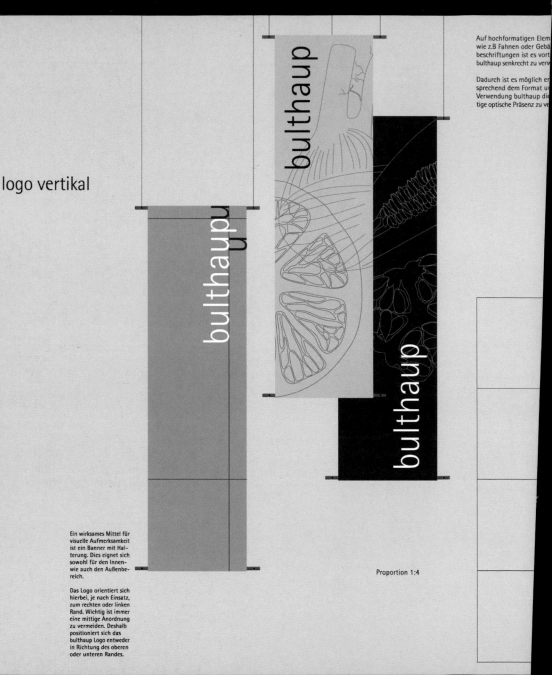

Auf hochformatigen Elem
wie z.B Fahnen oder Gebä
beschriftungen ist es vort
bulthaup senkrecht zu verv

Dadurch ist es möglich er
sprechend dem Format u
Verwendung bulthaup di
tige optische Präsenz zu ve

bulthaup

bulthaup

bulthaup

bulthaup

Ein wirksames Mittel für
visuelle Aufmerksamkeit
ist ein Banner mit Hal-
terung. Dies eignet sich
sowohl für den Innen-
wie auch den Außenbe-
reich.

Das Logo orientiert sich
hierbei, je nach Einsatz,
zum rechten oder linken
Rand. Wichtig ist immer
eine mittige Anordnung
zu vermeiden. Deshalb
positioniert sich das
bulthaup Logo entweder
in Richtung des oberen
oder unteren Randes.

Proportion 1:4

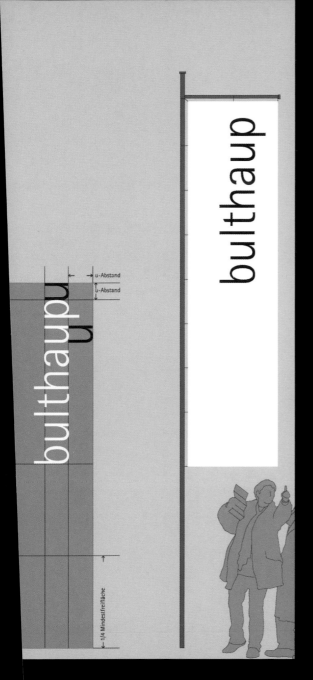

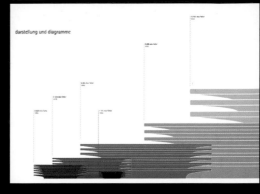

bulthaup

visuelles
menü

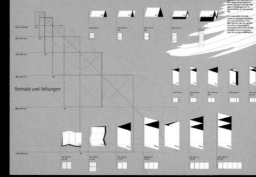

formate und faltungen

**Design manual for
Corporate Design Bulthaup**
Type position is influenced
not only by esthetics, but

also by such practical
considerations as paper
formats and foldings.

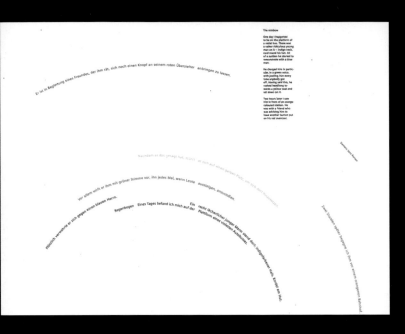

The rainbow

One day I happened to be on the platform of a violet bus. There was a rather ridiculous young man on it – indigo neck, cord round his hat. All of a sudden he started to remonstrate with a blue man.

He charged him in particular, in a green voice, with jostling him every time anybody got off. Having said this, he rushed headlong towards a yellow seat and sat down on it.

Two hours later I saw him in front of an orange-coloured station. He was with a friend who was advising him to have another button put on his red overcoat.

10

3

6

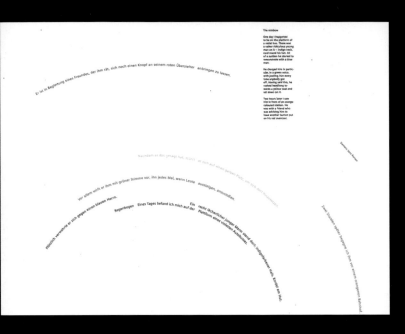

Interjektionen

Pst! he! ah!

oh! hm! ah! uff!

eh! nanu!

oh! bah! puh! hui!

uh! ei! eh! na!

he! pah!

Nanu! eh! bah! oh!

he! naja!

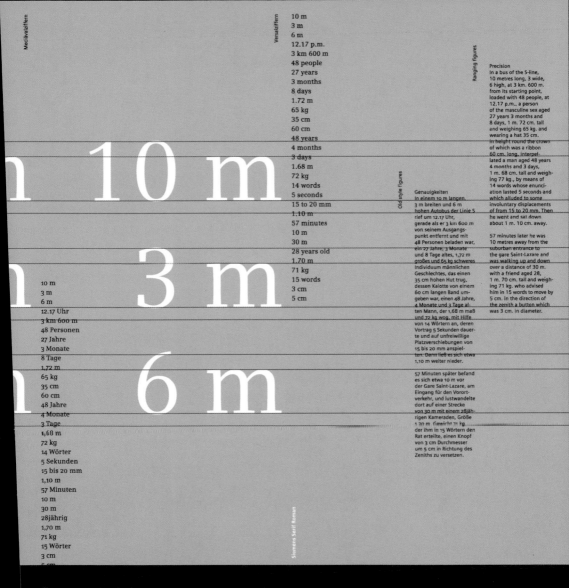

Corporate Design Book for Siemens
Baumann & Baumann developed the corporate design for Siemens AG. To accompany the design manual, they also designed a book, published by Siemens, which explained the thinking and ideas behind the design and implementation of Siemens' corporate identity.

HAIKU

SUMMER S LONG NECK

PLAIT HAT TOES ABUSE RETREAT

H   A   I   K   U

STATION BUTTON FRIEND

S   U   N   D   L   A   N   G   E   R   H   A   L   S

F   U   S   S   T   R   I   T   T   S   C   H   R   E   I   U   N   D

B   A   H   N   H   O   F   K   N   O   P   F   B   E   G   E   G   N   U   N

H A I

S

F   U   S

B   A   H

Siemens Slab Roman

Corporate design

Different modes of expression can transform the same set of facts to make completely different statements and to alter meaning. The sense of words and sentences can be changed through emphasis, arrangement, and punctuation. A visual rendering of language, typography enables us to communicate the same subject matter in different ways.

K
U
N
T
H

???

!!!

Hesitation

I don't really know
where it happened...
in a church, a dustbin,
a charnel-house? A bus,
perhaps? There were...
but what were there,
though? Eggs, carpets,
radishes? Skeletons?
Yes, but with their flesh
still round them, and
alive. I think that's how
it was. People in a bus.

Einem Autobus vielleicht?

But one (or two?) of
them was making him-
self conspicuous, I
don't really know in what
way. For his megalo-
mania? For his edginess?
For his melancholy?
Rather... more precisely...
for his youth, which
was embellished by a
long...

Leute in einem Autobus.

nose? chin? thumb? so-
neck, and by a strange,
strange, strange hat.
He started to quarrel, yes,
that's right, with, no
doubt, another passenger
(man or woman? child
or old age pensioner?)
This ended, this finished
by ending in a common-
place sort of way, prob-
ably by the flight of one
of the two adversaries.

nein: Hals, und einem seltsamen Hut, seltsam, seltsam.

I rather think that it was
the same character I
met, but where? in front
of a church? in front
of a charnel-house? in
front of a dustbin? With
a friend who must have
been talking to him about
something, but about
what? About what? about
what?

Zögern   Ich weiß nicht genau, wo ich das abspielte...   in einer Kirche, einer Mülltonne, einem Beinhaus?   Skelette?

Dort war...   aber was war dort noch?   Eier, Teppiche, Radieschen?   und lebendig.   Ich glaube, das wars.

ja, aber noch mit ihrem Fleisch dran

Aber einer davon (oder zwei) fiel auf, ich weiß nicht recht durch was,
Durch seinen Größenwahn?   Durch seine Schmierigkeit?   Durch seinen Trübsinn?

Nase? Kinn? Daumen?

Besser...   genauer...   durch seine Jugend, geschmückt mit einer langen...

(Mann oder Frau? Kind oder Greis?)

Er fing Streit an, ja, das ist es, mit einem anderen Fahrgast zweifellos

Das ging so aus, also, das endete damit, auf irgendeine Art und Weise zu Ende zu gehen,   wahrscheinlich durch die Flucht des einen der beiden Gegner.

Ich glaube, es war dieselbe Person, der ich wiederbegegnete, aber wo?

Vor einer Kirche?   Vor einem Beinhaus?   Vor einer Mülltonne?

Mit einem Kameraden, der ihm wohl irgendetwas erzählte,   aber was,   aber was,   aber was?

Cross-examination

At what time did the
12.23 p.m. ticket bus proceed to its destination
of the Porte du Champer-
ret arrive on that day?
At 12.48 p.m.

Were there many people
on the aforesaid S bus?
Bags oil set.

Did you particularly notice
any of them?
An individual who had a
very long neck and a plait
round his hat.

Was his demeanour as
singular as his attire and
his bearing?

At the very beginning, no,
it was normal, but in the
end it proved to be that
of a slightly hysterical pa-
rambic cyclothymic, in a
state of hypergamic incta-
pistic.

How did that become ap-
parent?
The individual in question
interpellated the man
next to him and award him
in a wheezing tone if he
was not making a point of
treading on his toes eve-
ry time any passengers
got on or off.

Had this reproach any
foundation?
Tue no idea.

Now did it the incident ter-
minate?
By the precipitance flight
of the young man who
went to occupy a vacant
seat.

Was there any sequel to
this incident?
Less than two hours later.

In what did this sequel
consist?
In the reappearance
of this person across my
path.

Where and how did you
see him again?
When I was passing the
Cour de Rome in a bus.

What was he doing there?
He was having some
some sartorial advice.

Im vorher Zeit fuhr der Autobus der Linie S, Richtung Porte Champerret, Abfahrtszeit 12 Uhr dreiundzwanzig, an jenem
Um 12 Uhr achtundvierzig.
Waren in dem Autobus...

Cartlidge Levene

Cartlidge Levene was founded in 1987 by Ian Cartlidge and Adam Levene. Its team of eight is committed to delivering communication design that is both functional and inspirational.

Located in London, it works for a wide range of client sectors including arts, design, corporate, government, retail, health, and leisure. It also works across a range of media applying its approach to branding, information design, literature, Web sites, environmental graphics, and wayfinding.

Cartlidge Levene believes that intelligently conceived, well-structured, and beautifully executed design can communicate and engage with the user in a powerful way. Its designs are founded on an understanding of the issues and problems that surround a design brief. It takes time to fully understand its clients' cultures and environments and engage with the key issues up front. Problem solving is key to its approach and this ensures that its designs are always relevant and effective, built on a solid understanding of the messages its clients want to communicate.

Typography is central to everything Cartlidge Levene does. It shapes the way the group communicates and creates the voice that talks to its varied audiences. It is the tool that Cartlidge Levene uses to create order, structure, and texture, and the medium it uses to create tone of voice and identity.

Cartlidge Levene thinks beyond surface appearance, working with its clients to ensure that the underlying structure of written information makes sense and helps to deliver the message in an intelligent, clear manner. This drives its approach to typographic detailing and layout, delivering information in a way that is appropriate to the audience.

Cartlidge Levene believes that typography is a powerful tool which can be used to shape and color the way it communicates. Well-designed communication can lift itself above the merely ephemeral to become meaningful, legible, user-friendly, and lasting.

"Its only a minority of young people who spoil it for the rest of us..." Young People's Workshop

"In certain areas there's a tendency to criminalise young people, but there is very little for young people to do... it's important that there are public spaces for young people to gather and do productive things." Citizens' Workshop

Government reports
Towns and Cities: Partners in Urban Renaissance is a set of five reports produced for the Government's Urban Summit to publicize the findings of research into urban regeneration carried out across 24 towns and cities in the UK. Aiming to make them feel friendly and accessible, the reports were designed around a simple, robust typographic system enabling complex information to be read and cross-referenced with ease. A series of photographs commissioned in each city provide a visual introduction to each volume.

You may not want to hear
You may want to hear
You want to hear
You may not hear
You may hear
You hear

The Unilever Series:
Bruce Nauman

A provocative audio installation
created for Tate Modern's Turbine Hall
Hear it to experience it
12 October 2004 to 28 March 2005
Free admission

MODERN
TATE

Exhibition catalog and marketing materials
Bruce Nauman: Raw Materials was held in the Turbine Hall at Tate Modern, in London. Cartlidge Levene were commissioned to design the exhibition catalog and marketing material. Nauman's installation consisted entirely of sound, with 20 spoken-word audio works playing simultaneously in the vast space. This provided an unusual challenge for the catalog as there was no visual aspect to focus on. The design response was to document the audio works as beautiful, typographic pieces, evoking the rhythm of the delivery and capturing nuances and inflections of the spoken words. The typography is bold and distinctive with an understated neutrality that doesn't overpower the content. Subtle changes in paper color and techniques such as foil-blocking were used to introduce a tactile element to the work alongside the simple, structured typographic approach.

OK OK OK

OK OK OK OK OK OK OK OK OK OK OK OK OK OK OK OK OK
OK OK OK OK OK OK OK OK OK OK OK OK OK OK OK OK OK
OK OK OK OK OK OK OK OK OK OK OK OK OK OK OK OK OK
OK OK OK OK OK OK OK OK OK OK OK OK OK OK OK OK OK
OK OK OK OK OK OK OK OK OK OK OK OK OK OK OK OK OK
OK OK OK OK OK OK OK OK OK OK OK OK OK OK OK OK OK
OK OK OK OK OK OK OK OK OK OK OK OK OK OK OK OK OK
OK OK OK OK OK OK OK OK OK OK OK OK OK OK OK OK OK
OK OK OK OK OK OK OK OK OK OK OK OK OK OK OK OK OK
OK OK OK OK OK OK OK OK OK OK OK OK OK OK OK OK OK
OK OK OK OK OK OK OK OK OK OK OK OK OK OK OK OK OK
OK OK OK OK OK OK OK OK OK OK OK OK OK OK OK OK OK
OK OK OK OK OK OK OK OK OK OK OK OK OK OK OK OK OK
OK OK OK OK OK OK OK OK OK OK OK OK OK OK OK OK OK
OK OK OK OK OK OK OK OK OK OK OK OK OK OK OK OK OK
OK OK OK OK OK OK OK OK OK OK OK OK OK OK OK OK OK
OK OK OK OK OK OK OK OK OK OK OK OK OK OK OK OK OK
OK OK OK OK OK OK OK OK OK OK OK OK OK OK OK OK OK
OK OK OK OK OK OK OK OK OK OK OK OK OK OK OK OK OK
OK OK OK OK OK OK OK OK OK OK OK OK OK OK OK OK OK
OK OK OK OK OK OK OK OK OK OK OK OK OK OK OK OK OK
OK OK OK OK OK OK OK OK OK OK OK OK OK OK OK OK OK
OK OK OK OK OK OK OK OK OK OK OK OK OK OK OK ...

Think Think Think

Think think think think think think think think think think
think think think think think think think think think think think
think think think think think think think think think think think
think think think think think think think think think think think
think think think think think think think think think think think
think think think think think think think think think think think
think think think think think think think think think think think
think think think think think think think think think think think
think think think think think think think think think think think
think think think think think think think think think think think
think think think think think think think think think think think
think think think think think think think think think think think
think think think think think think think think think think think
think think think think think think think think think think think
think think think think think think think think think think think
think think think think think think think think think think think
think think think think think think think think think think think
think think think think think think think think think think think
think think think think think think think think think think think
think think think think think think think think think think think
think think think think think think think think think think think
think think think think think think think think think ...

Bruce Nauman — Raw Materials

ISBN 1-85437-559-8

UK £11.99
US $21.95
Can $39.95

9 781854 375599

TATE

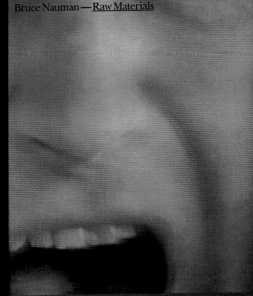

Bruce Nauman — Raw Materials

here are some
key challenges to
our board level
objectives...

board assurance
products for
good
governance
NHS

...and some prompts
to reassure us
we are making a
balanced response

Healthcare
Commission

NHS
Appointments Commission
Clinical Governance Support Team

NHS Governance cards

The objective of the Good Governance cards was to provide NHS Board members with the information they need to help them assess and discuss the challenges they face. Cartlidge Levene created a set of 24 cards secured with a binding screw. This allows individual cards to be referred to easily, while keeping the set together as a compact pack. The front of each card refers to a specific challenge that NHS Boards face while the reverse provides helpful prompts for solutions. A clear typographic hierarchy aids quick reference and a clear, jargon-free language aims to engage all users.

challenges

1 reduce serious
adverse events within
a given speciality

Key challenges

Can we assure ourselves that by examining clinical research and practices we do not have a serious problem with adverse events within the trust?

What is the preventable death statistic within the trust over the last 12 months and have we examined the cost to the institution?

With regard to corporate manslaughter are we discharging our duties corporately?

Have we involved patients within the trust in the examination of our adverse events cycle?

Have we got an effective clinical appraisal system for all doctors in relation to the delivery of care?

Have we reliable and meaningful up to date clinical information that is analysed, used and learnt from from which describes all aspects of the service?

here are some
key challenges to
our board level
objectives...

board assurance
products for
good
governance
NHS

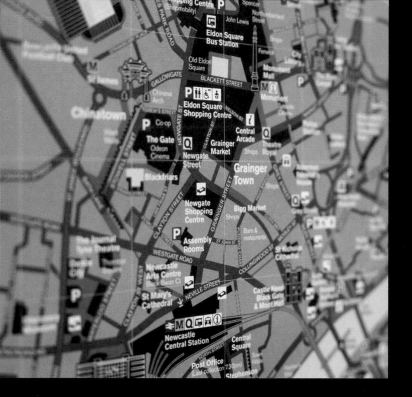

Tourist map

WalkRide is an information and movement strategy for NewcastleGateshead, UK. It is aimed at improving the visitor experience and presenting NewcastleGateshead as one destination. Cartlidge Levene collaborated with wayfinding specialists City ID to create a new range of maps integral to the city's overall WalkRide system. The content, design, and scale of each map was considered according to its function and audience. The range includes large-scale, heads-up maps located at bus stops, and a printed pedestrian map distributed by the visitor information centers.

David Jury and Fox Ash

I established the Fox Ash design and publishing studio in 1998, specializing in book design, writing, editorial, and letterpress printing. The idea was that commissions to write and design pay for projects that are both designed *and printed* "in-house." Only two projects have, so far, been completed: *In Darkest England*, about Mass Observation in the late 1930s (a boxed set of 23 sheets exploring the observers observations of the other observers!) and *Morocco*, a double-diary (the original and the self-censored version, set side-by-side) written by the photographer Humphrey Spender in 1934.

It was neither the printing nor the design of these projects that took so much time; it was finding the appropriate subject and completing the research. Having said that, Fox Ash publications *are* printed letterpress using a Vandercook proofing press. This means, taking *Morocco*, for example, that each (four-page) sheet had to be hand-fed through the press at least eight times to produce the two or more colors required per page. The process is slow, but wholly justified by the total control it affords.

I have not included *In Darkest England* here since it has been reproduced in numerous publications. Writing and designing for mainstream publishing is a very different, but equally exhilarating activity. The restrictions caused by budgets and deadlines being wholly justified, this time, by the mass audience made available.

In 1998 I became editor of *TypoGraphic*, the journal of the International Society of Typographic Designers (ISTD). Each issue is designed by a different, invited typographer or design studio, chosen for an independence of mind appropriate to the theme of the issue. In the circumstances, rigorous creative endeavor and a huge variety of craft performance should not be a surprise. It certainly ensures that every conceivable method of producing words on a page continues to be explored.

Book design
The aim of the design for *Letterpress: the allure of the handmade* was to give the reader as close an encounter with the physical nature of letterpress and its related materials as possible. The preliminary pages presented the raw materials: the 3-D type and the ink, followed by the resulting printed image. Full-bleed photographs were used regularly throughout.

Contents

A Rotovision Book

Produced and distributed by RotoVision SA
Route Suisse 9
CH–1295 Mies
Switzerland

RotoVision SA
Sales & Editorial Office
Sheridan House, 112/116A Western Road
Hove BN3 1DD, UK

Tel: +44 (0) 1273 72 72 68
Fax: +44 (0) 1273 72 72 69
Email: sales@rotovision.com
Web: www.rotovision.com

Copyright © Rotovision SA 2004

Designed by David Jury
Art Director Luke Herriott
Photography by Xavier Young and David Jury

Reprographics and printing in Singapore by ProVision Pte.
Tel: +65 6334 7720
Fax: +65 6334 7721

Introduction   Attitudes to letterpress

"The principles of typography are not a set of dead conventions but the tribal customs of the magic forest ..." **Robert Bringhurst**, *typographer and poet*

This book offers the opportunity to compare the work of artists, craftsmen, and designers. Although the subject is letterpress, the emphasis is not exclusively so. Instead, I have taken the opportunity to display and celebrate an eclectic range of typographic material, exploring the notions of craft and the underlying motivation of those using letterpress today.[1]

Letterpress, because of its remarkable commercial longevity — over 550 years — tends to be associated with tradition. The history of printing was driven by proven, sensible formulae within the print trade. Eventually, however, forces from outside the trade began to question established norms and to influence the appearance and the function of type.

Left: *Alphabete Sierschriften und Monogramme*, published by Fr. Bartholomäus in Erfurt, circa 1870s.

Right: A spread from *The Next Call*, edited and designed by H. N. Werkman in Grõningen, circa 1923.

Following page: Groß (sans serif) wood type.

people know next to nothing about Morocco, only the prices of hotels and hired cars; they blink at the idea of there being any interest outside the town.

President of the
Syndicat d'initiatives

Tangier
Casablanca

Chez Chic
Pullman-Bars
to Casablanca

undoubtedly clever, but he said he had been to the universities of Heidelberg and Edinburgh, a statement which could not be taken too seriously, when it later became apparent that he was entirely unable to read or write in Latin letters. He had a collection of visiting cards and letters written to him by English people whom he had picked up in the same way as he had picked up me; and these he occasionally produced and showed me, hoping that I would read them out to him. It was an extraordinary idea that when he received a letter from England he would probably not know what was written in it until gradually, over the course of perhaps two years, various people had read extracts aloud to him. I finally established his inability to read or write by asking him to write his name and address in my notebook; this he could only do in Arabic, and he was, for once, embarrassed and evasive when I asked him to write it in English. Amongst other lies, he told me that his wife had died eight years previously; I discovered later that he had never been married, although it was not until the last day or two of our acquaintance that he finally admitted that he really had dealings with men, as he put it.

Friday 18th
Inter-pm 10/-
hotel 20/-
horse-drawn vehicle to
(negociie) 20/-
bus to guide for whole day
and tips 30/-
Goa during stay, motion
in market 10/-
taxis 15/-

Ackmed, failed to turn up, and so I got into the big Pullman bus for Casablanca, where I was to present a letter of introduction to the President of the Syndicat d'Initatifs, which was actually the most unsurprising institution that I have every sought help from. The journey to Casa was dull. The bus was filled mainly with vaguely smart women who were probably the wives of French officers stationed in the interior; there were some wealthy Arabs, one very handsome. It seemed somehow inappropriate riding with these people across miles of arid desert in this comfortable bus, when only ten years ago it would have been a dangerous adventure to attempt the same journey, even with a car. Casablanca seemed to me unpleasant. It was full of French officers who swaggered and and of great boulevards with shady arcades and shops called Chez Chic ; the boulevards generally ended quite suddenly in heaps of old building materials and weedy sand-pits. The President of the Syndicate was very charming but entirely unable to do anything for me besides give me two letters of introduction to more distant president, and these letters turned out to be even more useless, for those

The drive to Casablanca, where I was to interview the President of the Syndicat d'Initiatives – the President of the Syndicat d'Initiatives – a most unenterprising institution — was comparatively busy, the occupants of the enormous Pullman bus being mainly French officers wives and some wealthy Arabs, one very handsome. It was slightly inappropriate rushing with these particular people across miles of arid desert which only ten years ago was a dangerous adventure to cross. But although these are two or three complete changes of scenic character there was nothing which compared at all with the wonders of the journey from Marrakech to Ouarzazate. Casablanca to Marrakech, this stretch was slightly more interesting, some exciting looking beehive villages appearing to left and right, but again nothing really exciting.

58

Book design

For *Morocco* texts are letterpress printed and the photographs printed litho and tipped-in. The texts consist of two versions of the same diary set by side-by-side to allow the reader to judge the moral climate of the time (mid 1930s). The book also includes 36 photographs, none of which had been previously reproduced.

Book and promotional materials for ISTD

TypoGraphic Writing (left) contains a selection of writings from 30 years of *TypoGraphic,* the journal of the International Society of Typographic Designers (ISTD). The typefaces are *Foundry Form Serif* and *Foundry Form Sans.* The poster (right) was designed as an in-store promotion for *TypoGraphic 55.* It illustrated the whole journal (designed by Attik) and used extensive quotes from each article. This was set entirely in Univers.

TypoGraphic 55 The real world issue Attik

TypoGraphic is the journal of the International Society of Typographic Designers (ISTD) and is published three times a year. Each issue is designed by an invited typographer with an international reputation and is dedicated to one aspect of typographic design.

Jannuzzi Smith

Michele Jannuzzi and Richard Smith are cofounders and Directors of Jannuzzi Smith, a design studio established in 1993, combining excellence in the disciplines of communication design and technology.

Jannuzzi Smith has an excellent knowledge of communication design across a broad spectrum of media enabling it to provide creative solutions that harness the possibilities of digital technology.

In designing communications for its clients, it works with them to provide strategic and creative thinking. It starts with their business needs and communication aims, helping them to decide how to tackle problems and realize their objectives. Economical and efficient solutions are often high on its list of priorities. Reaching target audiences in creative and stimulating ways is a prerequisite.

Jannuzzi Smith's creative skills are supported by proven technical experience and proficiency, including extensive programming skills in-house. It has developed applications including a suite of Web-based brand management tools, and easy-to-use, cost-effective systems that extend the benefits of database publishing from Web sites to printed items, automating the creation of anything from posters to complex brochures.

Its combination of energy, enthusiasm, and experience has fostered many long-standing client relationships in Switzerland, Germany, France, the USA, and the UK. Its staff are equally cosmopolitan.

Course brochures
Central Saint Martins College, London, needed to consolidate its visual presentation to better promote its services and products in an increasingly competitive education market. It was imperative that the course brochures did not appear "corporate." Interrelated items were fed by a common database which managed everything from factual and descriptive text to images illustrating the work and spirit of the college. The system exports content straight into Quark XPress and PDFs—fully formatted layouts with a high level of design detailing. The solution provides clearer, more consistent messages for readers in both printed and online media.

Central
Saint Martins
Directory
2005—6

Studying at Central Saint Martins

Apple Macs for Beginners

AppleBär for Beginners – Umsnap

BA (Honours) Criticism, Communication and Curation for Arts and Design

Alumni

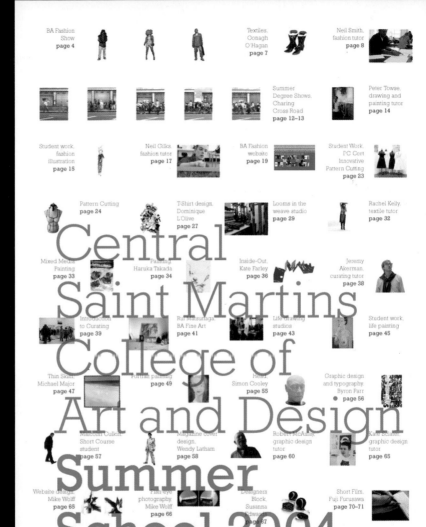

BA Fashion Show **page 4**

Textiles. Oonagh O'Hagan **page 7**

Neil Smith. fashion tutor **page 8**

Summer Degree Shows. Charing Cross Road **page 12–13**

Peter Towse. drawing and painting tutor **page 14**

Student work. fashion illustration **page 15**

Neil Gilks. fashion tutor **page 17**

BA Fashion website **page 19**

Student Work. PC Cert Innovative Pattern Cutting **page 23**

Pattern Cutting **page 24**

T-Shirt design. Dominique L'Olive **page 27**

Looms in the weave studio **page 29**

Rachel Kelly. textile tutor **page 32**

Mixed Media Painting **page 33**

Painting Haruka Takada **page 34**

Inside-Out. Kate Farley **page 36**

Jeremy Akerman. curating tutor **page 38**

Introduction to Curating **page 39**

Rui Matsunaga. BA Fine Art **page 41**

Life drawing studios **page 43**

Student work. life painting **page 45**

Thin Skin. Michael Major **page 47**

Portrait painting **page 49**

Head. Simon Cooley **page 55**

Graphic design and typography. Byron Parr ● **page 56**

Malcolm Culkin. Short Course student **page 57**

Magazine cover design. Wendy Latham **page 58**

Robert McAulay. graphic design tutor **page 60**

Kate Scuter. graphic design tutor **page 65**

Website design. Mike Wolff **page 65**

Fish-eye photography. Mike Wolff **page 66**

Designers Block. Susanna Edwards **page 67**

Short Film. Fuji Furusawa **page 70–71**

Christmas card illustration. Matthew Abbiss **page 74**

Alistair Steele. BA Arts, Design and Environment **page 75**

Anne Marie Hopkins. The Design Lab **page 77**

Queen of Hearts. Ruth Eisenhart **page 78–79**

Central
Saint Martins
College of
Art and Design
Summer
School 2004

Left: Degree courses template
Right: Brochure cover

Posters by Bruno Monguzzi for Museo Cantonale d'Arte, Lugano at Central Saint Martins College of Art and Design

THE NAKE WOR

Exhibition and catalog

The Naked Word exhibition consisted of a collection of posters designed by Bruno Monguzzi for the Museo Cantonale d'Arte in Lugano. The catalog is printed on Arctic Extreme stock and used stochastic screening to faithfully reproduce his sharp designs and use of color.

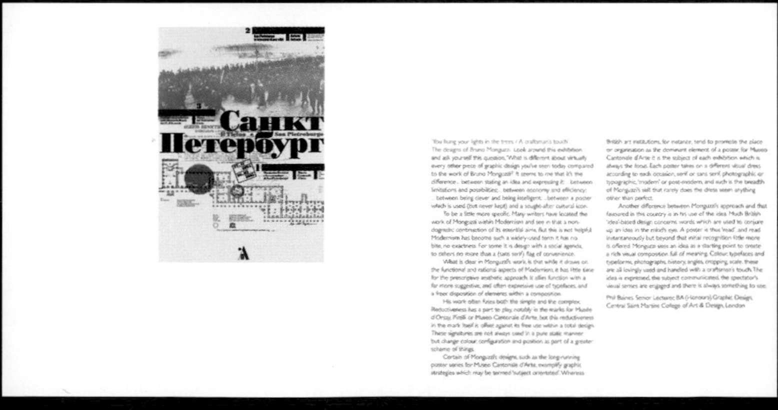

Thirteen

Thirteen is a graphic design company that was formed in Bristol, UK, in 1999. Thirteen has constantly sought to produce effective, well-crafted, and appropriate design solutions. Its clients include corporate, cultural, public body, and media organizations. Its projects range from brand consultancy and corporate communications to 3-D and screen-based information design.

Thirteen's company structure centers around a small core of designers and project managers who work under the creative guidance of Directors Danny Jenkins and John Underwood, both practicing graphic designers. Specialist consultants are brought in where necessary, depending on the scope of each project.

Thirteen strives to strike a balance in its work between the contrasting disciplines and objectives of its clients. It sees this diversity of experience as critical to bringing fresh approaches to projects.

For example, an approach or typographic solution born from a large-scale brand alignment project may influence and inform the direction of a small signage project.

If there is a common thread to be found running through Thirteen's work, it is one driven by its strong desire to produce meaningful work with an underlying clarity and simplicity, which clearly influences its typographic approach. Type is rarely used as decoration—typography works as a graphic framework in which messaging, image, and color content sit. Thirteen's work is not about typography; it is about the appropriate communication of message using typographic (and other) graphic elements.

Festival brochures and marketing materials
The brochures, flyers, and buttons shown are part of a range of communication materials for the Cheltenham Science Festival and the Cheltenham Festival of Literature. These formed the basis of an overall clarification of their communications, based on flexible and efficient typographic systems alongside a new identity for each festival.

Science for Schools

www.cheltenhamfestivals.org.uk
Bookings 01242 775822

Sponsored by QinetiQ

Wednesday 8 June

Robot Thought
S1 9.45–10.45am
Key Stage 1 and 2
Town Hall £4
If a fully-functional, thinking robot was developed would you consider it human? Explore the future of robot technology and find out if you can tell the difference between science fact and science fiction as you meet some of the robots of the future.

Space Adventure
S2 10–11am Key Stage 2
S3 12–1pm Key Stage 1
Town Hall £4
3, 2, 1 lift off! Buckle up for a flight through our Solar System where you make up the crew. Your interplanetary space flight will take in all the sights including giant planets, a reconstruction of Neil Armstrong's famous footstep, a hunt for alien life on Mars and a bombardment of large asteroids.

Prime Suspect
S4 2–3pm
Key Stage 3 and 4
Town Hall £4
Is there a code that could unlock the mystery of prime numbers? One million dollars has been offered to the person who can solve mathematics' greatest unsolved problem. Join mathematician **Marcus Du Sautoy** to explore the mysterious world of numbers and see if you can decipher the code.

Thursday 9 June

Science Physical
S5 9.30–10.30am,
S6 11am–12pm
S7 1–2pm
Key Stage 2
Nelson Thornes £4
Join our new high energy workshop and find out more about the physics of forces and the biology of muscles through our fun musical workout. Different games, animations, music and rap will give you a scientific experience you will never forget!

In association with Science – Physical

Sponsored by
nelson thornes

The Big Blue
S8 9.30am–10.30am
Key Stage 3
Town Hall £4
Did you know that sharks are not nearly the most dangerous creature in the ocean? Or that life thrives even in the icy waters of Antarctica? Dive in and discover the depths of marine life, both above and below the water with **Frances Dipper** and find out about a world of amazing creatures from giant cuttlefish to colourful coral.

Material World
S9 9.45–10.45am
Key Stage 3
Town Hall £4
Animals scream when hurt, plants go limp, but do rocks and metals feel pain? Join materials scientist **Mark Miodownik** to smash and break your way through lots of different materials to find out. Do they know if they are damaged, and if so can they heal themselves? Prepare to never to be able to look at a coat-hanger in quite the same way again!

Weird Science
S10 11.45am–12.45pm
Key Stage 3
Town Hall £4
Why does toast always land butter-side down? Explore the amazing world of Murphy's Law to prove that whatever can go wrong will go wrong. Find out if it is all in your mind through a magical show of illusions, sensory tests and mind bending challenges.

Plastic Fantastic
S11 1.45–2.45pm
Key Stage 3
Town Hall £4
What do disposable nappies, flat screen TVs, oil slicks and cress have in common? The answer is plastic! Join **Averil McDonald**, winner of Channel 4's Scrapheap Challenge to find out how to make your own slime... and discover how these wonderful polymers can make you a Nobel prize winner or a millionaire!

Friday 10 June

Blazing Science
S12 9.30–10.30am
S13 11.30am–12.30pm
Key Stage 1 and 2
Town Hall £4
Back by popular demand, Disney performer **Mik Jacobs** presents an unforgettable exploration of the science of fire live on stage. Why do fireworks explode? Why are stunt people told to drop and roll? Featuring fantastic facts and cinematic secrets, Blazing Science explores the exciting science of energy, matter and fire.

Brain and Body Show
S14 10–11am
Key Stage 2
Town Hall £4
Join the team from At-Bristol to take part in a lively game-show style look at our brains and how they interact with our bodies and the world around us. Find out if seeing is believing, how to improve your memory, or even if you're a super smeller!

Sponsored by ARUP

Big Bang
S15 1.30–2.30pm
Key Stage 4
Town Hall £4
Join Simon Singh, author of Big Bang, on an explosive journey through the story of the origin of the Universe. Meet some of the brilliant minds that deciphered the mysteries of the Big Bang and find out how the most important theory of all was unravelled in this rollercoaster story of curious incidents and peculiar characters.

Earthquakes
S16 3.30–4.30pm
Key Stage 3 and 4
Town Hall £4
Earthquakes can have a devastating impact. Join **Adam Crewe** to explore the causes and nature of earthquakes through live experiments, shaking table demonstrations, computer simulations and pictures of actual earthquake damage to find out what we can do to reduce their impact.

Daily 8–10 June

Lab in a Lorry
S17 Wednesday–Friday
10–11am, 11.30am–12.30pm,
1.30–2.30pm, 3–4pm
Key Stage 3
Town Hall £4
Enter the wonderful world of our Lab in a Lorry to discover the wonders of physics. Guided by practicing physicists and engineers each student will be able to conduct their own experiments. If Newton discovered gravity by accident see what you can come up with!

Sponsored by Institute of Physics

The Festival's Science for Schools programme takes place in the Town Hall and is open to members of the general public to book in the normal way. To request a full education pack, call 01242 775822.

Family Events

www.cheltenhamfestivals.org.uk
Bookings 01242 227970

Sponsored by UCAS

Saturday 11 June

F1 The Penguin
10–11am Town Hall
Age 5 to Adult £4
Adult penguins take over 30 miles to find food for their families, they can be expected to run and slide over the water when going at high speeds. Join **Pete Barham** for an interactive journey to find out more about these amazing flightless birds, and what makes so dirty look after them.

F2 Big Bang
10.30–11.15am Town Hall
Age 10 to Adult £5
Join Simon Singh, author of Big Bang, on an explosive journey through the story of the origin of the Universe. Meet some of the brilliant minds that deciphered the mysteries of the Big Bang and find out how the most important theory of all was unravelled in this rollercoaster story of curious incidents and peculiar characters.

Sponsored by

F3 Blazing Science
12.30–1.30pm Town Hall
Age 5 to Adult £5
Disney performer Mik Jacobs presents an unforgettable exploration of the science of fire live on stage. Why do fireworks explode? Why are stunt people told to drop and roll? Featuring fantastic facts and cinematic secrets, Blazing Science explores the exciting science of energy, matter and fire.

Supported by
The Daphne Jackson Trust

F4 Amazing Adventures
2–3pm Town Hall
Age 8 to Adult £4
From the highest mountains and deep through icy heartlands and temperate climates our world is a risky work for **Ben Saunders**. Find out what it really felt to become the youngest person to ski solo across the North Pole, how a sixty-five year old cabbage kept him alive and how he survived extreme temperatures, frozen rivers and thin ice and fear in some record region.

Sunday 12 June

F5 Talon Spotting
9.30–10.30am Town Hall
Age 5 to Adult £4
Come face to face with bald eagles, hawk, barn falcon and white-back vultures to experience the silent flight of the barn owl in our dramatic display of some of the most fearsome of nature's predators. Find out how these birds of prey hunt, track and dive as they are the Town Hall Arena. Just make sure you duck.

F6 The Lost Dragon
9.45–10.45am Town Hall
Age 8 to Adult £5
Unlocking the secret of one of the mythical beasts without creatures on this planet today. Join **Peter Hogarth** to reveal how the magical creatures could have looked like, where they might have lived, and what they could have preyed upon.

F7 The Secret Life of Electricity
11.30am–12.30pm Town Hall
Age 8 to Adult £4
Unlock the discovery electricity has been used to produce powerful and powerful phenomena as well as some bizarre inventions, such as the Catherine Bell – an 18th century birthday machine. Join **The Hustler** on an entertaining and revealing journey into the world of electricity from its beginnings to its amazing future.

Sponsored by Chelsea

Special Effects
F8 Special Effects
12.45–1.45pm Town Hall
Age 5 to Adult £4
Ever wondered how a volcano look like on a werewolf? Join **Max Van Der Hanks** hollywood make up artist, in this interactive show to uncover the secrets of special effects in films such as Lord of the Rings.

F9 How to be a Spy
1.30–2.30pm Town Hall
Age 8 to Adult £5
How are spies created and recruited? Who are the heroes and villains of the espionage world and how do modern spies catch the most dedicated? Former MI5 officer **Harry Ferguson** shows how to conduct an ultimate identity, check your house for bugging devices and drop your ice cover.

F10 Rough Science
1.45–2.45pm Town Hall
Age 8 to Adult £4
Join the Rough Science team to find out how subtle **Kate Humble**, if you feel like an earthquake through a volcano's hot house close from the bin. Live experiments, demonstrations and clips from the team will give your new insight into what you can do with the crab fish in your garden.

Food Explorers
Eggtastle
Waitrose Food Studio £5
F11 Age 9–7 10–11am
F12 Age 5–7 11.30am–12.30pm
F13 Age 8–12 1–2pm
F14 Age 8–12 3–4pm
Explore the chemistry of the kitchen and take home your own creation in these hands-on workshops. Parents do not need to stay for these events but must stay in the store during the workshop.

**Festival brochures
and flyers**
The challenge here was
to present dense program
information clearly and give
enough emphasis to festival
sponsors, without diluting
the overall impact of each
communication.

ENTER THE DISCOVER ZONE FEATURING THE
UK'S MOST EXCITING HANDS-ON EXHIBITIONS

DISCOVER ZONE
ACTIVATE 10AM–6PM
INNOVATE TOWN HALL
PARTICIPATE FREE

Abseil the wall of terror. Take part in
a musical megalab. Dig for a dinosaur.
Race a computer. Take the organic taste
test. Conduct your own experiments
and much more...

PLUS Robot Wars – meet the stars
of your favourite TV show and some
of the UK's most cutting-edge robots.

FESTIVAL AT A GLANCE

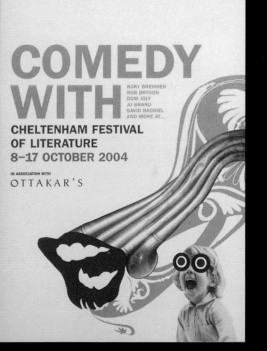

COMEDY
WITH

RORY BREMNER
ROB BRYDON
DOM JOLY
JO BRAND
DAVID BADDIEL
AND MORE AT...

CHELTENHAM FESTIVAL
OF LITERATURE
8–17 OCTOBER 2004

IN ASSOCIATION WITH

OTTAKAR'S

FREE
FESTIVAL
FUN AT

OUR MAMMOTH FESTIVAL TENT
IS THE STAGE FOR SOME SHORT
SWEET AND FREE TREATS,
SO JUST TURN UP AND STAY
AROUND – OR LOITER WITHIN
TENT, IF YOU WILL.

CHELTENHAM FESTIVAL
OF LITERATURE
8–17 OCTOBER 2004

IN ASSOCIATION WITH

OTTAKAR'S

Lucienne Roberts @ sans+baum

Lucienne Roberts remembers clearly the combined impact of reading Tschichold's *Asymmetric Typography* and her first typographic exercise as a student. It was reminiscent of postwar Swiss teaching. Take a short piece of text and lay it out four times using only one means of emphasis each time: type size, weight, color, and space. It was a revelation and still informs every typographic decision that she makes.

Roberts has allied herself with modernism because she finds it intellectually far-reaching: minimalism determined by a politically motivated belief in clarity and access for all. Considering graphic design to be fundamentally egalitarian, as most people see and use it, she feels that a designer has the responsibility to arrive at well-crafted, utilitarian design that respects the intelligence of the user.

Roberts coined the name sans+baum while sharing a studio space with a typographically orientated designer. Having worked alone for some time following this, she felt the need for a sympathetic colleague to bring a new dimension to her work. Bob Wilkinson has since become an associate. His interest in image-making and conceptual approach to design has opened up the remit of their work significantly.

Both signatories of the *First Things First 2000* manifesto, they now work both independently and together, along with their colleague John McGill, on a broad range of projects, from exhibitions to reports and books. Roberts initially looked for clients whose mission she was happy to endorse, so sans+baum have worked a great deal for charities and nongovernmental organizations (NGOs). Their clients also include organizations dealing in minority interests who are happy to be a little adventurous. Roberts considers herself primarily a typographer, so it is the written word and its visual representation that she holds most dear.

Above and following pages: Book design
Before World War II, the term "graphic design" did not exist. *Drip-dry Shirts: The Evolution of the Graphic Designer* celebrates the work of the practitioners who created this now familiar term. Each principal contributor has named a colleague or student over whom they feel they have had some influence. With the contributions of these secondary interviewees, the pieces are mini design-family trees and the symbiotic nature of work and teaching becomes apparent. Each of these "discussion" pieces opens with a self-portrait, and a soundtrack is suggested to evoke the designer's own chosen mood.

Rosmarie Tissi
self-portrait
'My faithful travelling
companion.'

Wim Crouwel

Wim Crouwel
scrapbook
[text too small to read]

Wim Crouwel
scrapbook
Amsterdam
[text too small to read]

Crouwel's recording
of Bauuniv. on the Beach in
on Sun Life from 1978 on
the Toronto Music Company
label, New York. The
accompanying booklet was
designed by Walter Allner.
The open was performed at
that time in Amsterdam.
Crouwel saw it and 'it made
a great impression'.

Rupert Bassett

16 selecting a college/
first impression of
Geoff White

Geoff White

17 early career choices/
getting a grant/
college experiences

18 breadth of learning/
the new typography/
painting and drawing

01 I retried all the other
London art colleges, but I
applied to Ravensbourne
out of pure instinct. I had
never seen anything like it
before. I immediately loved
the Minoan architecture,
rigorous signage system
and clean white open-plan
studios. It looked more like
a factory than an art college.
But mostly I loved the clear
similarity of the student
work, which looked like it
had been made by machines.
It was also obvious that the
teaching team shared a
modernist design philosophy.

I hadn't heard of Geoff White
before, but I met him in
the first year seminar room
on 29 September 1985, my
first day at Ravensbourne.
He seemed very quickly
spoken and unemotional
for an art teacher, much to
my relief, but he also seemed
to know something very
important. I wasn't sure
exactly what it was,
but I wanted to find out.

01 I dropped out of grammar school
when I was 15. The school was very
sports orientated, but I knew I was
more of an aesthete than an athlete
and wanted to try 'something
creative'. In the local library I found
the Artists and Writers Year Book.
I wrote to some of the studios listed
and thought myself very clever to
get a job as a junior and messenger
for 30 shillings a week.

The best part of this experience
was that we did one day a week day
release at Regent Street Polytechnic,
at the time the only art school I knew
in London. I had been impressed by
the work of the Design Research Unit
during the war – clever government
advertising and exhibitions – and so
I went along to see if I could study
graphic design at the Polytechnic,
but they didn't do it.

I eventually went to the Central
School of Arts and Crafts, almost by
accident really. Colin Forbes had
been a junior with me and it was he
who told me about it. I did my
national service prior to going, but as
my education had been interrupted
I was entitled to a grant of £2 a week
plus fees. All this may never have
happened as Colin and I narrowly
missed being blown up one lunch
hour by a 'doodlebug' that fell in the
Aldwych. We dived into a doorway
and the only injury I sustained
was made by a tiny particle of glass
that I dusted off Colin's jacket!

01 I was interviewed by Jesse Collins
and said I wanted to do graphic
design. Officially he was head of
the department of book production,
but I remember he'd address us as
'designers', which was good. Jesse
Collins had real influence on me.
He went around the studio with an
armful of books and introduced us
to everything... to designers we'd
never heard of like Paul Rand, and
to painters like Klee and Picasso.

He also brought in Anthony
Froshaug and Herbert Spencer
to teach typography. Apart from
Hans Schleger these were probably
the only two people in Britain
at that time who were doing what
they called new typography, or
continental typography.

Froshaug wasn't there for very long.
It was his first job. Years later he
told me at a party that he was really
nervous when he talked to us for the
first time. He fixed his eyes on one
student so he wasn't intimidated by
talking to 15 people, this student
turned all squirrelly, trying to avoid
Anthony's gaze! That was the first
I had seen of typography.

In the first year I got really
interested in life drawing and went
to do evening and day classes.
I found it confusing in that I really
liked the current way of painting
that was taught in the school – the
Euston Road School – and at the
same time I really liked the work of
people like Max Bill and El Lissitzky,
which was totally different. I wasn't
a good student at all in graphic
design because I used to sneak off
and do life drawing. I was a lousy
student really.

Rupert Bassett

Series of posters accompanying
the publication of Issues of
Britain/Abstracts modernity
finder magazine, 1992–94
[text too small to read]

Geoff White

In these recent Christmas
cards White continues to
explore modernist principles.

Karl Marx's poster, late 1970s.
White seized the opportunity
to produce this appropriately
angular piece of lettering.

In the end of this White went
to show evening life classes
a week. An exponent of the
Euston Road School he learnt
how to control paint to achieve
correct tonal values.

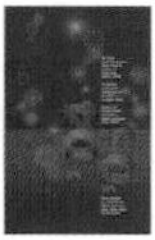

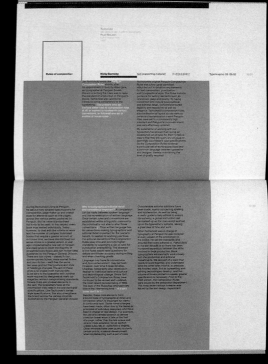

Above: Journal design

Designing for typographers is terrifying. The idea of so many beady-eyed professionals pouring over the kerning and so on is enough to paralyze the whole endeavor. For *TypoGraphic 59*, Roberts wanted the focus to be on typography and nothing else, so all images are contained within perforated, Chinese-bound pages. There is also a strong use of color.

Following pages: Exhibition poster

This poster was for the collaborative ISTD/26 exhibition held at the British Library as part of London Design Festival 2004. Twenty-six ISTD members were paired with a writer from the professional writer's body, 26. The brief was to write and design a poster using a letter of the alphabet. sans+baum hit problems early on with profound disagreements about content. The suggestion to produce a periodic table of the emotions led to a wonderful set of words from which Roberts made a final choice.

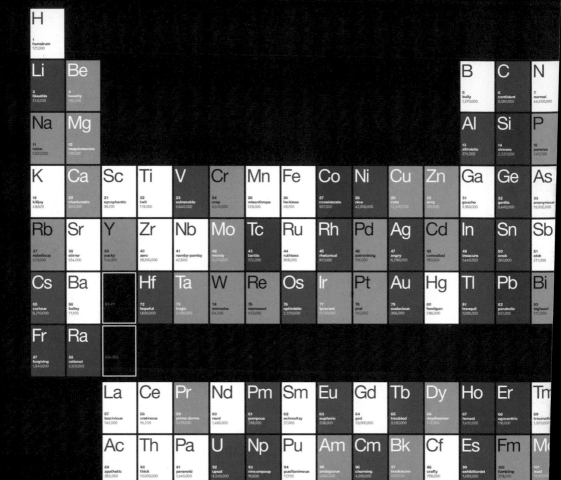

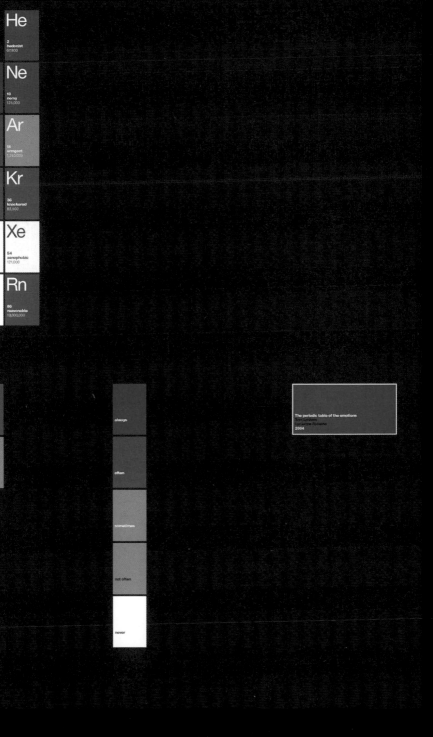

SAS

SAS, a London-based, integrated corporate design company, was established in 1989. Its diverse clients range from the Science Museum in London to big, blue-chip corporations.

At the heart of SAS's work is the belief that any good design solution should look as though it comes from the client, not from the designer. There is no house style at SAS—although it has a rigorous "house approach" by which it measures its work. Every piece must answer three questions: is the message clear?; is the tone of voice appropriate (to the audience and the brand)?; and will it be noticed and remembered? To achieve this, SAS works closely with its clients, often writing the brief in collaboration with them. Its approach to typography is about more than just making text readable. Its choice of typeface(s), size, leading, etc. all contribute to the tone of voice. SAS often uses typography to enhance the idea, albeit in a subtle way. Sometimes the grid takes its inspiration from the overall idea, sometimes words become the idea. There are certainly no "lorem ipsum" headlines at SAS. Instead, designers often write text themselves or in collaboration with a copywriter.

One of SAS's strengths is the different people, and the many different opinions they have. This makes for a lively, sometimes controversial debating culture which can take time to get used to, but which brings out the best in people. In the words of one designer "It's not for everyone, but if you like it here, it becomes a part of you."

Trustworthy

I'll do it straight away

No excuses.

We want people to believe that BT keeps its promises. This means that we need to do what we say we will.

Brand Value

You know where you are with BT.

It is honest, it delivers on its commitments, and it always offers good value for money.

People Value

We build open, honest and realistic relationships with customers and with each other.

We are reliable and act with integrity.

We do whatever it takes to deliver.

Why it's time to change

BT

Corporate brand book for BT

The BT brand book explains the reasons behind BT's change of identity and what BT wants to stand for going forward. But how can you make corporate values meaningful to 50,000 employees, ranging from the field engineer to the marketing executive? The answer: show it through simple, real-life examples. The typography is unimposing and is accompanied with illustrations that show how BT's values can be put into practice. Examples are chosen so that every employee can relate to them, regardless of their profession.

Trading Background

2004 saw strong growth in revenues for both of our businesses. In particular, the first half showed a significant improvement over 2003. From an external point of view, demand in our markets was good. Underlying profit before tax however was held back by the translation impact of the weakening US dollar and raw material prices – in some areas they reached a 20 year high. Underlying profit before tax for the year overall was similar to those in 2003, although on a constant currency basis it showed an increase of 5 per cent. It is interesting to note that in US dollar terms our underlying profit before tax has grown by 33 per cent since 2001.

We continued to generate strong free cash flows after investing £61.7 million in capital across the Group and after absorbing the cost of a significant restructuring programme in our engine repair and overhaul division.

We also continued our record of investing in value-adding acquisitions, principally in our Aviation division. Last year we acquired in total nine new companies, increasing and enhancing our service and product offering across the world. These acquisitions are expected to contribute some £120 million of sales in 2005 (9 per cent of our 2004 total).

AVIATION
£800m

MATERIALS
TECHNOLOGY
£572m

GROUP
REVENUES
(CONTINUING OPERATIONS)
£1,372m

Expansion of new and existing facilities
saw Signature's European network grow
significantly this year, with the number of
FBO's increasing from 5 to 19.

As the leading provider of FBO's, our portfolio
services and supports nearly one million aircraft
movements per year.

Annual report

This annual report was designed for the BBA Group, a focused, profitable holding company that owns several businesses in the fields of aviation and industrial fabrics. The approach of this annual report follows that of an art catalog, splitting the contents into three clear sections: "essays" (CEO and Chairman's letters), "plates" (pictures of BBA's businesses), and "appendices" (financial information). The design concept evolved around the theme "focus." All images converge toward a focal point in the center. The theme is then taken further in the layout: all spreads are composed from the center. Even the grid follows the same concept — the further away from the center the text starts, the smaller the size gets.

MONTSERR
EN COLABORAC

LUGAR

EL MUSEO N
CENTRO DE
REINA SOFÍ

FECHA

31 DE MAYO DE 2
A LAS 20:00 HORAS

Una nueva exposición creada en exclusiva para BT por la artista y fotógrafa Montserrat Soto será presentada en el Museo Nacional Centro de Arte Reina Sofía en Madrid. Esta es la segunda de una serie de proyectos artísticos comisionados.

TRACKING MADRID

Montserrat Soto

INVITACION

BT SOTO
ÓN CON BT

CIONAL
RTE

MADRID

¿Para qué necesitamos el arte en las ciudades? Un recorrido histórico permite decir que las artes, y en general los recursos estéticos, son necesarios no sólo por razones ornamentales sino en otros sentidos más decisivos. Encuentro al menos cuatro fines con los cuales el arte, la literatura y los medios masivos han intervenido e intervienen en espacios urbanos: para fundarlos y refundarlos, para celebrar, para espectacularizar y para nombrar u ocultar su pérdida. Néstor García Canclini.

Why do we need art in cities? If we look at history we can see that the arts, and aesthetic resources in general, are necessary not just for ornamental purposes but also for more important reasons. I can identify at least four motivating factors which underlie the continuing intervention of art, literature and the mass media in urban spaces: to create and recreate these spaces, to celebrate them, to make them more spectacular, and to pinpoint or conceal their loss. Néstor García Canclini.

PAISAJE URBANO Y MEMORIA.
MONTSERRAT SOTO PROYECTO TRACKING MADRID
JOSÉ MARÍA BERMÚDEZ DE CASTRO
MEMORY AND URBAN LANDSCAPE.
MONTSERRAT SOTO TRACKING MADRID

Arts catalog

The installation Tracking Madrid was a collaboration between BT and the Spanish Artist Montserrat Soto. The catalog had to be produced for the opening night and had therefore to be designed while the installation was still being planned. SAS made the most of this by designing a book about the process and thinking behind the project. Plans and sketches are juxtaposed with photographs and essays, and different paper stocks are used for different sections. The format is based on the proportions of Soto's images, allowing full-bleed printing without compromising the photographs. Columns are unusually wide, but the generous leading compensates for this and makes the text easy to read. The book is printed in two languages. The text is laid out in two horizontal columns, with the titles sitting between them. This saves the doubling up of elements that don't need translating (eg. the authors' names).

UNA (Amsterdam) designers

Language is the architecture of thought, the tool we use to fix our ideas in time and space. UNA's philosophy is based on the ideas embodied by the words present, presentable, presentation, presence.

The viability of any organization depends on its public presence. How a company presents itself determines the quality of that presence. Presentation is of the utmost importance. Like the presentation of a gift. Care and concern must be exercised in choosing its content. Sensitivity and attentiveness must direct how it is packaged. A well-chosen gift, presented with care, strengthens the bond between giver and receiver, and enhances the presence of one in the mind of the other.

The quality of any organization is reflected in the quality of its relationships. Having first formed a partnership in 1982, Hans Bockting and Will de l'Ecluse cofounded UNA in 1987. The studio has grown in stature since then, winning national and international acclaim for its design concepts. Intelligent, original, playful in combination with an eye for details are terms frequently used to describe the consultancy's work.

In addition to UNA's relationship with type designers, photographers, illustrators and authors, the studio touts long-standing relationships among the Netherlands' top production people: technical experts, prepress and digital professionals, printers, and binders. This means that, however complex, novel, or seemingly outrageous an idea may be, by virtue of its standing, UNA is able to count on experts willing to go the full distance to make an idea real. This kind of professional collaboration is invaluable, and often means the difference between convention and innovation.

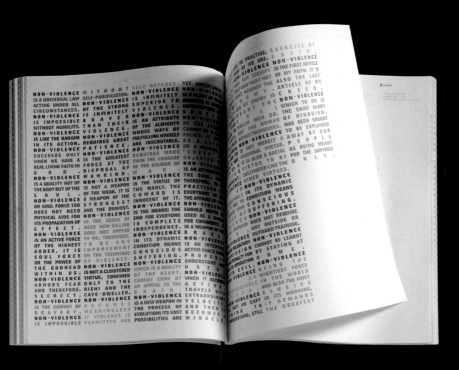

Diary
The concept behind this diary
was to celebrate the manifold
events, occasions, holidays,
and anniversaries marking time
around the world. Each week
commemorates a significant
holiday — religious, secular,
legendary, historical, political —
observed in that week by one
of the world's many nations.
A relevant story is told, visually
and verbally, in a sometimes
humorous, sometimes ironic
way. Collectively, the 52 stories
represent a unique and
provocative history of people
marking time. The diary
contains large amounts of

text, but has only a limited
amount of space available.
Bell Centennial, designed
for use in very small sizes,
provides the solution. *Bell*
also proved the perfect
typeface for the small,
embossed texts on the
cover. The diary uses three
of the original five versions
of the typeface.

Re-constructie van ons klimaat

nationaal**archief**

jaarverslag 2001: het nationaal **archief**
is grensoverschrijdend. het verkent
nieuwe gebieden, knoopt nieuwe
relaties aan en slecht de drempel voor
het brede publiek.

ARA 4 VELH 619.47

huisvestingsnotitie: ruimte voor een
breed publiek. het nationaal **archief**
vertaalt zijn ambities in concrete
plannen.

beleidsverkenning 2002 – 2005: het verleden
heeft een veelbelovende toekomst.
het nationaal **archief** ontvouwt zijn plannen
en ambities voor de komende jaren.

Magazine and annual report

The Nationaal Archief logotype always appears in conjunction with a text message that provides information about the archive's collection and facilities. The strong corporate identity helps to ensure that historical treasures contained in the collection are exploited and accessible to a society that knows very little about the Nationaal Archief.

The character of the chosen typeface, *FF DIN*, reflects the filing and standardization of the archive. In addition, the typeface can easily be combined with type that is visible in reproduced documents. In the 1990s, Albert-Jan Pool revised the original *DIN* to a typeface suitable for wider use. For the Nationaal Archief logo and all applications *FF DIN Alternate* is used with medieval figures.

Annual report

Delta Lloyd and OHRA Insurances are increasingly providing made-to-measure products for the insurance professional as well as the individual client. This annual report profiles some of Delta Lloyd's special consumer groups. *Swift* is a very economic and, in small sizes, very readable typeface, enabling a three-column grid for this annual report. *Swift*'s firm serifs avoid legibility problems in the printing of diapositive pages for graphs and annual accounts. For the illustrated segment, the sans serif *Corporate S* was chosen to create a strong contrast with *Swift*.

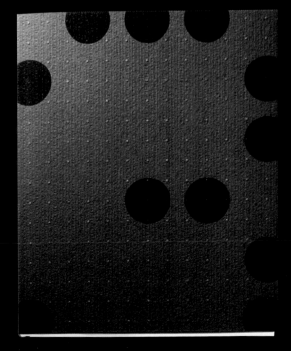

Diary
This diary visually accentuates the passage of time from one month to the next. Each month has its own Pantone color and these colors manifest themselves in various ways through the ciphers and paper inlays between the Japanese-folded pages. At the point where one month begins to lead into the next, subtle color changes become apparent and the ciphers belonging to the old month combine with the ciphers of the new, thus creating new color tones. In total, 15 different Pantone colors have been used. The introduction text is "cut" using a Filigran laser.

Webb & Webb Design

Webb & Webb start by assuming their clients want their publications to be read. They always ask what the client wants to say and who they want to say it to. The question they ask themselves is how best to convey that information — a legal publication will need to be clear, concise, not open to misinterpretation; an invitation can be entertaining, it can sneak up behind you and tap you on the shoulder; a letterpress job can involve all the senses, and be tactile as well as informative.

Their aim with every job is to involve the recipient and (hopefully) exceed the client's expectations. In the process this will stretch the imagination of everyone in the office.

Webb & Webbs' clients include financial companies, arts organizations, professional firms, and publishers. Projects range from corporate design, involving a wide variety of long-run printed material, screen-based design and building graphics, to letterpress jobs with tiny print runs.

Before starting Webb & Webb Design in 2003, Brian Webb was a designer and Director at Trickett & Webb. He has lectured at colleges and events around the world, assessed students and acted as a professional advisor at numerous colleges in the UK.

Trickett & Webb, founded in 1971, has received countless international design awards and has work displayed in many permanent museum collections including the Victoria and Albert Museum, London, and the Museum of Modern Art, New York.

Brian Webb is a Visiting Professor at the University of the Arts, London, Fellow of the University for the Creative Arts (Kent Institute/Surrey Institute), and was President of the Chartered Society of Designers from 2003 to 2005.

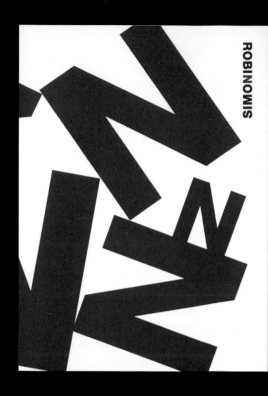

ROBINOMIS

Corporate publications, folders, and invitations
As part of law firm Robin Simon's identity program, Webb & Webb have designed a number of corporate publications including folders, new office announcements, and invitations to events. The type is printed in black and pink, with the pink N used as a design device.

A NEW
BIRMINGHAM
LANDMARK

INVITATIO N

Joseph Southall
1861–1944

Catalog
Joseph Southall was a major
Arts and Crafts artist. This
catalog of his paintings
includes a biographical essay,
along with essays on the
British Tempera Revival and
Southall's Quaker pacifist
activities. The typography uses
a limited number of type sizes,
a left-ranged measure, and
only one type weight; spacing
is used for emphasis. Without
attempting to be a pastiche,
the catalog follows the style
of earlier Arts and Crafts
publications produced by
presses including Doves
and Golden Cockerel.

Foreword
Mary Greensted,
Cheltenham Art Gallery & Museum

The acquisition of two important paintings by Joseph Southall, *Beauty Seeing the Image of her Home in the Fountain* and *Hortus Inclusus* (detail opposite), is a tremendous coup for Cheltenham Art Gallery and Museum. Cheltenham's Arts and Crafts Movement collections are acknowledged as being nationally significant by the award of Designated Status since 1998. The main strength of the collection is its furniture but it does include work by the Birmingham School most notably by Charles March Gere whose painting, *The Tennis Party* 1900, portrays Margaret Gere and Edith and Henry Payne among others. There are also examples of the distinctive jewellery produced by Southall's closest associates, Arthur and Georgie Gaskin, as well as paintings by William Rothenstein and other Arts and Crafts artists.

Cheltenham's lack of a significant example of Southall's work was recognised as a major omission because, of all the painters of the period, he epitomizes Arts and Crafts approach in his work. His strength and his interests were in the decorative – both in terms of composition and in the minutiae of the settings, costume and accessories. Influenced by John Ruskin he produced designs for Greek lacework which were made by his mother and featured in Arts and Crafts exhibitions. Some examples were given to Cheltenham in the 1980s including a design that is almost identical to the bodice lace worn by the model in *Beauty*. Southall saw the painting and its frame as a whole and regularly designed and carved his own frames. Above all his self-taught passion for the tempera technique was typical of the Arts and Crafts approach.

The acquisition of these two Southall paintings will ensure that the fine art of the Arts and Crafts period is well represented at Cheltenham. It will also be a fitting memorial to the late Margaret Bellwood of Chipping Norton, Oxfordshire who all her life derived great pleasure from looking at art and whose generous legacy, made through the Friends of Cheltenham Art Gallery and Museum, initiated this double acquisition. Additional funding came from the National Art Collections Fund and the MLA/V&A Purchase Grant Fund and we are very grateful to all these bodies, to the individuals involved, and to George Breeze and Peyton Skipwith for their support and assistance.

7

The British Tempera Revival
Abbie N. Sprague

A small exhibition of tempera paintings opened at Leighton House in the spring of 1901. John Roddam Spencer Stanhope (1829–1908), Christiana Herringham (1852–1929), and Joseph E. Southall (1861–1944) were among the contributors. With seventeen artists represented and forty works on display, including Southall's *Beauty Seeing the Image of Her Home in the Fountain* of 1897–8, (cat.no.4) this ground-breaking exhibition was the first solely devoted to contemporary works in egg tempera. Demonstrating that tempera painting was no longer a lost art, the exhibition heralded the resurrection of this ancient technique. The movement became the British Tempera Revival.

Cat.no.4. Joseph E. Southall (1861–1944)
Beauty Seeing the Image of Her Home in the Fountain (1897–8) (detail)

Egg tempera reached its zenith during the fifteenth century; however, as the *quattrocento* came to a close, oils were introduced from the North. With its ease of manipulation and preparation, this new medium quickly became the preferred technique. The labour-intensive craft of tempera painting slowly fell into disuse. Over three hundred years later, developing out of a fascination with ancient styles and techniques, tempera emerged out of obscurity. William Blake (1757–1827) was first among British artists to experiment with egg yolk as a binder for pigments. In a desire to find an alternative medium, Blake's experiments lead him to *Il Libro dell'Arte*, Cennino Cennini's treatise on renaissance techniques. Augmenting

Cennini's recipes with other materials, some of Blake's works have not had the lasting effect he desired. Nonetheless, he was instrumental in introducing alternative painting media and techniques to early nineteenth century British artists, including Samuel Palmer (1805–81) and George Richmond (1809–96). Oils no longer had the monopoly.

The project to decorate the Houses of Parliament in frescoes revived an interest in ancient techniques in the mid-nineteenth century. Providing the artists with a technical manual, Mary Philadelphia Merrifield (1804–89) published the first English translation of Cennini's treatise in 1844. Including recipes and instructions for gilding, fresco, and tempera, Cennini's *Il Libro dell'Arte* is regarded as the authority on early renaissance techniques. Though not her intent, Merrifield's translation provided the early revivalists with their first practical manual for working in tempera. Such is the significance of Cennini's treatise that through the next hundred years, additional translations were completed and published. Herringham's more complete version, with chapters based on her own experiences, was published in 1899; later in 1933, Daniel V. Thompson, Jr. (1902–80) published the most comprehensive and accurate translation to date. With each updated and improved version another generation of artists discovered the technique, creating a framework for the revival of egg tempera.

The tempera revivalists are often categorized as Pre-Raphaelite followers; understandably since they shared a common emphasis on religious and allegorical themes. However, the tempera artists took their work one step further as they mastered the medium and technique of early renaissance artists. Cognisant of ancient techniques, the Pre-Raphaelites reintroduced the white ground that was essential to their brilliant colours. By the time the British Tempera Revival gained momentum, most of the Pre-Raphaelites were nearing the end of their careers. William Holman Hunt (1827–1910) expressed his regret for not having discovered the medium sooner to a gathering of tempera artists, 'if I had my time over again I should be in the thick of it – one of you!' Nonetheless, the Pre-Raphaelites had a profound influence on the tempera revivalists and their

Fig. 5. Harry Morley (1881–1943)
The Young Bacchus (1930)
Tempera on board: 18 x 14 (46 x 36)
Private Collection

Royal Academy. Abstract paintings by Edward Wadsworth (1889–1949) were hung with works in memory of Herringham and Spencer Stanhope. The exhibition celebrated an innovative younger generation of artists while giving homage to the revivalists who came before them.

Cut short by war and the rationing of materials, the thirties ended for the tempera artists in 1938 with an exhibition in Birmingham. Similar to the Whitechapel exhibition, paintings with both modern and traditional subjects were shown. This time, however, the movement towards establishing tempera as a modern medium was more evident. Not only were younger artists deviating from the traditional technique as detailed in Cennini's treatise, they were absorbing the modernist influences from Europe. Surreal and abstract works by Wadsworth, John Armstrong (1893–1973), and Augustus Lunn (1905–86) were a stark contrast to the medieval tales and religious stories depicted in works by Southall, Gaskin and Batten. Wadsworth's *The Beached Margin* of 1937, an example of the dream-like marine paintings he created during this period, illustrates this departure from traditional subjects (fig. 6). As one critic described the

works, 'paintings which jerk us clean out of the allegoric and the subject picture rut... ...a picture that shouts in the company of its mild-mannered companions, but it is a good and heartening shout of genuine twentieth century origins.' As British artists recreated tempera for the twentieth century, American artists began to discover the medium.

Edward Waldo Forbes (1873–1969), later director of the Fogg Art Museum at Harvard University, developed a passion for early renaissance art during his travels to Italy. Beginning in 1909, he taught courses on Florentine painting to the Harvard community; by 1914, Forbes's courses were devoted solely to techniques, with special emphasis on tempera and fresco. As his students graduated, many took significant posts as scholars, museum directors, artists and conservators, dispersing the tempera technique throughout the United States.

The American translation of Cennini's treatise was published by Daniel Thompson, one of Forbes's devoted pupils. Though versions by Merrifield and Herringham found their way to the United States, Thompson's 1933

Fig. 6. Edward Wadsworth (1889–1949)
The Beached Margin (1937)
Tempera on linen on wood: 28 1/4 x 40 (71.1 x 101.6)
Copyright Tate, London 2005

*John's work projects a powerful iconography
that distinguishes his design and craftsmanship
– it is eminently collectable.*
Sir Peter Hall

Sand, contour au jour with ten drawers, including
a suede-lined writing surface. Soko apple ash.

*John Makepeace is second to none. From his
base in rural Dorset he produces furniture which
is classic and modern at the same time – and
represents workmanship at its very best.*
Sir Christopher Frayling.

John Makepeace Designer and Furniture Maker

The name of John Makepeace
has a special place in the world
of fine furniture design and
craftsmanship. He achieves a fusion
of innovation and experiment with
respect for tradition.

His work transcends the normal
perceptions of function and
structure, material and detail
with sensitivity and flair.
Individuals and organisations come
to John Makepeace to commission

luxurious and distinctive pieces,
mainly from indigenous wood, as
a creative statement and long
term investment.

Commissioning furniture is not an
esoteric or elitist activity. It is a
simple act of faith in the power of
art, craft and design to bring joy
and meaning to our lives.
Patronage of the arts has been a
conspicuous element of every
civilised society since time began.

Throughout history, commissioning
has been an aesthetic adventure
by patrons and artist leading to the
creation of lasting objects which
make their mark in contemporary
culture.

You can share in the simple
and satisfying experience of fine
furniture. John Makepeace
welcomes meeting prospective
clients in person to discuss
future projects.

Lower and right, Trine, one of a set
for an art nouveau interior. Reguam,
lapare of over waved and ring oak.

John Makepeace

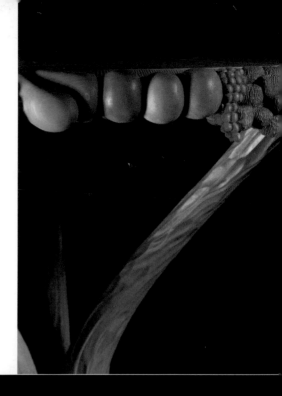

*The sublime effect of exquisitely chosen
materials, perfectly crafted to serve and
enhance the human body and soul, makes John
Makepeace's work overwhelmingly desirable.*
Rosalind Savill
Director of The Wallace Collection

English Fruits,

John Makepeace Furniture

Product brochure
To heighten the sense of
collectible craftsmanship and
tone down the sense of sales
pitch, Webb & Webb set John
Makepeace's collection of
testimonial quotations from
well-known museum directors
and clients in conversational
italics, without quotation
marks. The spreads show each
piece of furniture in situ and
as a full-page detail.

Sam Winston

Sam Winston explains that he began to use typography when he started to write. This may sound like a rather obvious statement, but he found writing incredibly difficult and the conventional formats restrictive. What resulted was a series of visual and linguistic experiments through his unconventional use of typography.

Winston's experiments came from looking at the structures of different kinds of literature, from storybooks to bus and train timetables. "Clearly the way one navigates a timetable is different from the way one reads a story. I wanted to take these different types of visual navigation and introduce them to each other: a timetable reordering all of the words to *Beauty and the Beast*, or a newspaper report on *Snow White*."

Despite the fact that the outcome of Winston's work is always self-published "graphic" material, interest in his work has come predominantly from galleries and collectors and the results have come to be called artworks.

Other works by Sam Winston can be seen in the special collections of the Museum of Modern Art, New York, and the Tate Galleries, Victoria and Albert Museum, and British Library, all in London.

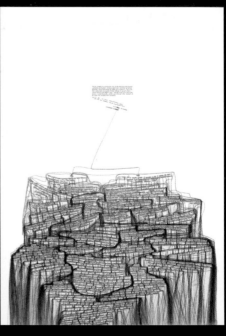

Posters

Winston's series of posters deconstruct well-loved stories and present them in a form that provides the reader with new insights into the author's preoccupations. "I wanted to play with the idea of sophisticated adult books meeting the more innocent children's books: a metaphor for some of the issues that need to be dealt with when growing up." In the main image (opposite) each individual word has been cut out and placed in a list on the poster, arranged alphabetically.

If you were to place an adult and child's world alongside each other you would see two extremely different landscapes. One is populated with facts and structure where as the other one is wild with make believe.

The bridge between these two happens in the grey place we call growing up. A place where facts aren't fully understood and fantasy completely tamed.

a made-up | true story

Even though books aren't human they still manage to have personalities beyond their authors. This starts when they leave the writer's desk and enter the world at large.

Take fairytales and rule books, they couldn't be more different from each other - fairytales have the agility to get away with whatever myth they see fit and are loved by children, while rule books bear the duty of getting things done precisely and correctly.

So what happens when a timetable, an encyclopedia and a newspaper approach some fairytales and hold them to account?

The beast, from Beauty and the Beast, felt a bump on the page and turned round to see his story change. The timetable had arrived.

The tree's bark was awaiting delivery, the stream had unforeseen delays and everyone was a little more confused because the 'who' 'why' and 'what' had been stuck together. The timetable had re-ordered his fantasy world so that everything fitted into a time line; here was a story in which the words had been arranged by their order of arrival. Starting with a and ending on z

References

What is typography?
1 By "universal" I am limiting the term to the "developed world." The growth of digital technology has been phenomenally rapid, but worldwide there are still estimated to be only 2% of the world's population directly connected to the Internet. See Alan Robertson, "Designing the Real World," *TypoGraphic* 55, International Society of Typographic Designers, 2000.
2 Joseph Moxon, *Mechanick Exercises: or, The Doctrine of Handyworks Applied to the Art of Printing,* 1683. This quote is taken from the second volume, from a paragraph headed "Some circumstances a good composter considers and observes in composing."
3 A key doctrine of the Dadaists in the 1910s was that the everyday world remains invisible until we are forced to see it differently. Art, it was said, is the primary means of "making strange" what we have always seen and always known.

The nature of typography
1 Gerard Unger, "Legible?" *Emigre*, No. 65, page 108, 2003.
2 Ibid.
3 Beatrice Warde, "Typography in Education," in *The Pencil Draws a Vicious Circle*, The Sylvan Press, 1955. "Flashy little stylists" is what Beatrice Warde, Publicity Manager for the Monotype Corporation and a great defender of the printing trade, called graphic designers.

Reading and typography
1 Miles A. Tinker, *Bases for Effective Reading*, University of Minnesota, 1965. Also, Michael A. Forrester, *Psychology of Language*, Sage Publications, 1997.

Writing and typography
1 Fernand Baudin, "Education in the Making and Shaping of Written Words" in *Computers and Typography*, compiled by Rosemary Sassoon, Intellect, 1993.
2 Ruari McLean, *Manual of Typography*, Thames & Hudson, page 50, 1980.
3 Rosemary Sassoon, "Handwriting or Calligraphy: An Attempt at Definitions," *TypoGraphic* 66, International Society of Typographic Designers, 2006.
4 I. A. McKinlay in the foreword to *The Handwriting File: Diagnosis and Remediation of Handwriting Problems*, Jean Aston and Jane Taylor, IDA, 1984.

Change and typography
1 "Does the World Need Another Typeface?", *George Hanson Critical Forum*, Department of Communication Art and Design, Royal College of Art, 2004.
2 Jaroslev Andel, "From a Feast for the Eye to an Economy of Means: Czech Avant-garde Graphic Design Between the Wars," *TypoGraphic* 63, International Society of Typographic Designers, 2005.
3 See Beatrice Warde's essay, "The Crystal Goblet" in *The Pencil Draws a Vicious Circle*, The Sylvan Press, 1955.

Authority and convention
1 The Campaign for Plain English also advocates the use of verbs rather than nouns or adjectives, short sentences with an average of no more than 20 words, short paragraphs with an average of 75 words or five lines or less. They also suggest that a line break between each paragraph is preferable.

2 For example, Fry & Steel's 1795 *Specimen* and Thorne's 1803 *Specimen books*.

Printing, composing, and house-style manuals
1 Horace Hart, *Hart's Rules for Compositors and Readers Employed at the Clarendon Press, Oxford*, Oxford, 1893.
2 H. W. Fowler, *A Dictionary of Modern English Usage*, Oxford University Press, 1926, and revised by E. Gowers, 1965.
3 Ruari McLean, *Jan Tschichold: Typographer*, pages 94 and 95, Lund Humphries, 1975.

Rules and conventions
1 David Jury, "Convention and Creativity in Typography" in *The Education of a Typographer*, Steven Heller (ed.), Allworth Press, 2004.

Craft and typography
1 Paul Greenhalgh, "The history of Craft" in *The Culture of Craft*, Peter Dormer (ed.), Manchester University Press, 1997.
2 Herbert Bayer, Walter Gropius, Isa Gropius, *The Bauhaus 1919–1928*, page 16, Exhibition catalog, Museum of Modern Art, New York, 1938.
3 David Jury, "Why Helvetica?", *Eye* magazine, No. 40, 2001.
4 William Morris would argue that in the Medieval Age (1066–1500) makers were attributed high status because there was no "technology," or at least, no technology which had not, of itself, been made entirely by hand.
5 David Jury, "Changes in the Relationship Between Printer and Designer: Craft Before, During and After Graphic Design" in *Computers and Typography 2*, compiled by Rosemary Sassoon, 2002.

Hypermedia
1 Robert Waller, "What Electronic Books Will Have to be Better Than," *Information Design Journal*, 5/1, 1986.
2 Joyce S. R. Yee, *The Role and Relevance of Typography in Screen-based Media*, PhD research project (in progress), Northumbria University, 2003.

Vision impairment
1 Peter Barker and June Fraser, *Sign Design Guide*, JMU Access Partnership and Sign Design Society, 2000.
2 H. L. Cohn, *Hygiene of the Eye in Schools* (translated by W. P. Turnbull), Simpkin & Marshall, 1886.
3 Quoted by Alison Shaw, *Print for Partial Sight: A Research Report*, Library Association, 1969.
4 Ibid.
5 For example, some of the research done before, and at approximately the same time as, this 1969 report: G. W. Ovink, *Legibility, Atmosphere-value, and Forms of Printing Types*, Leiden, 1938. Donald Paterson, Miles A. Tinker, *How to Make Type Readable,* Harper & Brothers, 1949. Sir Cyril Birt, *A Psychological Study of Typography*, Cambridge University Press, 1959. Miles A. Tinker, *Legibility of Print*, Iowa State University Press, 1965. Miles A. Tinker, *Bases for effective reading*, University of Minnesota Press, 1965. Herbert Spencer, *The Visible Word*, Lund Humphries, 1968. The ATypI Legibility Research Committee initial report (no named author), *Journal of Typographic Research*, 1968.

Business communication
1 Sue Walker, "How Typewriters Changed Correspondence: An Analysis of Prescription and Practice," *Visible Language*, XVIII 2, 1984.
2 David Jury, "The Typist and Her Typing Manual," *baseline* 49, 2005.
3 G. C. Mares, *The History of the Typewriter: Successor to the Press*, Post-Era Books, 1985.
4 John Westwood, *A Manual for Typists and Authors*, HMSO, 1975. (Westwood was Chief Graphic Designer for Her Majesty's Stationery Office.)

Rural communication
1 M. Lewis and D. Wray, *Writing Across the Curriculum: Frames to Support Learning*, Reading and Language Information Centre, 1998.
2 Sue Walker, *Typography and the Language of Everyday Life*, page 75, Pearson Education Ltd, 2001.

Urban communication
1 Sarah Whitcombe, "Sensation on the Street," *Penrose Annual*, Vol. 62, 1969.
2 Michael Twyman's introduction to Maurice Rickards, *The Encyclopedia of Ephemera*, The British Library, 2000.
3 Barbara Jones writing about the photographs of Herbert Spencer recording "typographic detritus or chance art" on the streets of London by in 1963, *Typographica* (new series), No. 8.

Semiotics
1 David Jury, *About Face: Reviving the Rules of Typography*, RotoVision, 2002.
2 Robin Kinross, "Semiotics and Designing," *Information Design Journal*, Issue 4:3, page 197, 1986.

3 Roland Barthes, *Mythologies*, Jonathan Cape, 1972.
4 J. P. Gumbert "'Typography' in the Manuscript Book," *Journal of the Printing History Society*, No. 22, 1993.

Linguistics
1 Rain. Nouns: cloudburst, deluge, downpour, drizzle, fall, flood, hail, mizzle, precipitation, raindrops, rainfall, rains, serin, shower, spate, squall, stream, torrent, volley. Verbs: bestow, bucket, deposit, drop, expend, heap, lavish, pour, spit, sprinkle, teem. Adjectives: damp, dripping, drizzly, hyetal, mizzly, pluviose, pluvious, showery, torrential. Taken from *Chambers Twentieth Century Thesaurus*, 1986.
2 Marshall McLuhan, *The Gutenberg Galaxy: The Making of Typographic Man*, Routledge & Kegan Paul Ltd, 1971.

Rhetoric
1 Walter Ong, *Ramus: Method and the Decay of Dialogue*, Harvard University Press, 1958.
2 Umberto Eco, *A Theory of Semiotics*, pages 227–228, Indiana University Press, 1976.
3 Robin Kinross, "Semiotics and Designing," *Information Design Journal*, Issue 4:3, pages 190–198 (particularly page 197), 1986.

Semantics
1 David Bartram, "The Perception of Semantic Quality in Type: Differences Between Designers and Non-designers." *Information Design Journal*, Issue 3:1, 1982.
2 David Crystal, *The Cambridge Encyclopedia of Language*, page 102, Cambridge University Press, 1988.

Readability

1 Ole Lund, "Why Serifs Are (Still) Important," *Typography Papers* 2, Department of Typography and Graphic Communication, Reading University, 1997.

Alphabets

1 Pepys' shorthand system was devised by the seventeenth-century translator, Thomas Shelton. The shorthand system contains reduced forms of letters, dots for vowels, abbreviated words, and 265 arbitrary symbols. There are also several "empty symbols" in an attempt to foil decoding. Pepys' diary remained secure until the early nineteenth century. David Crystal, *The Cambridge Encyclopedia of Language*, page 206, Cambridge University Press, 1988.

Linear texts

1 Michael Twyman, "Schema for the Study of Graphic Language" in *Processing Visual Language*, Vol. One, Plenum Press, 1979. Twyman's schema is presented as a matrix, consisting of 28 squares, seven across and four down. Across, the squares describe eight levels of linearity of a message, from pure linear (a single, uninterrupted reading route), through to nonlinear (most options open, offering multiple entry and exit points for the reader). Downward, the matrix describes four levels, from words/numbers through to schematic images. Linear interrupted occupies the second square across and this is the term Twyman gives to a text presented as "standard" lines on pages.
2 John Mountford, "'Text', 'Book', 'Writing', and the Medial Aspect of Language," *Information Design Journal*, Issue 3:2, page 117, 1982.

3 Wigger Bierma and Ewan Lentjes, "Dialogue/Typography," *Eye*, page 46, Issue 56, Winter 2004.

Ranged-left setting

1 T. L. De Vinne considered ranged-left setting not so much informal as "slovenly." *Modern Methods of Book Composition*, page 105, The Century Company, 1904.
2 J. H. B. Sandberg, "Must Line Length be Uniform?", *TypoGraphica* 5, 1952.
3 "… the need for unjustified setting to be elaborately specified, in terms of a given word space and treatment for word breaks; while justified setting can be understood and accomplished without further explanation." Paul Stiff, quoting Michael Twyman, "The End of the Line: A Survey of Unjustified Typography," *Information Design Journal*, Issue 8:2, page 130, 1996.
4 Paul Stiff, "The End of the Line: A Survey of Unjustified Typography," *Information Design Journal*, Issue 8:2, page 130, 1996.

Dividing words

1 Robert Bringhurst, *The Elements of Typographic Style*, page 42, Hartley & Marks, 1996.

Type on screen

1 Wim Crouwel, introduction to *TypoGraphic Writing*, David Jury (ed.), International Society of Typographic Designers, 2001.

Nonlinear texts

1 Information mapping was developed in the mid-1960s by Robert Horn.
2 R. Waller, *The Typographic Contribution to Language* (unpublished PhD thesis, University of Reading, 1987).

Quoted by Paul Stiff, "The End of the Line: A Survey of Unjustified Typography," *Information Design Journal*, Issue 8:2, 1996.

Information

1 The exception being the books by Edward R. Tufte, *The Visual Display of Quantitative Information* and *Envisioning Information* (1990), Graphics Press.

Ephemera

1 Maurice Rickards, *Collecting Printed Ephemera*, page 7, Phaidon/Christies Ltd, 1988. Whereas Rickards' definition of ephemera has gained widest currency, Rickards was fully aware of its shortcomings. Quoted by Michael Twyman in the introduction to Maurice Rickards, *The Encyclopedia of Ephemera*, The British Library, 2000.
2 David Jury, "The Rule-benders," *baseline*, Issue 46, 2004.
3 Maurice Rickards, *The Encyclopedia of Ephemera*, The British Library, 2000.

Novelty

1 A. G. Sayers and J. Stuart, *Art and Practice of Printing*, Vol. One, page 243, Pitman, 1933.
2 Nicolete Gray, *Nineteenth Century Ornamented Types*, page 7, Faber & Faber, 1976.
3 Ibid, page 8.
4 Ramon Perez de Ayala, *Belarmino & Apolonio*, Madrid, 1921. English edition: University of California Press, 1971.

Space around text

1 Donald Paterson, Miles A. Tinker, *How to Make Type Readable*, Harper & Brothers, 1949.
2 David Jury, "Publishing in the UK During the Second World War," *TypoGraphic* 61, International Society of Typographic Designers, 2004.

Glossary of punctuation and letter parts

An **apostrophe** (') signifies an omission: *it's*, for *it is*, or *tho'*, for *though*. It also signifies the possessive branch of the genitive case; *Rita's book*. It is also used in Irish names, as in *O'Brien* but is *not* used in abbreviated Scottish names. The apostrophe also forms the latter part of quotation marks.

The **brace** { } is used to connect, for example, two or more subtitles on different lines within a single, tabulated entry. The brace should always point towards its cross-referred entry.

A **colon** (:) signifies a pause; a turning point within a clause or sentence. Positioned within a sentence in which the preceding part is complete in sense while the following part is a statement or remark arising from it. The colon is also used to introduce a list of points, an example, or a quotation.

A **comma** (,) separates and defines the adjuncts, clauses, and phrases within a sentence. It should also follow each adjective except the last. A comma is also used to clarify high numbers—separating each set of three consecutive numbers from the right when there are four or more.

An **ellipsis** (…) is made up of three full points each separated by a short space (larger than that normally between characters, but smaller than a word space) and signifies the omission of a word. Where an ellipsis occurs at the end of a sentence a fourth full point should be added, its distance from the final full point of the ellipsis being the same as those within the ellipsis itself.

An **em dash** (—) is used in place of a comma or parentheses, offering the author a more dramatic pause where it is necessary for the construction of a sentence to be changed or even halted. It is also used to signify a faltering pause: "Well—perhaps…"

An **en dash** (–) is used (rather like a virgule) to connect two facts, such as dates (1968–1969) or to signify a partnership (Smith–Jones).

An **exclamation mark** (!) is used after words or sentences expressing a striking thought or utterance. It should be placed at the end of the exclamation, whether this occurs at the beginning, middle, or end of the sentence. It should not be followed by a full point if placed at the end of a sentence, or any other punctuation if in the middle of a sentence, except a quotation mark.

A **full point** (.) signifies the end of a sentence. Do not use a full point in titles, or subtitles.

A **hyphen** (-) is used to connect. When a word has to be broken at the end of a line a hyphen is used to signify its incompleteness and its connection to the second part of the word at the beginning of the following line. It is also used to connect words that represent a common idea, such as *mind-blowing*. Where two or more compound words have a common base this latter can be represented in all but the last by a hyphen as in *upper- and lowercase*. The hyphen is used to clarify meaning, as in *re-mark* (as distinct from *remark*). Generally, the hyphen should not be used at the end of more than two consecutive lines and must never be placed at the beginning of the second line. Also, avoid using a hyphen at the end of the last line of a page and in particular, the right hand (verso) page.

Parentheses ( ), like brackets (see *square brackets*), are used to separate additional remarks or responses within a text. The key to the practical relationship of brackets and parentheses is consistency. Where a remark in brackets requires a second remark to be isolated, then parentheses should be used and vice versa. If possible, avoid (words [words]).

A **question mark** (?) should follow each and every question, however short, if a separate answer is required, as in; What is type made of? How is it defined? Where did it start? A question mark should not be followed by a full point if placed at the end of a sentence, or any other punctuation if in the middle of a sentence, except a quotation mark.

Square brackets [ ], also called brackets or crochets, are used to separate comments, corrections, or explanations from the main body of text in which they appear.

A raised, **turned comma** (') is used in the abbreviation of the Scotch Mac (M'Donald). It also forms the first half of quotation marks.

A **double em dash** (——) is used to signify the interruption of a sentence or the omission of a word or part of a word, as in; "He called him a ——." Not often included in contemporary fonts, but easily composed by joining two em dashes together.

A **virgule** (/), also commonly called a forward slash, expresses the choice either or both. For example and/or and together/apart.

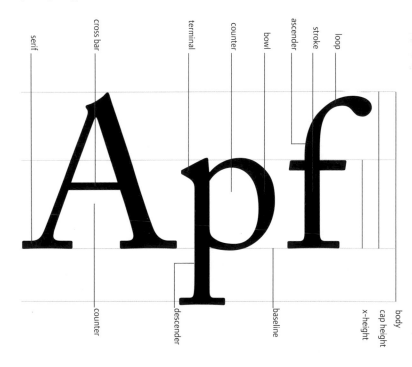

General glossary

accented Those letters with the various additional marks that indicate pronunciation and/or signal regional or social identity: áàâäåçéèêëíìîïñóòôöõúùûüÿ.

align To position letters, words, or images to fit on the same vertical line: "aligned left," "aligned right."

ampersand An abbreviation for *and*: &.

Arabic numerals 1234567890, as distinct from Roman (I II III IV V VI VII VIII X).

ascender Vertical stroke rising above the *x-height* in lowercase letters: b h k t.

ASCII A data or file format containing text and paragraph markers, but no formatting information.

auto-leading Default interline spacing in typesetting software. Generally set to an arbitrary 20% of the body height of type size. Should always be overridden.

baseline The imaginary line on which a line of letters sits.

baseline grid Lines at fixed, user-definable intervals on which the text can be made to sit.

bit-map A bit-map describes the location and binary state (*on* or *off*) of "bits," which defines a complete collection of *pixels* comprising an image or letterform.

black letter A general term used to describe letterforms originally drawn with a broad-nibbed pen.

body The rectangular area occupied by a letter.

body copy Continuous text, not including, for example, captions, page numbers, etc.

bullet A solid dot (•). Normally used to indicate the start of a new item, etc.

cap height Height from the top of a capital letter to its baseline.

capitals (or caps) Letterforms of even height, derived from the Roman "square capitals."

caps, small (SMALL CAPS) Capital letters of the same weight as lowercase letters and of a height designed to harmonize with them when set as text.

centered Symmetrical arrangement of type.

color The tonal value of a page of text.

copy Written material before it is typeset.

copyright © Legal right to control the use of intellectual property or created material.

counter The enclosed or semi-enclosed space within a letterform.

cursive Flowing, sloped letterforms (eg. italic or script typefaces).

descender Stroke falling below the baseline in lowercase letters: g j p q y.

design To plan an appropriate solution.

diacritic An *accent* or mark above or below a character.

digital The imaging of type on screen by use of *bit-maps* or outlines of letterforms stored electronically.

diphthong (æ Æ œ Œ) One *glyph* that represents two vowels.

display Monitor or screen.

display type "Headline" or "novelty" type designed to attract attention.

DPI (dots per inch) The resolution used to display an image.

expert set "Supplementary" font of characters extra to those provided in the standard font. Might include nonlining numerals, fractions, additional ligatures, etc.

font (originally fount in the UK) A set of characters (letterforms, punctuation, symbols, etc.) of a given typeface.

format The shape and size of a given project (book, poster, leaflet, etc.). Also a transitive verb describing the exact specification for textual area, size of type, typeface, leading, etc.

grammar The conventions of language.

glyph A single character, accent, or symbol.

H&J Hyphenation and justification.

indent Line of type positioned inward from the left margin. Usually used to indicate the start of a paragraph.

italic Cursive companion to a roman type.

justified Text set in lines of equal length requiring the adjustment of interword spacing for each line excepting the last line in each paragraph.

kerning Adjustment made to interword or intercharacter spaces. (Also called letter spacing.)

Latin The standard alphabet used in most Western European countries, based on Roman sources.

leading Interline spacing.

legibility Recognizability.

letterpress Printing method in which paper is brought into contact with raised, inked surfaces.

ligature (fi fl) Two (or three) letters combined into one character.

lining numerals Numerals that are all the same height (e.g. the same height as caps of the same font). 1234567890 ABCDE.

lowercase Small letterforms derived from handwritten letters (see *minuscules*).

majuscules Capital (or cap) letterforms.

measure The length of a full line of type (line length).

minuscules Lowercase letterforms.

Modern Class of typeface with extreme contrast in line thickness (e.g. *Bodoni*)

nonlining numerals (Old-style numerals) Numerals with ascenders and descenders. 1234567890

oblique A sloped letterform. Equivalent in some fonts to the italic.

Old style Class of letterform characterized by an angled stress and low to moderate variation in line thickness (e.g. *Garamond, Jenson, Caslon*).

Old-style numerals (or Old-style figures). See *nonlining numerals*.

orphan Simultaneously the last word of a paragraph and the first word on a new page.

phoneme A sound which is the smallest unit of speech within a language.

phonetics The study of sounds that make up human speech.

Pi characters Symbols and pictographs.

pictograph (or pictogram) A symbol representing a person or object.

pixel Screen dots used to render an image.

point size The means of "measuring" the *body* of the type. Type size is expressed in points; 72 points is equivalent to 1 inch.

preference box Dialog box that allows the user to change the software default settings.

ranged left Alignment of text with a vertical left- and a ragged right-hand edge.

ranged right Alignment of text with a vertical right- and a ragged left-hand edge.

resolution Density of pixels (or dots) in a specified area (e.g. dots per square inch, see *DPI*).

roman Upright (as opposed to italic) letterforms.

river Connecting white spaces running (usually vertically) through poorly set text.

sans serif Class of type with no *serifs*.

semantics The study of the meaning of language.

serif Accretion at the end of stems of roman letterforms. Styles include bracket, slab, wedge, etc.

set solid Text set with no leading (e.g. 10 on 10 point, or 10-point type on 10-point leading).

smart quotes The correct "curly" rather than straight quote marks.

soft return Line break instruction within a paragraph.

software Computer operating procedures and instructions that control hardware.

style (of type) Light, bold, italic, etc.

style sheet Sets of typographic attributes used to providea text with structure and clarity. By using style sheets all attributes can be styled at once and with consistency.

swash Decorative flourish added to a letter.

symbol See *Pi character*.

tabular numerals (or figures). See *lining numerals*.

textual Formal term for lowercase character set.

TIFF (or TIF) Tagged Image File Format. A file format used for scanned, high-resolution, bit-mapped images, and for color separation.

tracking Equal adjustment to spacing values applied to a line or page of text.

transitional Class of type stylistically between *Old style* and *Modern* (e.g. *Baskerville*).

type family Related variants in a font of type (e.g. light, bold, italics, small caps, etc.).

Unicode An international standard character set that will contain all the characters required by all the world's languages.

unjustified Column of text in which the interword space remains constant, usually ranged left or ranged right.

uppercase Capital letters.

weight The relative thickness of line or stroke in a letterform.

word break See *hyphen* in the Glossary of punctuation.

WYSIWYG (What You See Is What You Get) What you see on screen is what you get on paper.

x-height The height of the main part of lowercase letterforms (e.g. x).

Further reading

The following titles are just a few of the many helpful books concerned with various aspects of typographic matters. Not all are in print, but public libraries will be able to locate copies and specialist libraries will certainly have them on their shelves. The date provided is that of the edition I have; in many cases there will be more recent issues. I have listed each in only one category although there are a number that could comfortably appear within two, three, or all categories.

History (general)

E. EISENSTEIN, *The Printing Press as an Agent of Change*, Cambridge University Press, 1979.

L. FABVRE AND H.-J. MARTIN, *The Coming of the Book*, New Left Books, 1976.

R. KINROSS, *Modern Typography*, Hyphen Press, 1992.

S. MORISON, *Four Centuries of Fine Printing*, Ernest Benn Limited, 1960.

D. B. UPDIKE, *Printing Types*, two volumes, Oxford University Press, 1937.

History (twentieth-century typography)

H. BAYER, W. GROPIUS, I. GROPIUS, *The Bauhaus 1919–1928*, Museum of Modern Art, New York, 1938.

C. BURKE, *Paul Renner*, Hyphen Press, 1998.

E. GILL, *An Essay on Typography*, Lund Humphries, 2001.

R. KINROSS, *Anthony Froshaug*, two volumes, Hyphen Press, 2000.

M. LOMMEN (ed.), *Bram de Does*, Uitgeverij De Buitenkant Publishers, 2003.

R. MCLEAN, *Jan Tschichold*, Lund Humphries, 1975.

J. MORAN, *Stanley Morison*, Lund Humphries, 1971.

A. PETERSEN, *Sandberg, Designer and Director of the Stedelijk*, 010 Publishers, 2004.

H. SPENCER, *Pioneers of Modern Typography*, Lund Humphries, 1969.

J. TSCHICHOLD, *Die Neue Typographie*, Bildungsverband der Deutschen Buchdrucker, 1928. *Penrose Annual* First issue in 1895 (as *Penrose Work Year Book*), last issue 1973. These books constitute a unique record of the far-reaching changes in printing and designing for print. Individual copies are a common sight in secondhand bookstores.

History (typefaces)

M. ANNENBERG, *Type Foundries of America*, Oak Knoll Press, 1994.

G. DOWDING, *An Introduction to the History of Printing Types*, The British Library & Oak Knoll Press, 1998.

J. DRUCKER, *The Alphabetical Labyrinth*, Thames & Hudson, 1995 (for a wider account of the history of letterforms).

N. GRAY, *Nineteenth Century Ornamented Typefaces*, Faber & Faber, 1951.

A. LAWSON, *Anatomy of a Typeface*, Hamish Hamilton Ltd, 1990.

J. MIDDENDORP, *Dutch Type*, 010 Publishers, 2004.

J. MOSLEY, *The Nymph and the Grot*, Friends of the St. Bride Printing Library, 1999.

Book typography

J. BLUMENTHAL, *The Printed Book in America*, The Scholar Press, 1977.

C. EDE (ed.), *The Art of the Book*, The Studio Publications, 1951 (covers 1939–1950).

J. HOCHULI, R. KINROSS, *Designing Books*, The Hyphen Press, 1996.

J. LEWIS, *The Twentieth Century Book*, Van Nostrand Reinhold Co, 1967.

H. WILLIAMSON, *Methods of Book Design*, Oxford University Press, 1956.

Technology

M. TWYMAN, *Printing 1770–1970: An Illustrated History of its Development and Uses in England*, The British Library Press in association with Reading University Press, 1970.

L. W. WALLIS, *Typomania*, Sevenside Printers Ltd, 1993.

General reference

Numerous printers' "house-style books" can be found in secondhand bookstores along with:

F. H. COLLINS, *Authors' and Printers' Dictionary*, Oxford University Press, numerous editions.

H. HART, *Rules for Compositors and Readers*, Oxford University Press, numerous editions.

Type design

F. SMEIJERS, *Counterpunch*, Hyphen Press, 1997.

W. TRACY, *Letters of Credit*, Gordon Fraser, 1986.

Typography in a wider context

D. CRYSTAL, *The Cambridge Encyclopedia of Language*, Cambridge University Press, 1987.

M. A. FORRESTER, *Psychology of Language,* Sage Publications, 1997.

E. LUPTON, J. A. MILLER, *Design, Writing, Research*, Princeton Architectural Press, 1996.

M. MCLUHAN, *The Gutenberg Galaxy*, Routledge, 1967.

G. NUNBERG, *The Future of the Book*, University of California Press, 1996.

R. SASSOON, *Handwriting of the Twentieth Century*, Routledge, 1999.

I. WILKINSON, *Inclusive Design,* Joint publication between the Royal National Institute of the Blind and the International Society for Typographic Designers, 2005.

Journals

There are a number of excellent journals that have made a major contribution to our understanding of typography, although the majority of material is concerned with the nineteenth and early twentieth centuries.

Alphabet (1964)

Alphabet and Image (1946–1948)

The Fleuron (1923–1930)

Journal of the Printing Historical Society (since 1965)

Matrix (since 1981)

The *Monotype Recorder* (since 1902) The house journal of the Monotype Corporation, this provided an excellent and scholarly view of typographic history married to technical and trade issues. Its appearance has become very rare in recent years, but the centenary issue "One hundred years of type making 1897–1997" (new series, No. 10, 1997), is particularly useful.

Motif (1958–1966)

Signature (1935–1940 and 1946–1954)

Typographica (1949–1967)

Typography (1936–1939)

Typography Papers (since 1996) A recent welcome addition to this list, published by the Department of Typography and Communication at Reading University.

Contemporary journals that cover historical and current typographic issues are:

baseline (since 1970), published quarterly, www.baselinemagazine.com

TypoGraphic (since 1971), a triannual, www.istd.org.uk

Index